THE SEXUAL ECONOMY
OF CAPITALISM

CURRENCIES

New Thinking for Financial Times
STEFAN EICH AND MARTIJN KONINGS, EDITORS

The Sexual Economy of Capitalism

NOAM YURAN

STANFORD UNIVERSITY PRESS
Stanford, California

STANFORD UNIVERSITY PRESS
Stanford, California

© 2024 by Noam Yuran. All rights reserved.

No part of this book may be reproduced or transmitted in any form or by any means, electronic or mechanical, including photocopying and recording, or in any information storage or retrieval system, without the prior written permission of Stanford University Press.

Printed in the United States of America on acid-free, archival-quality paper

Library of Congress Cataloging-in-Publication Data

Names: Yuran, Noam, author.
Title: The sexual economy of capitalism / Noam Yuran.
Other titles: Currencies (Series)
Description: Stanford, California : Stanford University Press, 2024. | Series: Currencies | Includes bibliographical references and index. |
Identifiers: LCCN 2024016269 (print) | LCCN 2024016270 (ebook) | ISBN 9781503630277 (cloth) | ISBN 9781503640733 (paperback) | ISBN 9781503640740 (ebook)
Subjects: LCSH: Capitalism—Philosophy. | Sex—Economic aspects.
Classification: LCC HB501 .Y89 2024 (print) | LCC HB501 (ebook) | DDC 330.12/2—dc23/eng/20240514
LC record available at https://lccn.loc.gov/2024016269
LC ebook record available at https://lccn.loc.gov/2024016270

Cover design and pattern: Archie Ferguson
Typeset by Newgen in 10/15 Janson Text LT Std

In loving memory of Sivan
1963–2022

Contents

Acknowledgments ix

INTRODUCTION 1

1 WHAT IS SEXUAL ECONOMY? 20

2 SEX IN ECONOMIC THOUGHT 66

3 LOVE AND MARRIAGE 100

4 PROSTITUTION AND FINANCE 135

5 THE EROTICIZATION OF CONSUMPTION 166

6 WOMEN AND CAPITAL 195

Notes 219

References 223

Index 229

Acknowledgments

This book took me a long time to write, and many smart and kind people helped me along the way. I thank my friends Yuval Kremnitzer, Oded Shechter, Uri Eran, Keith Hart, and Liran Razinsky who read parts of the manuscript and gave me invaluable advice. I presented the ideas of this book in academic forums led by Shay Lavie, Shaul Setter, Ronnie Ellenblum, and Amin Samman and Earl Gammon. I enjoyed the lively discussions and learned from them a lot.

Near the completion of the work, my wife, Sivan Finesilver Yuran, passed away after a long illness. We were married for twenty-five years, and I miss her very much. I thank God that her departure was peaceful and that she lived every day to the fullest until the end. This book presents a theoretical critique of monogamy, but for me monogamy was the formative experience of my life.

I want to thank some of the many people who helped me go through the last year and half of grief. First and foremost, I thank my children, Itamar, Alona, and Omer. You are strong and wonderful, and my biggest wish is that you stay united. I thank my brothers Hanan and Nadav and their families. It is a great comfort to know you are there. Many friends kept visiting and calling, among them Michael Horovitz, Daniel Kish, Gonnen Harpaz, Yaron Egozy, Erez Schweitzer, and Uli Broido. Lastly, I want to thank Tahel Frosh. Your friendship gives me new life.

INTRODUCTION

WHILE I WAS WORKING ON THIS BOOK, many acquaintances inquired what I mean by the phrase "the sexual economy of capitalism." I often asked them in return whether they would like to hear the short and vulgar answer or a more refined one. Most of them preferred the former, so I will ask the forgiveness of more sensitive readers and start with it. In capitalism men do not buy women as wives, and this nonbuying is part of what shaped the economy. That marriage is no longer managed as an exchange, and that husbands no longer own their wives, are obvious fundamental facts about gender relations in liberal societies that distinguish them from traditional patriarchal ones. What tends to escape our attention, however, is that by the same token these are also basic facts about exchange, money, and ownership that distinguish capitalist economies from precapitalist ones. The nonbuying of women should be considered a positive property of the capitalist forms of money, exchange, and ownership, manifested in the eroticization of economic life. Advertising is but the most conspicuous manifestation of this. From the perspective afforded by advertising, capitalism seems to be an economy where wives are not owned, at least not formally, yet everything one buys is a woman. This book takes the transformation in gender relations as a starting point for an economic theory of capitalism, addressing ostensibly gender-neutral questions: What is capitalist money? What is its relation to finance and capital? What is economy? What is the difference between an economy encompassing wives alongside things such as lands, tools, and houses, and one that consists, formally at least, only of things?

For a more detailed presentation, let me turn to the tactlessness of economics. It is sometimes of great intellectual merit that, regardless of their answers, which are often off the mark, economists pose tactless questions—not unlike speaking about money at a dinner party. Such a tactless question has attracted the attention of some economists lately regarding the institution of monogamous marriage: why is it that rich men in affluent societies do not marry more than one wife (Adshade 2013)? The significance of this question is highlighted by an assumption shared today by both economists and many of their critics, namely that market relations have come to dominate society as a whole. The manifestation of this assumption within economics is usually called "economic imperialism," a term that designates the belief that the concepts and tools of the discipline can be applied to any sort of human behavior, including marriage. On the critical side, a similar assumption informs the study of neoliberalism, which is understood as a political agenda aiming to reshape society to the form of the free market. So that is the full meaning of the economists' tactless question: if social life is indeed increasingly permeated by market logic, why is it that rich people still marry only one wife? They can afford more than one, some of them may want more than one, and if they are rich enough, we can speculate, they might find women who would share them as husbands with other wives.

It goes without saying that the solutions that economists provide to the riddle are misguided, yet they are nonetheless worth reading. For one thing, they underline how the basic fact of marriage poses a challenge to the mainstream economic worldview and suggests the need for an alternative. More importantly, at the root of these failed explanations one notices a shadow: a notion of ownership that still haunts monogamy, a shadow which economics can neither contain nor dismiss. Marina Adshade cites two economic explanations for the persistence of monogamy. The first one is formulated with populations in view: "If there are equal numbers of men and women in a polygynous society, then it is a mathematical reality that some men will be disenfranchised from the market for marriage (and possibly sex) because of that institutional arrangement" (Adshade 2013, 115). Monogamy laws, according to this view, are instituted by rulers and governments to pacify the masses: "Being a poor man in a country in which other men are extremely rich is one thing, but being a poor man who will never be able to marry while other men have many wives is quite another" (126). This should be read carefully. From this specific economic perspective one answer to the question of why capitalist societies stick to monogamy is that they are not capitalist *enough*. They can withstand huge inequalities in the allocation of things and money, so long as in marriage they maintain a socialist regime that entitles any man to precisely one wife.[1]

As this explanation draws on laws, politics, and rulers, Adshade maintains that it does not fully solve "the mystery of monogamy," namely, its persistence in industrial societies. She supplements it with a further explanation more strictly economic in nature. As income gaps widen in affluent societies, so do the gaps in human capital. Richer men want children with higher capabilities to support them in old age, and for that purpose they need wives with higher human capital. Let us quote Adshade's formulation, with its intentional or inadvertent dismissal of the demands of political correctness: "Monogamy has emerged as the dominant marriage institution because the demand for high-quality children has increased the value of high-quality women in the marriage market, making it difficult for even wealthy men to afford more than one wife" (Adshade 2013, 128). (Now, just imagine the supreme quality of Jeff Bezos's wife!) In this further explanation, it is not laws and politicians that sustain the socialist regime in the allocation of wives, but market forces themselves. They maintain its basic principle—one wife for one man—while attenuating its egalitarian nature by inscribing differences between women.

Why should we dwell on these economic explanations? Noneconomists would probably dismiss them as sexist fantasies masked in the rhetoric of a sober science and offer instead a host of commonsensical explanations drawing on notions of religion, tradition, or love. Marriage is a religious institution, which the Judeo-Christian tradition sanctioned in a monogamous form. Modern societies have indeed gone through processes of secularization, but the persistence of monogamy shows that these processes were never completed. Moreover, notions of love and romance, which substituted for marriage's religious justification, are also colored by monogamy. They present an ideal of marriage as a union of two souls, and they too have their form of persistence. We can put these objections aside for the meantime, because above all the economic explanations make a categorical mistake regarding the meaning of institutions. Adshade explains that monogamy "has emerged as the dominant marriage *institution*" because of the forces of supply and demand of wives. Yet to claim that a free market in marriage leads, by itself, to a monogamous pattern would mean precisely that monogamy is *not* an institution. The concept of institutions, after all, is called for to explain patterns of human activity that are irreducible to individualistic motivations. Such patterns persist regardless of, or even in contrast to, individuals' egoistic motivations. Accepting the economic explanation for the persistence of monogamy would only make the fact that the *law* sanctions monogamy all the more mysterious.

The economic explanations of monogamy are important precisely because of their overtly fantasmatic nature. Addressing them, one should keep in mind that the concept of social institutions does not by itself provide a full explanation for the persistence of monogamy. At least not an interesting one. Although human reality is patterned by institutions, these do not always designate a simple form of persistence. Institutions do not refer to things that simply "remain as they have always been," but more importantly to things that persist throughout changing historical contexts. It is indeed important to draw attention to the institutional nature of monogamous marriage, but only as a backdrop for a further set of questions: What is it exactly that persists with monogamy? How does it persist? What meanings of it persist and what new meanings does it acquire while traveling through different historical contexts, as diverse as slavery, feudalism, and capitalism? It is against this background that the economic explanations acquire their significance. They spell out the economic meaning of marriage in free-market societies, which can appear *only* in a fantasmatic form, because they aim to subsume within the ahistorical economic mindset an institutional inheritance which is essentially foreign to it. Read as a fantasy, Adshade does a good job in formulating two complementary aspects of the economic meaning of marriage today: wives are the most prized possessions of men, and they are prized because they infringe the regulation of private property through the free market.

Regarding the first aspect, the economic explanations of monogamy recapitulate the strand of feminist thought that couples the history of the family with that of private property. Friedrich Engels put forward this line of thought in *The Origin of the Family, Private Property and the State* (1902), and Simone de Beauvoir developed it further in *The Second Sex* (1956). They trace the origin of the family to the agrarian revolution. Cultivated lands required ongoing intensive investment of work, for which the family was essential. Lands and tools also constituted the first goods to be transmitted across generations. The strict regulation of sex under monogamous morality was the means to ascertain that a man passes his property to his own sons. This speculation perfectly demonstrates the difference between a historical outlook and the dominant economic one. Whereas economists aim to *solve* the mystery of the persistence of monogamy, the historical speculation explains the persistence of monogamy *as a mystery* (that is, as a vestige of the past, not fully comprehensible in the official language of the present). Engels and de Beauvoir do not dissolve the mystery of monogamy, but juxtapose it with another mystery, that of private property. The need to ascertain the right of inheritance does not solve the mystery of monogamy because it only raises a further one: why do men toil so hard to cultivate their property only to bequeath it to their true sons? This overlapping of mysteries is not a fault in argumentation. Rather, it suggests that mystery is part of the substance of history: what it transmits through time is precisely what transcends the individualist horizon. De Beauvoir is more aware of this than Engels. She points out that the juxtaposition of the questions of the family and of private property brings about a further mysterious association: between property and *immortality*. The owner of property, she writes, "transfers, alienates his existence into his property; he cares more for it than for his very life" (de Beauvoir 1956, 106). Engels and de Beauvoir do not provide a solution to the riddle but answer the question with another question. Inheritance mediates the relation of fatherhood in terms of property relations, but the inverse is also true: blood relations confer meaning on private property. Private property provides an answer to the question "How is a man the son of another?" He is a son, among other things, as a future inheritor. But in the same manner, fatherhood provides an answer to the question "How is a piece of land one man's property?" It is property as a future inheritance to one's sons. In both cases, a question is summoned as a reply because each of the questions rests on an insoluble uncertainty. Fatherhood is an uncertain relation: monogamy partially solves the factual aspect of this uncertainty, and inheritance provides it with content. Yet private property is also an uncertain relation, and that is what its coupling with monogamy brings to the fore. Property is also tainted with mystery, insofar as it transcends the horizons of individuals and their selfish motivations. To identify its origin with the need to regulate inheritance means that private property is a mysterious social arrangement from the outset. Engels's reference to biology in his theory, with the invocation of the uncertain status of fatherhood, might mislead us to read it as proposing a natural basis for ownership. In truth, biology, precisely because in the case of fatherhood it designates uncertainty, is invoked to denaturalize ownership from its very beginning. The reformulation of Engels's and de Beauvoir's views in the language of contemporary economics proves a crucial point: private property still must be rethought once the economic perspective encompasses the family. Engels problematized it through the association of property with the patriarchal tradition which encompassed wives in the circle of ownership. Adshade shows how a patriarchal fantasy keeps informing property relations in societies that have formally left patriarchy behind.

The second aspect of the economic meaning of monogamy we find in Adshade pertains more specifically to capitalism. She explains that in preindustrial nations, where the goal of marriage is to "produce as many children as possible . . . potential wives are not so different from each other" (Adshade 2013, 128). It is in capitalism that women, in their unique individuality, become a prized possession, and they assume this role precisely because they infringe the dynamics of private property regulated by the free market, through the socialist monogamy regime. This vulgar idea, too, has its partial parallel in critical thought. In her wonderful book *Family Values*, Melinda Cooper shows how the question of the family became the site of the strange convergence between neoliberalism and social conservatism.

Moreover, she shows how the family assumed this role because of its externality to the market. Her argument goes against a commonsensical yet misguided trend in critical thought that sees neoliberal capitalism as destructive of family life. One can immediately see the logic that drives this trend: long-term family obligations stand in contrast to flexible labor relations, to the notion of the self as an entrepreneur, to the pervasive nature of the calculating frame of mind, and so on. Reasonable as it may appear, this critical trend ignores the apparent fact that some of the most important champions of neoliberalism, including Ronald Reagan, Margaret Thatcher, and Milton Friedman, were also avowed spokespersons for family values. The root of this shortsightedness of critical thought, according to Cooper, is a tendency "to conflate capitalism itself with the logic of the market" (2017, 14). In her view, by contrast, the family is "internal to the dynamic of capital" (15) precisely in its externality to the market. From a Marxist perspective the dynamic of capital, in its limitless process of generation and accumulation of value, is indeed destructive of all traditional social formations. Yet it must also reassert such formations as a condition for the realization of value in the form of private wealth. The standard view takes literally the popular theme of "the crisis of the family" as a sign of its coming dissolution—a position which locks critics in a nostalgic view of traditional family values, as an anchor of a critique of neoliberal capitalism. Cooper, by contrast, portrays the crisis as a mode of the ongoing existence of the family, a symptom of the need to "reinvent" it: "If the history of modern capital appears on the one hand to regularly undermine and challenge existing orders of gender and sexuality, it also entails the periodic reinvention of the family as an instrument for distributing wealth and income" (17).

Cooper grounds her critique on Marx's *Grundrisse*, but for the meantime it may be useful to illustrate it with a simpler text, which is also closer to the canonical tradition of economics. In "The Backward Art of Spending Money," published in 1912, Wesley C. Mitchell posed a naïve question, in the most illuminating sense of the term. Modern societies have developed systematic knowledge about making money. Why is it, then, that knowledge about spending money remains rudimentary in form? His answer to the question portrays the family as a site of constitutive anachronism. The contemporary economic role of the family is defined by its lagging behind economic transformations, its persistence beyond its traditional economic roles. In preindustrial societies "the family was the unit in large measure for purposes both of producing and consuming goods" (Mitchell 1912, 269). With industrialization, production was transferred to bigger units, more susceptible to rationalization and systematization. Consumption, by contrast, remained confined to the family home under the direction of the housewife, due to "our race-old instincts of love between the sexes and parental affection, long since standardized in the institution of monogamy." For that reason, from the economic perspective, "the art of spending lags behind the art of making money" (270–71).

The concept of lagging is crucial. It is the mode of existence of the family as a residue, a remnant of the past, articulated economically in monetary practices. In Cooper's terms, lagging is how the family is reinvented. It does not designate simple persistence in the sense of remaining the same. The family changes, reinvented, precisely because it now appears lagging, a vestige of the past. "Reluctantly we have let the factory whistle, the time-table, the office hours impose their rigid routine upon our money-making days; but our homes we have tried to guard from intrusion by the world of machinery and business" (Mitchell 1912, 271).

We should not let Mitchell's sentimental tone mislead us. Sentimentality is part of how the family is reinvented. When the family was the locus of both production and consumption—when it directly assumed the form of a basic economic unit—there was presumably less need for a sentimental view of it. This sentimentality, however, does not designate the family as external to the economy. That would be an absurd position if we keep in mind that "making money and spending money are strictly correlative arts" (Mitchell 1912, 269). Because a dollar spent is a dollar earned, the sentiments that mark the economic backwardness of the family are a supplement of rationalized money making. The family thus marks an internal split within the economy. It is a gendered split, between masculine and feminine roles, articulating different economies underlying money making and money spending, production and consumption, the family home and the business enterprise.

Some of the reasons Mitchell lists for the impossibility of rationalizing the art of spending money are inherent to the tasks of the housewife. These are more varied than those of engineers and managers ("She must buy milk and shoes, furniture and meat, magazines and fuel, hats and underwear, bedding and disinfectants, medical services and toys, rugs and candy. Surely no one can be expected to possess expert knowledge of the qualities and prices of such varied wares" [Mitchell 1912, 271]). More importantly, her tasks differ from that of the businessman in that they entail an ethical dimension, a consideration of ends. The businessman has a clear and measurable aim: "to make money becomes an end in itself." The housewife's goals are inherently incalculable: "to spend money involves some end beyond the spending." The housewife cannot avoid questions of what constitutes the good life: "She can tell herself that she seeks the happiness of her husband and herself, the fair development of their children. But before these vague statements can serve as guides in the intensely practical problem of spending money, she must decide what happiness and development mean in concrete terms for her particular husband and children" (277). In Weberian terms, the difference between the art of spending money and the art of making money is not an opposition between rationality and sentimental irrationality, but between two forms of rationality. The masculine art of making money obviously follows Weber's notion of formal rationality, based on value-free, goal-oriented calculation. The feminine art of spending money involves substantive rationality, which takes into account values and ends rather than focusing solely on the means to achieve ends (Weber 1978, 85).

Other causes for the backwardness of the art of spending money are rooted in the social organization of the family as a "separate sphere." Mitchell points them out through an amusing thought experiment. Despite the numerous obstacles, "a surprising number of women achieve individual successes" in their art. "If housekeeping were organized like business," he concludes, "these efficient managers" would have been promoted to senior positions and "supervise the work of many others to the advantage of themselves and the community." The privacy of family life, upon which "we jealously insist," makes this possibility absurd. Even advice to inefficient neighbors, let alone supervision, is not welcome in this respect: "These neighbors, and even the husbands of these neighbors, are prone to regard critical commentaries upon their slack methods, however pertinent and constructive in character, as meddlesome interferences" (Mitchell 1912, 274).

That is an early version of the logic underlying Adshade's explanations of monogamy. Wives are a prized possession precisely because the family infringes the dynamics of the free market. The jealously guarded privacy marks the family home both as exception to the logic of the market and as exceptionally valued. Mitchell, however, is an institutional economist, a favorite student of Thorstein Veblen, and in his intellectual environment economics and history are not exclusive of each other but complementary perspectives. This can explain why love, so conspicuously absent from the arguments of contemporary economists that Adshade cites, finds a place in his economic analysis of the family. In the historical dimension of his argument, love is the form of persistence of monogamous marriage beyond its patriarchal origin, which entailed direct or indirect ownership of women. In its economic dimension, love designates a bifurcation of economic rationality, where the family home, as an integral part of the economy, deviates from the rational calculating spirit of the free market. Love also gestures at a shift in the subject matter of economic history, from men and women to masculinity and femininity. Traditional patriarchal families consisted of men owning women. The modern family, as a residue of this past, transposes the gender distinction into contrasting and complementary gendered economic categories, articulating an inner split within capitalist economy: a masculine rational art of making money and a feminine irrational art of spending money.

The family and the economy have kept on changing from Mitchell's time. Women have entered the world of business and labor, and the term *housewife* has become offensive, replaced by the gender neutral *homemaker*. The "crisis of the family" recurrently invoked since the 1970s rendered Mitchell's sentimental attitude obsolete. The matrix he outlined, though, still informs our imagination, as exemplified by the reality TV series *The Real Housewives*. The participants in this prolific franchise are rich women, and while many of them do have careers, the shows focus on their social lives and their lavish money spending. A price tag—aimed at sustaining the shock value of the show—appears on screen whenever a purchase decision is considered. The "real" in the show's title, however, is not a simple euphemism for "rich." It is the real of reality TV, opposed as it is to realism: the unbelievable real, the scandalous real, or the impossible yet necessarily real. Money and women confer this sense of "unreal reality" on each other. The participants are "real housewives" insofar as they are preoccupied with spending money, and more so because the vacillations regarding how to spend are not ameliorated but worsened by having a lot of it. Their money is the real and crazy money of lavish spending, as opposed to the calculating rationality of money making.

Another television series, *The White Lotus*, presents with mathematical precision the gendered nature of money. A plotline in the first season revolves around the relationship of a rich heir with his fortuneless fiancée. The second season presents a mirror image in a plotline about a rich heiress and her new husband. The relations of the protagonists to their money are diametrically opposed. The male heir has entered the family business, and his relation to his money is natural. He expects everyone to treat him as a rich man and is constantly annoyed when reality does not align with his expectations. The question of whether his fiancée wants him for his money or for his personality is meaningless for him because his money is a part of who he is. The female heiress inherited her fortune from an abusive father and has no idea about business and money management. Her money is an uncanny object, a foreign body which defines her yet is incomprehensible to her. It is hers but also alien to her. She cannot know whether people around her, including her husband, want her for herself or for her money. Her money drives her crazy and keeps her out of touch with reality.

The family is lagging behind the market economy. This lagging lies in the background of the alarm about the crisis of the family, which envisions a future when the temporal gap will close and sexual life and procreation will be completely overtaken by market logic. As Cooper notes, this idea confers on the prevalent critique of the juncture of economy and the family its sentimental, and unwittingly conservative, undertone. What should be added, however, is that critics alarmed by the possibility of the market overpowering the family disclose a historical shortsightedness. There actually was a time when sex and procreation were fully submerged in the economy. It is called traditional patriarchy. In that historical context, monogamy was directly both a private property regime and a sexual regime, without any tension between the two dimensions. The family is lagging in the sense that monogamy has persisted beyond its economic underpinning. In this sense lagging is not an ominous sign but simply the mode of existence of the family in capitalism. Maybe monogamy will indeed disintegrate eventually. But then again, if it does, maybe capitalism will also evolve to a different economic regime.

Groundbreaking feminist writers, like de Beauvoir, Betty Friedan, Shulamith Firestone, Carole Pateman, Arlie Hochschild, and many others made us see how capitalism confers new forms on the patriarchal tradition of marriage: how the family retains a patriarchal kernel within the liberal world which is formally foreign to it. This book aims to contribute to this tradition through a reversal of perspective, shifting the focus to capitalism rather than patriarchy. For the feminist cause, it was important to expose a secret dimension of continuity between patriarchal and liberal societies. Feminist writers showed in different ways how ownership of women is encoded in liberal societies' notions of love and romance, of the happy family, of male and female forms of labor, and even of intercourse. What they often stopped short of is exploring the consequences of their discoveries for an economic theory proper to capitalism. The very notion of private property must be rethought if ownership of women is still encoded in various ways in our societies. Private property is not the same institution when it encompasses women *and* things, or, as economics believes, *only* things, or, as is the case with capitalism, *formally* only things and *informally* also women. This book therefore argues that the whole theoretical infrastructure of economic theory must be reworked once sex and the family are included within the economy. A whole set of ontological economic questions needs to be rethought in that light: What is ownership? What is money? What is a market exchange? What are goods and commodities? What is capital? What is finance? Mitchell's argument provides a localized demonstration of this need in the context of money. Economic common sense conceives of money as a universal equalizer: a means to other ends, a standard measure of value that makes all things quantitatively commensurable and supports an all-encompassing sphere of calculability. The family bifurcates this picture. On the side of its making, money is indeed an equalizer that supports comprehensive calculability, although *against* economic common sense in this context it is also an end in itself; on the side of its spending, money is a means to external ends, but these are marked by incalculability and incommensurability. As we shall see, Mitchell's view is too naïve, as the bifurcated aspects of spending and making infiltrate each other. Yet it suffices to demonstrate the aim of this book. By conceiving of money and other economic objects in their entanglements with sex and gender, it proposes the notion of sexual economy as an economic theory appropriate to capitalism.

Why Sexual Economy?

In recent years there has arisen a renewed interest in the idea of libidinal economy. Developed in different versions by thinkers such as Marcuse, Deleuze and Guattari, and Lyotard, libidinal economy designates a psychic counterpart of capitalist economy. It points to structures of desire and eroticism supplementing the workings of capital and underpinning consumer culture. I share this basic motivation of the framework of libidinal economy, yet this book approaches it from the starting point of sexual economy. It is a more concrete starting point. In contrast to libidinal economy, sexual economy refers to the direct entanglements of sex and gender with the economy, beginning with relatively simple questions: Are wives owned? Is marriage a form of exchange? Which economic exchanges between men and women are legitimate, and which are obscene? Why is it obscene to exchange sex for money, and what does it imply about capitalist money? Why is prostitution abhorred in sexually liberal capitalist societies, and how does this abhorrence differ from precapitalist stigmas of prostitution? The turn to such questions aims to fill a gap left open in the framework of libidinal economy. This framework leaves open the question of mediation: how does an economic regime come to be inscribed on the psyche? This question should be answered in terms of an economic theory. If capitalist economy is distinguished by its unique forms of desire, it must be because it is also distinguished by the forms of its basic objects and concepts:

because money, goods, exchange, and ownership have uniquely capitalist forms, distinguished from their precapitalist versions.

To address the various dimensions of the uniqueness of capitalist economy, this book turns to the history of economic thought, which during the twentieth century went through an intellectual catastrophe. From a discipline submerged in philosophical controversies—as it was during most of its modern history, and as it rightly should be, since it addresses the insoluble question "What is a human being?"—economics became a technical field (which does not mean that it lacks a philosophy, but only that it misperceives its own philosophy as a factual truth). In Thomas Kuhn's terminology it became a natural science, organized around a paradigm, which dictates not only how questions are answered, but also which questions can be posed.[2] Sometime during the second half of the twentieth century, economists stopped arguing about the building blocks of the economy, namely, about the proper conceptualizations of money, goods, capital, exchange, and private property. To understand the extent of this intellectual catastrophe, imagine a situation where sociologists unanimously agree on the question of what society is, and literary scholars agree on the question of what literature is. The unpleasant odor of a technocratic society accompanies such imaginings.

My turn to the history of economic thought is thoroughly biased. What the discipline has left out during its crystallization as a science is, as a rule, much more valuable and interesting than what it has kept in. At least for the questions of this book. Marx and Veblen are the most important pillars in the alternative conceptualization of economy I present. Alongside them are three thinkers that once belonged to the field of knowledge of the economy but are no longer present in the discipline: Weber, Sombart, and Mandeville. At first sight, the views of these thinkers seem to differ widely. Once grouped together as alternatives to the mainstream, some similarities in basic principles arise. All of them, in different manners, pave ways to conceive of capitalism as a historical economic regime. They surpass, in different manners, the now established dichotomy between history, colored by notions of contingency, and economics as an abstract and general theory. Their historical sensitivity is expressed in numerous differences from standard economic theory. Without going into details, two general distinctions are paramount. First, these writers open the question of the delineation of economy, of what subject matter belongs in the scope of economic inquiry. A central contested subject is gender relations: the inclusion of the family, marriage, love, sex, and prostitution within the compass of economy. The second distinction of these writers is less apparent and rarely explicitly mentioned. They all provide ways to conceive of what money cannot buy as a crucial economic concept. That is a central axis of the argument in this book: specifically in capitalism, the relation of money to what it cannot or should not buy must be a part of its economic definition. What money cannot buy does not denote something noneconomic, but rather a unique economy that pertains specifically to capitalism. It is positively expressed in economic life: in economic motivations and ends, in the movements of money, and increasingly in the nature of consumer goods (again, a superficial look at advertising confirms this: everything we buy can hold the promise of providing something that money cannot buy).

These two facets provide a compact formulation of my argument: the exclusion of gender relations from the sphere of exchange with the twin rise of liberalism and capitalism did not result in an economy consisting exclusively of inanimate objects. Rather, it transformed the economy, reorienting it around what money cannot buy. It is expressed in the eroticization of various aspects of economic life: of money, goods, capital, and ownership. Their eroticized versions distinctly differ from their standard economic conceptualizations.

Overview

The first chapter of the book presents some basic concepts for a study of the sexual economy of capitalism. These concepts are summoned to outline the unique *topology* of capitalist economy, a strange map in which the family assumes a place of an external inside. The family is external to the market yet internal to the economy. Critical thought tirelessly reiterates the idea that capitalism involves an expansion of market logic to all spheres of life. It is a misleading idea which deeply damaged critical perspectives on capitalism. From a broad historical perspective, the anxiety about the expansion of markets in fact reflects a *narrowing* of the sphere of exchange.

An economy where all things are given to exchange is closer in form to what anthropologists used to call a primitive economy. In such an economy, there is nothing despicable about exchange. It is a noble and uniquely human deed. The capitalist free market was shaped by the exclusion of some things from the sphere of exchange, most notably marriage. This exclusion conferred on the market its odious form, as a context of human activity governed by selfishness and cynicism. A double movement shapes this form: that what is outside the market is now conceived as noble is the flipside of the fact that economic exchange appears ignoble. If these ideas sound strange, consider the cliché that in capitalism everything has a price. What it means is not that the market expands to swallow the whole of social life, but precisely the opposite: that capitalist economy is *not* identical to the market. That everything has a price means that there are things which are related to money, and maybe acquired by money, not through market exchange. The chapter argues that this distinction is relevant to our understanding of the market itself because its outside is reflected inside it, rendering it different from its standard view as a tool of universal leveling, a mechanism that makes all things commensurable. Another linguistic peculiarity, often used in advertising, demonstrates this: the word *priceless* does not necessarily mean "noneconomic." Often, and most typically in advertising, it means "expensive." Again, this does not simply mean that "everything can be bought," but rather that the standard concept of price as grounded on exchange of equivalents is unfit for capitalism.

The second chapter addresses the question of sex in economic thought. What would economics have looked like if it had included sex in its scope? Strangely enough, the question is not at all hypothetical. Two seminal texts from the beginning of modern economic thought allow us to pose it concretely. Adam Smith imagined an economy populated with artisans, laborers, rentiers, and capital owners. His provocative predecessor Bernard Mandeville portrayed a gaudier landscape, consisting also of husbands and wives, prostitutes, and mistresses. The chapter shows that much more than a question of vocabulary is at stake. Two completely different sets of foundations for economic thought, distinguished by the presence or absence of sex, were laid down by Smith and Mandeville. Much later, with the emergence of economic imperialism, sex reentered the scene. The chapter shows that this reemergence of sex is but a completion of its disavowal, which began with Smith's prudish rewriting of Mandeville. It reflects not an interest in sex, but an erotic attachment to economics: a conviction that its models can explain *everything*, that they can explain sex in exactly the same manner that they explain food consumption.

The third and the fourth chapters address, respectively, the twin topics of marriage and prostitution. It is specifically in capitalism that these topics are indeed twinned: when marriage is supposed to be motivated exclusively by love, any pragmatic motivations for marriage (and is there one completely free of them?) might cast on it a suspicion of prostitution in disguise. The chapters explore respectively the economies underlying love-marriage and prostitution as two mirroring forms of what money cannot buy: a sublime form and an obscene one. The third chapter presents the economy of love as subverting the accepted hierarchy between luxuries and needs. Revisiting Sombart's claim about the origin of capitalism in the rise of illicit love, alongside readings of nineteenth-century realist novels and of some courting practices, the chapter shows that love designates an economy where luxury assumes a necessary form. The fourth chapter focuses on the weird monetary aspect of prostitution. If, for male clients, prostitution is a sexual experience mediated by money, it is, at the same time, an experience of money mediated by sex: a monetary experience of sex and an erotic experience of money. As such, prostitution is a symptomatic exception of capitalist economy, diverging from the standard understanding of everyday exchanges, but also embodying a disavowed aspect informing them. Prostitution consummates the fact that in capitalism money can buy *everything*. This fact informs, in one way or another, everything that we buy, but is obscured by the limited nature of those things. As the chapter shows, this status of symptomatic exception explains the prevalent cultural association between prostitution and finance.

The fifth chapter moves from specific contexts of sexual economy to a broader view of the eroticization of consumption as a whole, beyond its direct entanglements in interpersonal gender relationships. For that purpose, it follows the transformations in the economic expressions of what money cannot buy throughout the twentieth century. Its theoretical anchor is Veblen's theory of the leisure class, which provides the most concise tools for understanding what money cannot buy as an economic concept. This concept is embodied in the difference between conspicuous leisure, associated with the lifestyles of old money, and conspicuous consumption, associated with the nouveaux riches. The refined practices of conspicuous leisure are, by definition, what the nouveaux riches strive to imitate but cannot buy. During the twentieth century conspicuous leisure lost most of its economic significance. The chapter shows, however, how a new figure has taken its place: the cool attitude or cool person. These were originally associated with counterculture and rebellion, rather than with social elites, yet the cool attitude inherited the basic features of the social phenomenology of conspicuous leisure: inimitability, effortlessness, and nonchalance, supporting a silent judgmental and exclusionary mechanism. Moreover, in its use in marketing, cool replicated the economic function of conspicuous leisure, as embodying what money cannot buy. Buying something cool is precisely what practically makes it uncool. The rise of cool requires an ontological inquiry into the status of modern consumer goods. Conspicuous leisure could embody what money cannot buy due to its immaterial nature. Set against mere material consumption, it acquired a spiritual quality. In parallel to the dissolution of conspicuous leisure, goods have become increasingly spiritual. The rise of cool in marketing presents a paradox: things that money buys embody also what it cannot buy. They have become ephemeral objects: desirable at one moment but threatening to become a source of embarrassment.

The sixth chapter offers a reversal of perspective: instead of considering the economy from the vantage point of sex, it takes a look at contemporary sexual culture to uncover its economy. Dating practices, hook-up culture, and pornography show how financial logic increasingly informs mainstream versions of male desire and female eroticism. Like the rest of the book, this chapter focuses exclusively on normative heterosexual relations. The omission of any reference to nonheterosexual relations may require an explanation. It results from the historical perspective underlying the argument. Heterosexual monogamy was for centuries a cornerstone of property regimes. Understanding capitalism as a historical economic regime means locating the lines of change, persistence, and most notably persistence-through-change that connect it to these property regimes.

Nonheterosexual relationships did not play an equivalent role in precapitalist economies. That is not to say that the sexual economy of capitalism is irrelevant to contemporary forms of nonheterosexual relations. The demand for the right to marry, which plays a central role in agendas of many gay movements, suggests otherwise. However, it falls outside the scope of the argument of this book to inquire into this.

ONE

What Is Sexual Economy?

THE TERM *SEXUAL ECONOMY* AS I use it in this book comprises two interrelated aspects. The narrower aspect is "the economy of sex." It refers to the economy that informs gender relations and is articulated in courting, love, marriage, prostitution, and more. All these types of relationships between men and women are entangled with economic relations, transactions, and exchanges. They give rise to various economic questions: Who owns or governs the family property? Who pays for a date? Who oversees the family income and consumption? What types of exchange are legitimate and what types are obscene in relationships between men and women? The broader aspect of sexual economy is "the eroticized economy." It refers to the ways goods and money are gendered beyond interpersonal relations—to the manners in which goods are eroticized or invested with sexual and gendered meanings. Commodities are gendered in the simple sense that there are feminine and masculine types of some consumer goods. More broadly, it seems that all goods—iPhones, ice cream, sneakers, cars—can in some sense be eroticized, and as such they require a different understanding than is afforded by the utilitarian, gender-neutral framework of orthodox economics. As eroticized objects they are not just needed or simply enjoyable, but also desired, which is a completely different matter. Even money, despite its abstract and empty nature, or maybe because of it, can be eroticized. As *Billions* protagonist Bobby Axelrod tells Wendy Rhoades, his psychiatrist and the wife of his nemesis: "Being a billionaire, when you walk into a room, is like being a woman with a perfect set of tits." The basic argument of this book is that these two aspects of the sexual economy of capitalism are indeed interrelated: the economy underlying interpersonal gender relations is articulated and expressed in the broader economic sphere, in the eroticization of goods and money. The far-reaching implication of this argument is that fundamental economic objects and concepts assume unique forms in capitalism: capitalist money, goods, and exchange are different from their precapitalist versions, and this difference has to do with their roles in a sexual economy.

The Economy of Sex

The narrower aspect of the topic, namely the economy of sex, can be more easily presented. Let me outline its trajectory in broad strokes, which will be elaborated further on in the book. Every historical economic regime includes an economy of sex. The way societies reproduce their means of subsistence, consume them, and pass them on to subsequent generations is always entangled with the family and the structures of ownership it entails. Economic regimes usually involve gendered divisions of labor within the family and beyond it, as well as legitimate and illegitimate exchanges between women and men. A central distinguishing feature of the economy of sex for any historical economic regime seems to lie in the question of whether wives are owned by husbands. Regarding this question, two narratives outline a break of modern societies from the patriarchal tradition that preceded it. A liberal narrative points to a gradual process through which wives were freed from the explicit or implicit legal status of property of their husbands. Along the lines of what Henry Maine (1861) described as a comprehensive social and political shift from status to contract, marriage came to be perceived as an agreement between two free and autonomous individuals. Another narrative complicates the picture. It is what Stephanie Coontz (2006) calls "the love revolution." According to this narrative, the long-lasting tradition of arranged marriage gave way to marriage motivated by love. In precapitalist patriarchal societies marriages were arranged by family fathers, according to economic considerations in the broad sense of the term: fabricating ties between families, maintaining the economic stability of the household. Starting with the eighteenth century and during the nineteenth century, this tradition gradually lost its dominance to marriage motivated by love between a man and a woman. The story of the love revolution does not contradict the liberal narrative of the shift to contractual relations, but it does pose a certain challenge to it. Our notions of love, and more specifically those of "falling in love," imply a certain loss of conscious will which undermines the idea that marriage can be formalized as a contract.

Some powerful ideas from the feminist tradition suggest a simple explanation of this tension: love is a continuation of patriarchy through other means. Love is indeed alien to the language of contracts, and the gap between them suggests that marriage is an exception to shift to contractual relations. Shulamith Firestone has shown how the language of love and romance encodes relations of domination of women (1971, 146–55). Betty Friedan demonstrates a similar claim with a quote she found in one marketing research report: "The modern bride seeks as a conscious goal that which in many cases her grandmother saw as a blind fate and her mother as slavery: to belong to a man . . . to choose among all possible careers the career of wife-mother-homemaker" (1963, 210). The extensive marketing research she studied had little theoretical intention, yet one finds in it a concise formulation of historical persistence through change. Love did not abolish patriarchy but paradoxically invested it with emotional attachment. Love disavows the patriarchal tradition of ownership of wives at the same time it gives it a new form, in a transformation from a blind fate to something consciously willed. A further advantage of this quote is that it inscribes the persistence of the notion of marriage as possession of a wife on the particulars of the home economy of the 1950s—the reports which Friedan cites at length were oriented toward maintaining the "crucial function ... that women serve as housewives" which is *"to buy more things for the house"* (197).

Other feminist writers have shown how the patriarchal notion of possession of women permeates, in practical and imaginary senses, various aspects of everyday life. Andrea Dworkin has shown how intercourse is imagined, in literature and everyday discourse, as an act of taking possession of a woman. Although the man (meaning his penis) "is buried inside another human being. . . surrounded by strong muscles," it is the woman who is imagined as being possessed: "The normal fuck by a normal man is taken to be an act of invasion and ownership" (Dworkin [1987] 2007, 79–81). That is a blunt formulation, yet the question is whether economics can simply ignore it when it conceptualizes ownership. It would certainly be a difficult task to incorporate it. Arlie Hochschild has argued that women do more "emotion work" than men—both as paid work in the labor market (in professions such as flight attendants) and as unpaid work at home. In the latter case an implicit transaction is involved: women typically depend on men for money, and one way of "repaying their debt is to do extra emotion work—*especially emotion work that affirms, enhances, and celebrates the well-being and status of others*" (Hochschild 1983, 165). It is an "unseen effort, which, like housework, does not quite count as labor but is nevertheless crucial to getting other things done. As with doing housework well, the trick is to erase any evidence of effort, to offer only the clean house and the welcoming smile" (167).

For the feminist cause, it was important to highlight a continuum between patriarchy and liberal societies, to expose those secret lines of infiltration through which patriarchal characteristics keep informing our reality. To apply these feminist insights for an exploration of the unique economy of sex in capitalism, however, a different challenge is at stake. It is not to deny the continuity between capitalism and patriarchy but to trace a clear line of demarcation along this continuum. Love, which in its monogamous form carried the patriarchal worldview into capitalism, also designates the clear economic difference between capitalism and its predecessors. In both capitalist and precapitalist societies, marriage is an important economic institution, with the family being a primary locus of consumption and of the intergenerational transfer of wealth. The clear difference is that in precapitalist societies it was also directly *conceived* in economic terms, whereas with the parallel advance of capitalism and liberalism this possibility has gradually become obscene. An economic theory of capitalism should therefore encompass both love and obscenity.

If we follow Lévi-Strauss's theory of kinship, the tradition of arranged marriage was an instance of the practice of exchange of women, as old as civilization itself. Marriage, for Lévi-Strauss, is not just an economic practice, but the originary form of exchange. The incest taboo, which forbids some women—daughters and sisters—for any man, also makes some other men's daughters and sisters potential wives. This first step away from nature into culture makes possible connections between groups. But let us recall some unsettling formulations of Lévi-Strauss: "Marriage by purchase is a special institution only in its form. In reality, it is only a modality of that basic system analysed by Mauss, according to which, in primitive society and still partially in our own, rights, goods and persons circulate within the group according to a continual mechanism of prestations and counter-prestations" (Lévi-Strauss 1969, 63). Further on the terminology becomes even more scandalous: "It would then be false to say that one exchanges or gives gifts at the same time that one exchanges or gives women. For the woman herself is nothing other than one of these gifts, the supreme gift among those that can only be obtained in the form of reciprocal gifts" (65). What's important in such formulations is the instinctive recoil they arouse in us. We feel offended by the matter-of-fact reference to women as "gifts." Yet, there is something misleading about this recoil. It hides from our sight the fact that we cannot imagine a society where the notion of marriage as an exchange or a purchase of women *does not appear obscene*. It goes without saying that this notion belonged to a patriarchal order, but what makes it alien to our gaze is that it did not necessarily involve a humiliation or degradation of women in the personal sense of those terms. For us, the notion of a purchase of a woman cannot but invoke disturbing sexual associations of sadism, domination, and bondage. These associations belong, of course, to our own gaze. When marriage was directly conceived as an exchange, there were no obscene erotic undertones to it. Faramerz Dabhoiwala quotes Bishop Burnet denouncing fornication and adultery in terms of harms to property: "Men have a property in their wives and daughters, and so to defile one, or corrupt the other, is an unjust and injurious thing" (Dabhoiwala 2013, 119). This inclusion of "wives and daughters" together within the notion of ownership attests that ownership over women does not carry at this stage an erotic meaning, at least not in any way that resembles our own notions of eroticism. It gestures at a *double* transformation between capitalism and traditional societies: a change in the nature of ownership and exchange alongside a change in eroticism.

Lévi-Strauss inserts some observations on modern Western societies, but it seems that in these cases his structuralist creed misleads him. "Not so long ago it was the custom in our society 'to ask for' a young girl in marriage, and the bride's father 'gave' his daughter in marriage." And also: "The 'wedding presents' of our society are obviously to be included in the group of phenomena studied above" (Lévi-Strauss 1969, 63). Wedding gifts or asking for the hand of a girl from her father are indeed vestiges of the notion of marriage as an exchange. That is precisely how they articulate the capitalist difference: they are vestiges. Wedding gifts are no longer a part of a system of exchange but closer to the modern notion of an offering that demands no return, at least not explicitly. In this sense they should more properly be seen as a disavowal of the notion of marriage as exchange.

Love, Marriage, and Prostitution

Mary Wollstonecraft famously described marriage arranged for the sake of convenience as "legal prostitution" ([1790] 1995, 21). That is a uniquely modern idea which captures a conceptual triangle that distinguishes the economy of sex in capitalism: love, marriage, and prostitution. Love is the axis of this triangle. It is within the ideology of love that marriage motivated by practical considerations (and is there a marriage completely free of them?) is suspected as a form of prostitution in disguise. The suspicion is addressed mainly at women. The *Oxford English Dictionary*, for example, defines a "gold-digger" as "a person who dates others purely to extract money from them, in particular a woman who strives to marry a wealthy man." This triangle expresses the economic meaning of marriage today. Marriage is obviously still an economic institution. It may be one of the most important factors that shape people's economic fate. The point is that marriage must not be directed at its economic effects. If it does, it colors the relationship with obscene undertones and renders it akin to prostitution.

To complete the preliminary portrait of the unique economy of sex in capitalism, we need to consider a transformation in the economic status of prostitution that accompanied the change in the economic status of marriage. It is a semi-invisible yet crucial change, which brings us closer to our goal, as it entails a change in the nature of money. Oddly, in relation exclusively to capitalism, money cannot be fully theorized without reference to prostitution. Prostitution was abhorred in many societies. Its prohibition was usually patriarchal in thrust, suggesting anxiety about female sexuality. In precapitalist societies, however, the condemnation of prostitution belonged to the broad realm of sexual ethics, prescribing legitimate and illegitimate sexual practices. Prostitution was often listed together with adultery and fornication and was not clearly distinguishable from them. With the twin progress of capitalism and liberalism, the realm of sexual ethics dramatically narrowed down. Adultery and fornication are no longer obvious moral issues, yet the popular abhorrence of prostitution remains intense. The term *whore* is still an unspeakable insult directed at women. The repugnance toward prostitution went through an invisible shift in its moral backdrop. The grounds for its popular abhorrence today are purely economic, in the broad sense of the term. It is not sex itself that is abhorred but its exchange for money. Strictly speaking, the condemnation of prostitution no longer belongs to the realm of sexual ethics, but to the realm of monetary ethics, specifying what should or should not be done with money. We obviously cannot pinpoint this transformation, but Dabhoiwala provides us with some key coordinates. In the seventeenth century, the popular discourse about prostitution still focused on sexuality: an extensive report on the topic by the journalist John Dunton attempted to prove that whores "gave in to their corrupt nature" (Dabhoiwala 2013, 154). In the eighteenth century, money entered the discourse, when discussions started to present prostitutes as innocent victims of financial necessity. In this new theme, prostitution expresses a certain corrupting power of money.

In our sexually permissive societies, the obscenity still attached to prostitution has to do with money. It is an obscenity of money and should therefore be included in any theoretical definition of money in capitalism. This is highlighted by the suspicion that the male experience of commercial sex, whether pleasurable or shameful, is inherently related to money, and thus signals a unique use of money, different from its use as a means of exchange. A scene in Lauren Greenfield's documentary *Generation Wealth* demonstrates how the pleasure of money is involved with commercial sex. It takes place at a striptease club in Atlanta: the male clients stand amidst the naked dancers, within touching distance, but without actual touch, showering dollar bills on them while they dance. One of them explains the thrill of this masculine experience: "It's the fact that I can throw money on a person . . . and she likes it. There's a rush." Then he adds: "It's no finesse." That is obviously an understatement, yet the question remains of where the unique obscenity of the scene lies. Judged strictly as a sexual practice stripping may in fact seem in some senses a more refined form of sex work: no touch is involved, the earnings are high, and an interviewed dancer explains she is happy with her work ("being average has never been an option for me"). What actually heightens the sense of obscenity is the monetary aspect: the fact that for the customers throwing money is *itself* the sexual pleasure. They find pleasure in the monetary aspect of prostitution without having sex. That money can provide sexual excitation suggests again that capitalist and precapitalist money are not exactly the same kind of object. Moreover, the uniqueness of capitalist money that surfaces here has to do with the way it diverges from the commonsensical economic conception of it as a means of exchange. The obscenity of the striptease show is economic in nature, in the sense that it presents a use of money that cannot be understood in terms of exchange. The money which the male clients frantically throw at the dancers is not paid against a pleasure: it is the thrill itself.

The view of money through its relation to prostitution may pertain to capitalist economy as a whole. The best evidence for this is the prevalent derogatory use of the term *prostitution* to describe economic conduct that is not strictly sexual. People are said to "prostitute themselves" when they sell something that should not be sold. In this metaphorical expansion of the term, sex emerges as the paradigmatic form of the obscene nature of money as such.

What Money Can't Buy

This preliminary outline of the economy of sex already points at a possible way to theorize capitalism in its distinction from precapitalist economies. It is best described in terms of topology: in capitalism, marriage was excluded from the sphere of exchange, as this sphere has become subsumed under the concept of the market. Yet marriage still belongs to the economy in the broad sense of the term, namely the organization of social production, consumption, and regeneration. Gender relations occupy a position of an external inside of the economy: external to the market but nonetheless internal to the economy. Here lies the challenge that the economy of sex poses for economic theory. Capitalist economy includes an obscene supplement: a realm of economy which must not be named as such, a realm where the functioning of the economy depends on its remaining partly masked. The family is the prototype of this realm. The boundaries of this realm, however, are unclear, and as we shall see it keeps infiltrating the market economy, whenever sex and eroticism emerge there. Economists model their views of money on the market, where it can be conceived (erroneously) as a neutral medium and a universal equalizer. Outside the market, in its involvement with sex, love, and eroticism, this very same money is an obscene object, which calls for a different economic conceptualization.

This description goes against the familiar tendency to portray the capitalist market as an ever-expanding swamp threatening to swallow the whole of society. In *What Money Can't Buy*, Michael Sandel argues that in contemporary societies "almost everything can be sold and bought" (2013, 5). The market economy, he writes, generated unprecedented affluence and prosperity, but the problem is that the sphere of market relations constantly expands and seeps "into aspects of life traditionally governed by nonmarket norms" (7). Sandel explores a wide variety of ethically suspicious goods, from the right to skip the queue for security check at the airport to blood donations. Commoditizing things that should not be bought impairs their integrity and authenticity. One can buy today traditional tokens of friendship, such as a wedding toast, but one cannot really buy a friend: "The money that buys the friendship dissolves it, or turns it into something else" (94).

It is certainly true that money cannot buy real friendship, yet why this is so may be less simple than Sandel seems to think. Is it because of the nature of friendship or because of the nature of money? Set against a broader historical perspective, the antithesis between money and friendship emerges as a distinct consequence of the way capitalist money has restructured the sphere of exchange to its current form of the market. In some sense, capitalism should in truth be defined as an economy where *not* everything is up for sale. A society where everything is susceptible to exchange is closer to what anthropologists call a primitive or gift economy. As Marshall Sahlins explained, "What are in the received wisdom 'non-economic' or 'exogenous' conditions are in the primitive reality the very organization of economy." The circulation of things in a primitive economy is inseparable from the noblest forms of social relations. It is entangled with relations of loyalty, honor, and reciprocity. Exchange also fashions social relationships: "If friends make gifts, gifts make friends" (Sahlins 2017, 169). It is in the primitive economy, rather than in capitalism, that there is no outside to the sphere of exchange. The unimaginable variety of commodities in capitalist economies gave rise to the idea that in capitalism everything can be sold and bought. The correct historical formulation is that in capitalism one can buy many things but not everything, while in precapitalist economies one can purchase much fewer things but can exchange almost everything. That can be the case because exchange and reciprocity are indeed venerable human capacities. In other words, it is not exchange as such that is antithetical to friendship. After all, friends still exchange gifts, although usually not monetary. It is the form that modern money has conferred on exchange, the form of the market, that is opposed to friendship. In the primitive economy the exchange of things concerns more than the things exchanged. Things exchanged are also tokens of friendship, reciprocity, loyalty, honor, and more. That these noble things appear to us as antithetical to the world of exchange should be considered a fundamental fact about our own notions of exchange, dominated as they are by the twin concepts of markets and money. It suggests that capitalist money is entangled with a fundamental transformation of the human notion of exchange. Economists refer to money as a neutral means of exchange. The truth is that, for some reason, in capitalism money is a means of debasement of exchange, and in that sense, we can speak about "capitalist money," which is distinctly different from precapitalist means of exchange.

The title of Sandel's book calls for a second thought. "What money can't buy" can prove to be a most useful phrase provided one reads it correctly. In Sandel's use, this phrase refers to "things"—those things that money can't buy. There are things that money cannot buy because of their inherent qualities. From a broader historical perspective, the phrase should be understood as referring to capitalist money. There are things that money cannot buy, because of some qualities of money no less than of these things. A full definition of money in capitalism should include its relation to both what it ordinarily buys and what it cannot buy. To view what money can't buy as a positive characterization of money, we should note the range of modalities the phrase denotes, which includes impossibilities alongside ethical and social prohibitions. This range points at various manners in which money may be practically involved with what it can't buy: money should not buy X but maybe it does; maybe it acquires it without buying; money may be *suspected* as buying what it should not; it cannot buy X but it may buy a substitute, and so on. That is the meaning of the cliché that in capitalism money can buy everything. The cliché does not mean that everything is marketized. Quite the opposite. It means that the *capitalist economy is not identical with the capitalist market.* Things outside the market are nonetheless included in the economy and as such may involve nonmarket relations with money.

As this book will demonstrate further on, a diverse selection of economic theories, mainly outside the canonical tradition, gestures at the crucial significance of the category of what money can't buy in capitalism. Although it is not often mentioned explicitly, it plays an important role in the economic thought of Marx, Veblen, Weber, and Sombart and appears more incidentally but symptomatically in the works of Adam Smith and Alfred Marshall. In all those cases it emerges as a marker of an economic theory radically different from the orthodox economic framework. To start with a simple example, a direct reference to what money can't buy is found in Marx's early work, in a section about "the power of money" in the *Economic and Philosophical Manuscripts*: "I *am* ugly, but I can buy for myself the most beautiful of women. Therefore, I *am* not *ugly*" ([1959] 1977, 130). The invocation of "buying" here is obviously ironic. It aims to highlight the obscenity of things that money acquires *without* buying: an effect of money beyond exchange. It refers to what the rich man acquires by *having* his money rather than by giving it away in exchange. This claim belongs to the early work of Marx, before the full development of his concept of capital. Yet something of the nature of capital is already foretold here. Capital, for Marx, is not a sum of money, but a process of ongoing increase of value. Capital is value "greater than itself." This notion is foreshadowed in a view of the power of money to acquire a surplus not through exchange. We will return to this idea from various perspectives throughout the book: eroticized money is in some senses already capital. Marx's claim may seem simplistic, yet it entails a theoretical bifurcation of the concept of money. Money modeled on the market is different than money in an economy that includes an obscene supplement to the market. The former is a medium of comprehensive equivalence. The latter subverts the possibility of equivalence.

A strange semantic feature of English captures the wider resonance of this logic in a nutshell: the word *priceless* literally refers to things beyond the economy, but it may also refer to things that are exceedingly, indeterminately, or luxuriously expensive (in advertising, *priceless* typically means luxurious or, more simply, expensive). This semantic oscillation between the economic and the noneconomic senses of the word does not mean that in capitalism everything has its price, but rather that there are economic things that fundamentally subvert the very notion of price.

To clarify the specific relevance of what money can't buy to capitalism and to anchor it in sexual economy, we should turn to the huge gap that the irresponsible comparison between market economy and primitive economy has left open. The European feudal economies that preceded capitalism were also structured around what money can't buy. As an economic category, it referred mainly to lands and class status. In addition, sumptuary laws articulated class distinctions by limiting the purchase of various clothing articles to specific ranks. In this sense what money can't buy was already an economic category before capitalism. But its meaning in feudal economies was diametrically opposed to its meaning in capitalism. In feudalism it referred to the *things* rather than to *money*. There was a specific group of things that money could not buy. And since the prohibition on selling and buying them was unequivocal, this group denoted a *real limitation* on the potential power of money. It denoted an economy consisting of two separate classes of things—things that money could buy and things that it couldn't—with no considerable interchange between the classes. Before capitalism, "what money can't buy" characterized an economy that was not yet fully monetized. In capitalism the same phrase has the opposite significance, denoting an indefinite expansion of the potential power of money. It is a paradoxical form of expansion, which progresses through limits that are inherently traversed. In this lies a further affinity of eroticized money to capital. In the *Grundrisse* Marx presents this form of expansion as a defining feature of capital: "Capital is the endless and limitless drive to go beyond its limiting barrier. Every boundary is and has to be a barrier for it . . . If ever it perceived a certain boundary not as a barrier, but became comfortable within it as a boundary, it would itself have declined from exchange value to use value, from the general form of wealth to a specific, substantial mode of the same" (1973, 334).

The relation of sex to the unique topology of capitalist economy involves some sense of overdetermination. Sex is certainly a primary manifestation of what money can't buy in capitalist economy. This might seem to suggest a causal relation between the exclusion of marriage from the sphere of exchange and the restructuring of this sphere around what money can't buy. But the relation is more complex because the realm of sexuality also provides a distinct *name* for the widespread presence of this category in capitalist economy *beyond* matters of sexuality. This name is prostitution. As a metaphor, prostitution refers to the selling of what should not be sold (one's integrity, values, reputation). This sexual metaphor captures an obscenity inherent in money as such, beyond sexuality: the suspicion that it buys what it should not buy. It is the slippage between the metaphorical and the literal use of the term that characterizes the unique sexual economy of capitalism.

In this slippage sexuality functions as the model for equivocal types of prohibitions entailed with money in its capitalist form, that is, prohibitions implying ways of infringing, bypassing, or overcoming them. In different ways, both Freud and Foucault viewed sexual prohibitions as generative. In psychoanalysis that is a unique characteristic of human sexuality as such. The introjection of the oedipal prohibition can give rise to a series of substitutes which govern the adult's love life (Freud [1910] 1981). In Foucault the generative character of sexual prohibitions is rather a historical phenomenon, characteristic specifically of modern sexuality and manifested most clearly in its entanglement with scientific, political, and juridical discourses. Premodern sexual regimes addressed forms of illicit conduct which could be theoretically, even if not practically, eliminated. Prohibitions of consanguine marriages or the condemnation of adultery attempted to reach their objectives through an "asymptotic decrease" (Foucault 1978, 41). By turning attention to new definitions of illicit conduct, modern practices of power have a unique effect of intensifying what they aim at: the extraordinary effort to suppress manifestations of children's sexuality, for example, "leads one to suspect that what was demanded of it was to persevere, to proliferate to the limits of the visible and the invisible, rather than to disappear for good" (42). Notice that this Foucauldian distinction between premodern and modern power is analogous to the distinction in the significance of what money can't buy between precapitalist and capitalist economies: in the former it limits the uses of money, in the latter it expands them.

Freud and Foucault provide a background to the overdetermined character of the relation between sex and capitalist money. A notion of overdetermination is called for because we cannot answer the question of whether the exclusion of sex from the sphere of exchange has made money obscene, or the other way around: an obscenity of money excluded sex from the realm of legitimate market exchanges. A similar question applies to sex and its prohibitions: is there something unique in sexuality that conjures generative prohibitions? Or is it the opposite: do generative prohibitions sexualize things? In Foucault, the slippage between the two options wears the form of *"perpetual spirals of power and pleasure"*: in its modern form, the power directed at sexuality becomes itself eroticized. "Pleasure spreads to the power that harried it" (Foucault 1978, 45). Some writings of Freud seem to suggest a different view, namely, that sexuality conjures generative prohibitions. *Three Essays on the Theory of Sexuality* shows how mature, genital sexuality is shaped through the introjection of prohibitions on infantile polymorphous perversity. Other works, however, point in the opposite direction. Freud's short, and somewhat comic, essay "On the Sexual Theories of Children" presents the fanciful ideas that children invent to answers questions that their parents evade, like where babies come from. The adult evades a direct answer because matters of sexuality are obscene and unfit for children. The theoretical point, which makes the essay more than anecdotal, is that for the children it is the other way around: things are sexual insofar as they are, for some reasons unknown to them, obscene. Their first interest in sex is summed up in not knowing anything about it but that it is shameful. A similar slippage characterizes prostitution in capitalism, as both a monetized experience of sex and a sexual experience of money. More broadly, this slippage expresses the relation between the two aspects of the sexual economy of capitalism: the way the economy of sex is articulated in an eroticized economy.

From the Economy of Sex to Eroticized Economy

As noted, the main argument of this book is that the economy of sex in capitalism is expressed in a broader context, in the eroticized economy: the way economic objects carry sexual meanings beyond interpersonal relations. The short discussion about prostitution has already led us to a point of contact between the economy of sex and the eroticized economy. In prostitution money is eroticized. The crucial point, however, is that eroticized money behaves differently than the economists' money. Catherine MacKinnon provides, perhaps inadvertently, an elegant formulation of the difference. Prostitution, she argues, is not strictly about male sexual gratification but about sexual domination. In prostitution "some men sell women to other men for intimate access to and power over them" (MacKinnon 2011, 294). MacKinnon qualifies the monetary transaction involved with prostitution with a peculiar phrase: men in prostitution, she writes, "pay for paid sex" (274). This strange phrase expresses the aspect of domination in prostitution abuse. Paying for paid sex means that men pay for "'you do what I say' sex" (294). We should not ignore, however, the peculiar economy that the phrase "paying for paid sex" denotes. It diverges from our most basic concepts of monetary exchange, where one thing, money, is given in return for another thing, a good. In prostitution, if we follow MacKinnon, money appears *on both sides* of the exchange. It is a means of exchange, paid against sex, but it also qualifies the thing it buys. Although aberrant in relation to our most basic economic concepts, MacKinnon's insight is almost tautological in nature (in relation, that is, to capitalist economy): paying money for sex does indeed change dramatically the thing paid for—it turns it to prostitution. The presence of money on both sides of the exchange means, in other words, that prostitution abuse entangles a sexual and a monetary experience: it is an experience of sex shaped by monetary relations, and at the same time an experience of money expressed by sex. On the one hand, it is an experience of sex as a form of domination, expressing the fantasy of full control over a woman. On the other hand, it is an experience of the universal power of money: its power to buy everything, *including* sex.

Prostitution manifests an aberration in relation to the economic outlook. It is important for economic theory, however, because it is not at all an aberration in relation to capitalist economy, but actually closer to its rule. Strange as it may seem, we often, if not always, pay for paid things. Eroticized money and the perverse economy it entails are important keys to the eroticization of the economy as whole, *beyond* interpersonal relations, that is, beyond the relatively focused perspective of the economy of sex.

To demonstrate how, let us consider, at some length, a sexist Jaguar commercial, a somewhat refined version of the vulgar advertising theme of "cars and women." It consists of a series of scenes, alternating between images of Jaguar cars and images of women in various luxurious and high-society settings. A luscious voice-over repeats the word "gorgeous," referring, presumably, to both the car and the women. It lists the qualities that make something "gorgeous": "Gorgeous demands your immediate attention. Gorgeous makes effort look effortless . . . Everyone cares what gorgeous says . . . Gorgeous can't be ordinary even if it tries . . . Gorgeous doesn't care at all what others are doing. Gorgeous was born that way."

The overt sexism of the commercial should not blind us to its accurate exposition of a perverse economic logic. The word *gorgeous*, as the voice-over cares to explain, designates the singular, exceptional, and incomparable. That is the real reason why the commercial conjures images of women to begin with. The Jaguar car, although expensive, is nonetheless a commodity. As such, it is *thoroughly comparable*. It has a price, which measures its value in monetary terms and makes it quantitatively comparable to all other commodities. If we say, for example, that it costs as much as two or three or ten "ordinary" cars, then that's exactly what we do: we compare it. People, in contrast, can be incomparable. The images of women are thus summoned for a paradoxical yet crucial task, namely, *to render the expensive incomparable with the cheap*. It is a paradoxical task because for economic common sense, *expensive* cannot be other than a purely quantitative and comparative term. It is nonetheless crucial if we believe, in contrast to economics, that the economy is theoretically inseparable from society. Any account of the social aspect of economic life must acknowledge that for some reason expensive things signal qualitative distinctions. The images of women in the commercial perform this task of converting *expensive* from a purely quantitative term into a qualitative one. What this means is that they render expensiveness one of the qualities of the car, and presumably its most important one. MacKinnon's paradoxical formula "paying for paid X" recurs here, beyond the economy of sex, in the wider context of eroticized economy. If expensiveness is one of its qualities, then in buying a Jaguar one "pays for a paid car." In the prostitution exchange, it seems as if money subverts standard economic concepts because it is involved with sex. Here the relation is reversed. A perverse form of exchange eroticizes commodities.

Eroticization indicates the workings of a unique economy, featuring relations between goods and money, which markedly differ from ordinary economic conceptualizations. When price is a quality of the commodity, money and goods are not as clearly distinguishable from each other as suggested by their conceptualization through the means-ends dichotomy. They permeate each other. If price is a quality of a commodity, then in some sense that commodity should be considered a quality or a visible form of money. Such a commodity confers visible qualities on abstract money. Eroticized economy necessitates a break with the familiar idea that money homogenizes things through processes of commodification. Even Marx contributed to fashioning this false impression: "Just as in money every qualitative difference between commodities is extinguished, so too for its part, as a radical leveller, it extinguishes all distinctions" (1976, 229). That was Marx's way to indicate how monetary relations infiltrate the social fabric and transform the foundations of social life. Eroticization points at the opposite way in which money transforms social life: not by flattening and erasing qualitative differences, but by turning quantities to qualities.

It is in Marx, however, that we can also find the grounds for theorizing the relation between money and commodities in the eroticized economy. In the third chapter of *Capital*, Marx describes this relation with some erotic metaphors: "Commodities are in love with money" (1976, 202), prices are "wooing glances cast at money by commodities" (205), and the use value of commodities "attracts the gold" (203). The Jaguar commercial seems to explicitly stage these metaphors, showing a car in love with money: images of women standing for the way money permeates the commodity. Yet for Marx these were still only metaphors. In *Capital* he does not have much to say about love, wooing, and attraction (although these recur as metaphors for capital). The metaphors are nonetheless important because they accompany a conceptual claim, which Marx presents as distinguishing his own thought from the work of economists. Economists subsume the relation between money and goods in the concept of exchange. Their exclusive focus on it obscures another relation, which evades them: "If we keep in mind only this material aspect, that is, the exchange of the commodity for gold, we overlook the very thing we ought to observe, namely what has happened to the form of the commodity" (199). Throughout the chapter, Marx uses a host of terms to refer to this other aspect of exchange: "a change of form," "metamorphosis," "conversion," and even "transubstantiation." In what he terms "the material aspect of exchange" things remain what they are and only change hands. But exchange should also be conceived as a change of forms that happens on both sides: on the seller's side a commodity *becomes* money, and on the buyer's side money *becomes* a commodity. "The process of exchange is therefore accomplished through two metamorphoses of opposite yet mutually complementary character—the conversion of the commodity into money, and the re-conversion of the money into a commodity" (200).

To understand how Marx's erotic metaphors came to be visualized in contemporary advertising, we need to inquire into the conceptual claim that accompanies them. It, too, might be dismissed as merely metaphorical. After all, money does not *really* become a commodity in exchange. To understand why Marx sees it as a dividing line between his thought and the work of economists it is crucial to figure out how the idea of conversion can be read literally. If we focus on "the material aspect" of exchange, as Marx writes, we miss the aspect of transformation. That is obviously true: viewed as material objects, money and goods remain exactly the same during exchange. The economists' exclusive focus on this aspect simply means that they conceive of the economy as composed of material objects: everyday discrete objects, identical to how they appear to subjects. This conception of economic objects is the obverse of the conception of the economic subject as autonomous. Discrete objects and discrete subjects imply each other. For Marx, by contrast, the basic object of capitalist economy, namely the commodity, is not a material object. It is always embodied in a material object, but it is not identical to it. It is a commodity, and not simply a good, insofar as it has a "dual character," split due to the concept of value. Commodities have their intrinsic qualities, marked by the concept of use value, which designates what they are for subjects. But their economic fate is determined by the concept of value: the amount of abstract social labor required for their production. In Marx, this concept of value functions like an X-ray photo, unearthing the real economy, foreign to its appearance to people in everyday goods. The idea of a change of form, of "transubstantiation," relies, however, on a further insight of Marx. Value is the innermost principle of capitalist economy, but it does not exactly reside *in* commodities. It takes effect only insofar as it is represented by an external object, namely money. It is an internal principle that governs the movement of commodities while residing outside them. The economists Marx refers to see the market as consisting of two discrete kinds of objects: material goods and money. Goods are exchanged for the money-object simply because it is money. In an X-ray photo of the economy, this relation is reversed: a certain object is money because all other commodities express their value in it. What the economists do not see because of their focus on exchange is "that gold, as a mere commodity, is not money, and that the other commodities through their prices, themselves relate to gold as a medium for expressing their own shape in money" (Marx 1976, 199). The fact that a certain object is money is a fact about the economy as a whole. It resides outside the money object, in the relations of all other commodities to it. From this perspective the notion of "transubstantiation" makes perfect sense. To focus on material exchange is to see money and goods as existing independently of each other. This ignores the fact that what confers on objects their respective roles in exchange, as either money or commodities, is a relationship between them that precedes exchange. From this perspective exchange is also change in the form of appearance of value: at one time as commodity (whose value resides in money) and at another as money (whose moneyness resides in the relation of all other commodities to it). This perspective explains also why Marx uses erotic metaphors to illustrate his argument. To speak of "love" between commodities and money is to turn attention to the prior relation between them which makes each of them what it is, and is therefore realized, consummated, in exchange.

The visualization of Marx's metaphors in advertising suggests, however, that there is more to it, and maybe more than what Marx himself intended. Maybe love, too, is not "just" a metaphor. The dividing line between Marx and the economists can be described in terms of economic subjects and what drives their actions. The economists' focus on discrete material objects is the counterpart of an economy driven by subjective needs. People more or less know their needs and know which objects can satisfy them. Desire is another matter. It can be opaque to the subject possessed by it. For that reason, Marx's theory can incorporate desire alongside needs. As value resides beneath the immediate appearance of economic things, contrasted to their use value, it points at a human drive beyond subjectivity. As value is a quality of commodities residing outside them, it points to a motivating force of the subject that appears external to it. More specifically, Marx's idea of "a change of form" opens the way to conceive of the workings of libido, desire, and eroticism in the economy.

Psychoanalysis perfectly clarifies this distinction. The term *libido* was introduced by Freud through an analogy to hunger: libido is to sex as hunger is to food ([1905] 1981, 135). The analogy, however, fails at its starting point. Libido quickly became distinguished from hunger, as an *energetic* perspective on sexuality (Laplanche and Pontalis 1988, 239–40). The analogy to the concept of energy is most significant, provided, that is, that one completely ignores its scientific aura. In science, energy refers to something that is discernible only insofar as it completely changes its form. It is this conceptual kernel that confers meaning on the idea of libido as energy. Libido is distinguished from hunger in that it has no fixed object that satisfies it but is articulated through transformations. Lacan made this point most explicitly: "The fact that a man may ejaculate upon seeing a slipper does not surprise us . . . But surely no one imagines that a slipper can serve to abate an individual's hunger pangs." Sexual behavior is defined by this susceptibility to transformations. "The element of displacement is an essential mainspring of the set of behaviors related to sexuality." That is what distinguishes sex from other appetites and satisfactions. "The subject's illusory satisfactions are obviously of a different order than the satisfactions that find their object purely and simply in reality. A symptom has never sated hunger or slaked thirst in a lasting manner" (Lacan 2013, 12–13).

This distinction between hunger and libido clarifies the difference between Marx and the economists. For them, the economy consists of objects that are what they are, or in the words of Lacan, of satisfactions "that find their object purely and simply in reality." It is an economy modeled on hunger and eating. In Marx, objects are transitory moments in an unceasing change of form. For that reason, they occupy a dual position, suspended between two conflicting principles of needs and desires. While an economy of needs is grounded on a view of money and goods as discrete objects, libidinal economy relies on a mutual permeation that undercuts their discreteness.

Capital and Its Mirror Image

The potential of a libidinal view of economy is reflected in Marx's conceptualization of money. Throughout *Capital*, Marx repeats the idea that a commodity assumes the function of money by being "excluded" from the world of commodities. This formulation seems similar to the familiar economic myth of the emergence of money from barter. Adam Smith, for example, writes that "every prudent man in every period of society" must have kept "a certain quantity of some one commodity or other, such as he imagined few people would be likely to refuse in exchange for the produce of their industry" ([1776] 2007, 15). Marx's version is distinguished from this in two complementary aspects: first, in his use of "exclusion" to describe the process. The commodity that becomes the general means of exchange is "excluded from the ranks of all other commodities, as being their equivalent" (Marx 1976, 162); and second, this exclusion is performed not by people (Smith's "prudent men") but is the product of a social action of the commodities themselves. "The social action of all other commodities, therefore, sets apart the particular commodity in which they all represent their values" (180). These are complementary aspects of what distinguishes Marx from the economists. Exclusion designates the foreignness of value to subjectivity. It means that a commodity becomes money, the universal embodiment of value, by *casting off* use value. An object is money due to what it lacks, and what it lacks is a connection to immediate lived experience enfolded in the concept of use value. That this process is performed by commodities rather than by people is another reflection of the foreignness of value to subjectivity. Commodities, of course, are but inert objects and cannot perform any "social action." Their so-called action is in truth a unique form of human action: a social action mediated through objects that is irreducible to subjectivity, and thus appears *as if* it is the action of objects. That is the root for a libidinal view of money: money as representing a human drive which cannot be fully subjectivized, an internal drive that remains opaque to the agents themselves.

The conception of money as foreign to subjectivity may seem to imply that Marx's theory lacks a notion of human agency. The truth is that it is a theory of agency uniquely appropriate to sexual desire, which paradoxically tends to appear to active subjects (especially male) as overpowering them. That his conception of money is open to a formulation in terms of desire is evidenced by the fact that money does have a use value, only of a different order than ordinary commodities. In reality, Marx writes, gold is exchange value. "Its use-value appears only ideally in the series of expressions of relative value within which it confronts all the other commodities as the totality of real embodiments of its utility" (Marx 1976, 199). It is a use value of the order of potential, namely the fact that money can buy *everything*. Further on in the chapter, Marx makes explicit the connection between potentiality and desire, arguing that a boundless drive to hoard is embedded already in money. Qualitatively, "money is independent of all limits": a sum of money may be exchanged for an almost unlimited scope of goods. Yet any sum is quantitatively limited: practically, it can purchase a limited choice of objects from its indefinite scope. The contradiction between "the quantitative limitation and the qualitative lack of limitation" is what drives "the hoarder back to his Sisyphean task: accumulation. He is in the same situation as a world conqueror, who discovers a new boundary with each country he annexes" (230–31). A further look at the Jaguar commercial is in place here. The images of women in the commercial attest that the car is a form of appearance of money. Women stand for the use value of money: they stand for "everything" that money can buy. And they stand for it because women are excluded from the sphere of exchange.

The hoarder, however, is not a capitalist. The former hoards wealth simply by avoiding consuming or spending it, while the latter repeatedly throws his wealth to the market to receive it back increased. His action is also mediated through objects which designate its foreignness to subjectivity. In the shortest description possible, capital is the manner in which the lack of use value becomes a positive quality of money. As is well known, capital is first defined as a series of exchanges, or rather transformations, between money and commodities, designated M-C-M: "The transformation of money into commodities, and the re-conversion of commodities into money" (Marx 1976, 248). It is opposed to the "direct form of the circulation of commodities," C-M-C (247). The comparison between the two highlights the fact that in the capital circulation the beginning and end point are qualitatively indistinguishable. "They are both money, and therefore are not qualitatively different use values, for money is precisely the converted form of commodities, in which their particular use-values have been extinguished" (251). For that reason, this form of circulation would be "purposeless and absurd" unless a *quantitative* change occurs, in the form of a bigger sum of money extracted from it: M-C-M'. The lack of use value of money is therefore positively expressed in a drive for limitless accumulation. Capital obviously cannot accumulate by itself, without people managing it. Yet its objective existence necessarily implies agents who act *as if* they are submitting themselves to an alien drive emanating from the objects themselves. It cannot be otherwise, because of the nonhuman drive of capital: endless movement of growth, lacking a possibility of an ultimate goal. That is why Marx refers to the capitalist as a passive medium through which capital realizes its own endless movement. In his first appearance in *Capital*, the capitalist is described as "capital personified and endowed with consciousness and a will"; "His person, or rather his pocket, is the point from which the money starts, and to which it returns" (254). This may be read as a description of capital as a purely impersonal phenomenon. Its impersonal nature is rather a specific form of agency and desire. The capitalist has a subjective purpose, but it is colored by objectivity: "The objective content of the circulation we have been discussing—the valorization of value—is his subjective purpose" (254). His subjectivity is objective in a double sense: first, it is implied from a circulation of objects and for that reason appears as originating outside him; second it marks his desire as a foreign body: an internal drive which cannot be fully subjectivized.

The capitalist's desire is defined through a double negation: neither things nor money are his goal ("Use-values must therefore never be treated as the immediate aim of the capitalist; nor must the profit on any single transaction" [Marx 1976, 254]). It is rather the constant transformation between money and things that defines the capitalist's desire, in an endless movement oriented to "ever more wealth in the abstract" (254). One last look at the Jaguar commercial: eroticized consumer desire mimics the movement of capital. It is not a desire for this or that consumer good. Rather, it is woven into a conversion between money and commodities. Money is the underlying principle of this movement. It is a transformation of money between its abstract and qualified forms; between its form as money proper and as a commodity qualified by its price, a qualitatively expensive commodity. That is money as a libidinal object, desired through its constant change of form. Whereas the capitalist aims neither at money nor at use values, eroticized consumer desire is aimed at both: commodity as embodying the use value of money. It is, of course, a mirror image of capital. While the movement of capital is aimed at the accumulation of abstract wealth, eroticized consumer desire is defined by abstract waste. Buying a commodity whose price is one of its qualities is a pure form of waste. It converts money to a visible form which has lost its primary feature, namely universal exchangeability.

Metaphors, as a rule, play a significant role in Marx's thought. Recall that the pivotal concept of commodity fetishism is grounded on a metaphor, a religious one. "To find an analogy" to the way the products of human labor confront people as independent of them, Marx writes, "we must take flight into the misty realm of religion" (1976, 165). The erotic metaphors of love relations between money and commodities may be unique in that Marx himself does not seem to take them literally. That they are literalized in contemporary consumer culture suggests that metaphors have to do with his unique concept of capitalist economy. It may be that the plurality of metaphors is grounded on the metaphorical nature of money itself, as holding a double relation with commodities: exchange as well as substitution.

Economy of Consumption and Erotic Monogamy

Eroticized consumer desire reflects in an inverted form the drive of capital. Significant implications of this are that consumption may also be an object of economic knowledge and that the economy of consumption is related to that of production. This would have been a trivial observation but for the fact that the canonical tradition of economic thought, as well as Marx, disregard it. For this tradition consumption is the end of economy, located beyond the limit of economic knowledge. This is most evident in relation to the neoclassical framework, which has built an immense theoretical apparatus based almost exclusively on the assumption people buy things because they provide them with "utility" (i.e., pleasure). Utility could have played such a role in this theory on the condition that it is not, in any way, itself an object of economic knowledge. Economists cannot explain what the specific utility of a certain object is. This limitation is not coincidental: it is what allowed the theory to treat price as fully equivalent to utility. Marx shares this self-limitation in the scope of economic knowledge. "It is not what is made but how, and by what instruments of labour, that distinguishes different economic epochs," he writes, and adds in a footnote: "The least important commodities of all for the technological comparison of different epochs of production are articles of real luxury" (Marx 1976, 286). For Marx, when something is bought for consumption, it stops being a commodity: it no longer bears a "dual character" of value *and* use value but becomes solely use value, a useful thing.

The drawback of excluding consumption from the scope of economic knowledge is more evident in relation to Marx. In contrast to mainstream economics, Marx aspired to formulate a historical perspective on the economy, an economic theory pertaining specifically to capitalism. This aim is jeopardized by an exclusive focus on how things are produced, disregarding what is produced. It is as if capitalism exists only in the factory and not all around us: in the shops, inscribed on the things we buy and use, on our desires for them, and more. An exclusive focus on production imposes a limit on the possibility of understanding capitalism as a historical epoch, characterized by its unique ways of life. It is this limit that Walter Benjamin aimed to break in his excursions into nineteenth-century consumer culture in his *Arcades Project*. In one of the theoretical statements scattered through this huge compilation of quotes and details Benjamin explains his motivation. Marx, he wrote, showed how the economy fashions culture—what Benjamin calls "the causal connection between economy and culture." His own mission, in contrast, is to follow what he calls the "thread of expression." "It is not the economic origins of culture that will be presented, but the expression of the economy in its culture" (Benjamin1999, 460).

This notion of expression requires rethinking the concept of economy and its delineation. The traditional Marxist approach to culture through the lens of ideology posits culture as external to the economy as the relatively well-defined realm of the social organization of production (economy that concerns how things are produced rather that what is produced). Expression, by contrast, points to a more internal connection between economy and culture and entails more diffuse boundaries between them. On the one hand, it suggests that there is a sense of economy permeating phenomena we tend to categorize as cultural. On the other hand, the concept of economy also requires reconfiguration to address this function of expression. That is especially true regarding consumer culture. To account for expression, a new type of object must be added to the economic cosmos. What is economy if it includes objects whose function is neither use value nor exchange value but expression? The mirroring of capital in eroticized consumption shows one implication of such objects: they sustain an economy informed not by thrift and accumulation but by pure waste.

Among his explorations of the expression of the economy in its culture, Benjamin follows the erotic undertones of new commercial spaces and practices in nineteenth-century Paris. Some of his insights provide a link between the eroticization of consumption and broader changes in eroticism. In wording that might appear offensive today he writes that "under the dominion of the commodity fetish, the sex appeal of the woman is more or less tinged with the appeal of the commodity" (Benjamin 1999, 345). Following this, a further claim is by now but a trivial observation about advertising: "The modern advertisement shows, from another angle, to what extent the attractions of the woman and those of the commodity can be merged" (345). The importance of these claims lies in their conjunction. The first claim speaks of an objectification of women (and might be suspected as itself objectifying women). The second claim, however, completes its meaning, and should be read as a condition of the possibility of the first. We are accustomed today to speaking of objectification, to the extent that a riddle that surrounds it disappears from our sight: how can objectification be associated with desire? How can treating a woman like an object channel desire rather than mark the end of it? Taken together, the two claims propose an answer: female eroticism can be objectified insofar as the world of objects has become erotic. Objectification of women is possible against the background of feminization of commodities. Attributing an erotic meaning to the fetishism of commodities, Benjamin, in a way, goes both beyond Marx and into Marx. Today it is almost impossible for us to unthink the erotic associations of fetishism, yet for Marx, the concept carried no such meanings, as demonstrated by the unsexy selection of commodities he summoned to demonstrate the concept: a table, linen, iron, coats, and boots. Eroticism, however, emerges by expanding the notion of economy beyond the narrow boundaries of production.

The relevance of Benjamin's view is apparent in the contemporary use of the adjective *hot* for women. This one-dimensional measure gestures already at the presence of economy in eroticism. The structure of commodity fetishism, however, is evident in the adjective *hottest*, such as in a typical list of "50 Hottest Hollywood Bachelorettes."[1] Ubiquitous as it is, the word *hottest* portrays the strangest form of desire, impossible to translate to ordinary terms of interpersonal relations: it interweaves the whole world as mediating the relation to an object of desire. To desire the "hottest" is to desire a woman as embodying all womanhood. The desire for the "hottest" speaks of a drive of limitless increase, which like the drive of capital seems to cancel the possibility of an object of desire. Moreover, the logic of capital is reflected in the indeterminacy of value that the adjective expresses. A list of the "hottest women" is not really meant to reassure us that there are absolutely no "hotter" ones outside it. In this media context, women cannot be simply "hot". To be "hot" they must be described as "hottest" (much like Marx's description of capital as a value greater than itself). Underlying these peculiarities is a social form of male desire. Desire for the hottest cannot but be a desire for what "everybody" desires. The captions that accompany the photographs in this example from MSN spell this out explicitly, inserting "everybody" between the viewer and the object of his desire: "Every guy wants to date her, and every girl wants to friend her"; "Who wouldn't want such a catch on their arm?"; "[her] svelte body has put [her] on everybody's radar again." That is a precise demonstration of commodity fetishism informing eroticism. In Marx, fetishism produces "socio-natural properties" of commodities, where social relations mediated through objects appear as properties of these objects (Marx 1976, 164–65). Price is the most basic example. The price of a commodity is in truth a social relation, expressed as a relation between two objects—a money object and a commodity. The quantitative relation between the two objects encodes a social relation because it reflects the amounts of abstract social labor required for the production of each.[2] In commodity fetishism, price appears not as a relation but as an objective property of the commodity, a "socio-natural" property of it. This inversion accounts for the mystery that commodity fetishism is invoked to explain: how is it that human-made objects confront human beings as external objective forces, shaping their destinies. The same structure of fetishistic inversion applies to the eroticism of the hottest women: their desirability is socially produced as if it is a property of them—as if they are desirable "in themselves," regardless of whether the reader indeed desires them. The captions suggest that they are desired by everyone because they are so "hot," while in truth they are produced as hot when presented as desired by everyone.

Shulamith Firestone argued already in the 1970s that the eroticization of women is a last line of defense of patriarchy. "Women are the only 'love' objects in our society, so much so that women regard *themselves* as erotic" (Firestone 1971, 148). Rather than a quality of *relationships* between people or of human activity, eroticism has become a quality of women. In Firestone's terms, this new type of eroticism is the mode of persistence of patriarchy facing a possibility of a "liberation of women from their biology." Her explanation rests, paradoxically, on a puritan kernel at the heart of an apparent intensification of erotic culture. On the part of men, the erotic regime she presents rests on channeling all sexual pleasures and emotional needs to genital sexuality: "People must never touch others of the same sex, and may touch those of the opposite sex only when preparing for a genital sexual encounter."[3] An exception to this tormenting physical isolation is that a man can sometimes hug children, but they naturally must be *his* children. In other words, what Firestone described can be termed *erotic monogamy*. In place of traditional monogamy articulated in terms of property lineages and procreation, erotic monogamy is folded into formations of passions and desires. It could be distinguished from traditional sexual monogamy along the lines Bataille distinguishes between eroticism and sex. Eroticism, which is unique to human sexuality, is an inner experience (Bataille 1986, 29). It is marked by detachment from the biological function of sex: "a psychological quest independent of the natural goal: reproduction and the desire for children" (11). Strange as it may seem, the raunchy obsession with the "hottest" is but a promiscuous expression of the same puritan kernel that informs erotic monogamy: the hottest woman stands for the whole of the female sex. To desire the hottest is to desire to have all women in one. The lewd, hypersexualized terminology of the "hottest" is not a counterweight to the stale tradition of patriarchal monogamy but its intensification.

The erotic version of monogamy can be conceived as a mode of its persistence beyond its traditional form. It emerges when women are not explicitly owned. In precapitalist monogamy, eroticism tended rather to be conceived as antithetical to marriage. That was the case when monogamy was both a sexual regime and a property regime. In this historical context Montaigne, in a comment that would appear absurd to us, equated a too passionate relation to one's wife with nothing less than incest. "Men do not marry for themselves . . . they marry as much or more for their posterity and family," and therefore "it is a kind of incest to employ in this venerable and sacred alliance the heat and extravagance of amorous licence"

(Montaigne 1958, 646). A woman who cannot be owned is the object of erotic monogamy. The loosening of the immediate connection between sex and property regimes marks the emergence of eroticism. The detachment from an economic-sexual goal (reproduction, children, succession) is, to follow Bataille, the starting point of eroticism. But eroticism does not mean that sexuality is excluded from the economy. It could have been, had it replaced monogamy, rather than infiltrating into it. Erotic monogamy designates the inclusion of eroticism within the economy, but in a different form. Its detachment from a goal marks its affinity to capital. Hotness is the manifestation of this affinity: a woman can always be hotter; a man can strive to get the hottest.

On the part of women, the erotic regime Firestone describes results in what she calls "sex privatization": the "confusion of one's sexuality with one's individuality." Female inferiority is maintained by instilling in women the belief that what they have in common with other women is precisely what makes each of them different. That is how a woman's sexuality "becomes synonymous with her individuality" (Firestone 1971, 149). The logic of value permeates this form of eroticism, grounded on commensurating the incommensurable. Being "erotic" means excelling in being a woman. It both expresses and conceals the logic of value by sustaining a notion of individuality grounded on generality.

Eroticization of Ownership

That wives are not owned means that ownership in capitalism is eroticized. A perfect demonstration of this is found in Walter Benn Michaels's illuminating reading of Leopold von Sacher-Masoch's *Venus in Furs*. At the heart of the novella lies a contract: a contract that fulfils the wish of the male protagonist Severin to become a slave of his beautiful lover Wanda. Contractual relations between free individuals also form the basis of the capitalist organization of production and distinguish capitalism from feudal economies. As Marx notes, to sell labor-power as a commodity, its possessor, the worker "must have it at his disposal, he must be the free proprietor of his own labour-capacity, hence of his person" (1976, 272). In Michaels's reading, the slavery contract between Severin and Wanda is not an aberration in relation to liberal society but a consummation of the modern notion of contract. In a society grounded on contractual relations, any external limitation on contracts is perceived as restricting the freedom of contract. This freedom must include the right to forfeit freedom itself. Within legal discourse this paradox emerged around the question of peonage, which conferred a contractual form on slavery, by compelling ostensibly free workers to pay off debts with work. Legal arguments for limiting peonage contracts on grounds of human rights could be interpreted, and at times were indeed interpreted, as restricting the rights of individuals to freely forfeit their rights. In a society grounded on contract, as Michaels writes, freedom is an end in itself and for that reason susceptible to turn into tyranny.

The masochistic contract is a unique expression of this paradox, mapping it onto the terrain of pleasures and desires. Allegedly foreign to the legal discourse, it thus constitutes a unique vantage point on it. It discloses a secret language of capitalism: "The masochist loves what the capitalist loves: the freedom to buy and sell, the inalienable right to alienate" (Michaels 1987, 133). Masochistic pleasures mark an axis of both continuity and break with precapitalist society, a historical narrative of persistence through change. Wanda's imagination is excited by the thought of the pleasures that slavery afforded in the ancient world, but Michaels notes that the pleasure of domination portrayed in the novel is thoroughly different than these. "The ancient world's freedom of pleasure made possible only by slavery has been transmogrified into a pleasure available to no one in that ancient world, the pleasure of buying and selling in a free market" (129).

In Michaels's reading the masochistic contract is symptomatic of the contractual society. To see how it expresses the eroticization of ownership, let us consider closely the story of Severin's enslavement. The first encounters between Severin and Wanda are replete with philosophical discussions about the nature of love, marriage, sensuality, freedom, and more. At first sight, these might be dismissed as superficial rationalizations obscuring Severin's masochistic desire. But along the lines of Žižek's maxim that "the Unconscious is outside, not hidden in any unfathomable depths" (1997, 1), it is in these discussions that the real of history expresses itself in Severin's desire. His reasoning appears formal in nature, but it unearths the historical background against which his perversity makes sense.

Wanda is a free spirit and despises Christian morality, hostile to "nature and its innocent instincts." Her libertine attitude excites Severin even more ("Yes, madam, you belong on Mount Olympus"), but it also deters him ("The idea of sharing a woman with others" is "revolting" to men). This manifestation of bourgeois mentality by Severin only intensifies Wanda's scorn of institutions and men who seek "to bury woman like some treasure." No ceremonies, oaths, and contracts can secure the permanence of love, "the most changeable element in our transient lives" (Deleuze and von Sacher-Masoch 1989, 159–60). As their encounters proceed, however, Wanda softens her attitude and offers a compromise: she will give Severin a year trial, throughout which they will live as husband and wife, and if during that time he wins her love she will belong to him for life. In their next meeting, ten days later, Severin confronts Wanda with the choice, to take him as either a husband or a slave. "I love you with all my soul, with all my senses. You are necessary to my very existence, you and all that emanates from you. You must choose: make of me what you will, your husband or your slave" (171).

This should be read in the most literal way: in Severin's formulation, masochism is second best to marriage. It is not a revolt against bourgeois mentality. In a sense, Severin's true desire is to marry Wanda, and masochism is a compromise, an indirect way to realize his desire. It is a solution to a problem raised by the entanglement of love and marriage. Severin wants the unconditional ownership that marriage traditionally provided, but he wants it cast in the form of love and sensuality ("the most changeable element in our transient lives" in Wanda's words). Giving himself as a slave is his only way to integrate the two conflicting demands of unconditional ownership and love. The impossibility of unconditional ownership confers on ownership its erotic quality.

After deciding on the slavery choice, it is Wanda who demands that they sign a contract. Initially she plans that they travel to Constantinople, where slavery is still in custom. Later she changes her mind and decides that they will stay in Europe. Her explanation deserves close attention because it shows how eroticism expresses the historical change in the ownership regime entailed by capitalism: "What is the point of having a slave in a country where slavery is common practice? I want to be the only one to own a slave. If we live in a cultivated, sensible, Philistine society, then you will belong to me, not by law, right or power, but purely on account of my beauty and of my whole being. The idea is most exciting" (Deleuze and von Sacher-Masoch 1989, 197).

The slavery contract assumes its erotic meaning to the fullest in Europe rather than Constantinople. In Europe it consummates the exclusivity inherent in ownership as such: having what no one else has. Moreover, the contract is erotic (a "most exciting" idea) when contractual relations mark a break with the past. It is erotic when it is severed from the traditional historical arrangements that maintained slavery like law, right, and power. Wanda's desire encodes the grand historical transformation from feudalism to capitalism. In Žižek's reading, Marx analyzes this transformation in terms of repression: "With the establishment of bourgeois society, the [feudal] relations of domination and servitude are repressed" ([1989] 2008, 22). Domination is formally abolished in a society where everyone is equal before the law, yet people still live off the work of others, in mechanisms mediated through the market, money, and commodities. The eroticism of the slavery contract marks a return of the repressed. It brings to the fore the historical legacy that contracts maintain through repression.

Severin eventually learns his lesson. When the narrator of the novel meets him, Severin already possesses his own female slaves whom he whips when they are not quick enough to obey his commands. In his last words to the narrator, he explains why: "There is only one alternative: to be the hammer or the anvil. . . . whoever allows himself to be whipped deserves to be whipped" (Deleuze and von Sacher-Masoch 1989, 269). But immediately preceding this blatant truth is a didactic feminist idea, which against the background of this story of cruelty cannot but strike the reader as highly artificial: "Woman, as Nature created her and as man up to now has found her attractive, is man's enemy; she can be his slave or his mistress but never his companion. This she can only be when she has the same rights as he and is his equal in education and work." This too should be taken at face value: relations of domination are embedded in the ways men find women attractive, because love does not mark a break with the patriarchal tradition but its reformulation in erotic terms.

The latest blockbuster in BDSM literature, E. L. James's *Fifty Shades* trilogy is of a lesser literary value than von Sacher-Masoch's work. This may result from the fact that it brings the economic background of sexual domination too close to the surface. Embedding it in the atmosphere of consumer culture also highlights the connection of sexual domination to mainstream culture. The publishing industry has baptized the trilogy with the strange diminutive "mommy pornography"—a phrase that refers to its suburban female readership and to its strange mix of schmaltzy romance with the language of submission contracts. It also qualifies the trilogy as somehow lesser than "proper pornography." It can be read, however, as a fine example of pornography of money and finance. As James has revealed in an interview, her books were originally written as fan fiction of the vampire series *Twilight*. In the published version, the handsome vampire Edward Cullen is replaced by the young billionaire Christian Grey ("the epitome of male beauty" as Anastasia "Ana" Steele, the heroine and first-person narrator of the book, describes him) thus echoing the familiar image of finance as a parasite.

"It's too erotic. I'm going to combust" (Ana, thinking of eroticism during sex). Throughout the novel, Ana is in a constant state of hyperexcitation and shock: of Grey's "breathtaking" beauty, of her attraction to him, of his obscene demand to make her his property. More or less the same vocabulary is used to express her shock and excitation of commodities: of the gifts he gives her (most of them mentioned as their brand name: a two-door compact Audi; a MacBook Pro, "sleek and silver and rather beautiful"; "What has Christian sent me now? . . . It's a BlackBerry. My heart sinks further" [James 2012, 266]); and of the signals of wealth surrounding him—his helicopter, his plane, the design of his office and apartment, his cars (when they're riding in his "sleek" Audi R8 Spyder, people stare at them. "For a moment, I think it's at him . . . and then a very paranoid part thinks everyone is looking at me because they know what I've been doing during the last twelve hours, but finally, I realize it's the car" [135]). The monotonous erotic tension of the book is the counterpart of Ana's sexual innocence. It is produced by her as a naïve narrator, unable to understand her own feelings, as well as the atmosphere of sexual domination blended within her own descriptions of Grey's economic power.[4]

The first encounter between Ana and Grey takes place in his spacious office, at the top the twenty-floor building of his company. On her way there Ana must pass through three young blonde women: the first blonde is very attractive and groomed and, wearing "the sharpest charcoal suit jacket and white shirt I have ever seen," she "looks immaculate"; the second blonde is "dressed impeccably in black and white"; the third blonde is "elegant and flawlessly dressed." As she gets beyond the blonde harem and finally meets Grey, they shake hands: "As our fingers touch, I feel an odd exhilarating shiver run through me. I withdraw my hand hastily, embarrassed. Must be static. I blink rapidly, my eyelids matching my heart rate." Coming out of the building Ana explicates the intermingling of eroticism and economic power, just in case some readers haven't noticed it already: "No man has ever affected me the way Christian Grey has, and I cannot fathom why. Is it his looks? His civility? Wealth? Power? I don't understand my irrational reaction" (James 2012, 11).

To see the intermingling of eroticism and economy, consider an awkward foreshadowing of the plotline in the first encounter between Grey and Ana. She has arrived at his office to interview him for the student newspaper of her university. She doesn't know much about him and volunteered to come in place of her friend, the newspaper's editor who fell ill. She mostly reads to him the questions her friend prepared in advance. At the end of their interview, Ana asks Grey whether he has a philosophy:

> "I don't have a philosophy as such. Maybe a guiding principle—Carnegie's: 'A man who acquires the ability to take full possession of his own mind may take possession of anything else to which he is justly entitled.' I'm very singular, driven. I like control—of myself and those around me."
>
> "So you want to possess things?"...
>
> "I want to deserve to possess them, but yes, bottom line, I do."
>
> "You sound like the ultimate consumer."
>
> "I am." He smiles, but the smile doesn't touch his eyes. Again this is at odds with someone who wants to feed the world, so I can't help thinking that we're talking about something else, but I'm absolutely mystified as to what it is. I swallow hard. The temperature in the room is rising or maybe it's just me. (James 2012, 9)

We readers know perfectly well what this "something else" is that they are talking about. Grey's confession that he wants to possess things is an awkward foreshadowing of his perverse desire to possess women. He wants to possess women as things, or maybe not exactly as things: he wants to "deserve to possess" them, a strange phrase which receives its meaning throughout the main plotline of the book—the tiring negotiations between Ana and Grey over the contract through which she will intentionally make herself his property ("The Submissive accepts the Dominant as her master, with the understanding that she is now the property of the Dominant, to be dealt with as the Dominant pleases during the Term generally but specifically during the Allotted Times and any additional agreed allotted times" [James 2012, 89]). Simplistic as it is, or rather because it is so simplistic, this moment deserves a second look. How can a banal confession of the "ultimate consumer's" desire to possess things foreshadow the perverse desire to dominate women? When the book is read as a pornography of money, the question disappears. The desire to possess things can foreshadow a perverse erotic desire because from the perspective of economics this desire is itself obscene, a theoretical perversion. The desire to own things may seem ubiquitous in everyday consumer culture, but the telling point is that it is unintelligible from the perspective of mainstream economics and economic common sense. Ownership of things grants us the legal right to use and enjoy them—enjoyment that at some stage in the history of economics was euphemistically termed "utility"—but for that very reason it cannot be desired for itself. Economics keeps telling us that we want to own things in order to enjoy them, not as an end in itself. This omission is entailed in the basic theoretical choices of economics: its individualistic framework and the distinction between economy and society. Accounting for a pleasure in ownership must insert a social dimension into our relation to our belongings: it cannot but be grounded on the exclusivity of ownership, as a pleasure of the fact that others do not have what we have. It is a pleasure of our things situated beyond them.

The strange phrase that Grey uses, "to deserve to possess things," underscores the impossible status of the pleasure of ownership. To deserve to possess means that possessions are situated in the moral and social realm. It expresses a too intimate relation to things and sets them against a horizon of expectations they cannot fulfill. To deserve to possess things means that things are supposed to affirm one's internal worth and value. Exaggerated as these expectations are, they do capture an essential aspect of contemporary consumer culture. That is precisely how Don Draper defines the promises of happiness in advertising in *Mad Men*: "It's a billboard on the side of the road that screams with reassurance that whatever you're doing, it's okay. You are okay." Luxury advertising, in particular, spells out the ethical promise of consumption in countless variations of a basic formula: "You deserve it!" To read the *Fifty Shades trilogy* as a pornography of money is to take Grey's insinuation literally: he is, indeed, "the ultimate consumer." It is not that he wants to possess women as things. He wants to possess things in the full and impossible sense of the term, and only women can fulfill his expectations from things. Only women can want to be possessed by him: reassure him that he deserves to possess them and that perverse as he is, he is okay.

Sexual Economics

How do we conceptualize the sexual economy of capitalism in terms of economic theory? In their entanglement with sex, love, marriage, and eroticism, basic economic objects and practices, such as money, commodities, and exchange, differ from the way they are conceptualized in the commonsensical orthodox economic framework. How can we account for them within the confines of an unorthodox economic theory?

To advance carefully it is best to start from the relatively narrow question of the relation between money and prostitution, in the literal and metaphorical senses of the term. Marx sometimes considers money in this metaphorical register: "Prostitution is only a particular expression of the universal prostitution of the worker" (1988, 100), and money "is the common whore, the common pimp of people and nations" (138). Benjamin focuses on the literal aspect, claiming that in prostitution money has a "dialectical function," different from its everyday uses. The exchange between clients and prostitutes, he writes, cannot be apprehended if money is thought of only as a means of payment. "It buys pleasure and at the same time becomes an expression of shame." In the exchange involved "impudence throws the first coin onto the table, and shame pays out a hundred more to cover it" (Benjamin 1999, 492). One pays for sex and pays more for the shame of paying for sex. A streak of romanticizing prostitution separates Benjamin form MacKinnon's view of prostitution as a form of domination (one thinks of the stereotype of the good-hearted whore initiating shy youth into the world of sex). Yet both of them point at the same way prostitution diverts money from its standard conceptualization. They point at different forms of "paying for paid sex."

To develop a conceptualization of money from the perspective of prostitution, I want to start with a strange argument of Adam Smith. The next chapter addresses Smith at length, demonstrating the effects that the disavowal of sex had in shaping the mainstream economic outlook. As Albert Hirschman has shown, Smith ignores the workings of passions in the economy, substituting them with the bland concepts of interests and advantages (1977, 19). This, however, may be the reason why in a rare reference of his to the topic, one finds in Smith the most concise formulation of sexual economy. The term *prostitution* appears twice throughout *The Wealth of Nations*. The first occurrence is metaphorical and invoked in order to explain away an exception to the law of value which holds a pivotal place in Smith's thought—the claim that economic value reflects the amount of labor invested in the production of goods. The exception Smith refers to is the "exorbitant rewards" paid to opera singers, dancers, and players, which bear no proportion to the amount of labor they invest in performance and practice. Let me quote the argument in full, since with it Smith comes closer to understanding capitalism more than anywhere else in his book:

> There are some very agreeable and beautiful talents, of which the possession commands a certain sort of admiration, but of which the exercise, for the sake of gain, is considered, whether from reason or prejudice, as a sort of public prostitution. The pecuniary recompence, therefore, of those who exercise them in this manner, must be sufficient, not only to pay for the time, labour, and expense of acquiring the talents, but for the discredit which attends the employment of them as the means of subsistence. (Smith [1776] 2007, 70)

A strange economy surfaces here, radically different from the rest of Smith's own theory. To put it in a nutshell: there are things that should not be sold for money, and *therefore* they are expensive. Why does Smith use the term *prostitution* as a metaphor for professional art performance? The passage does not address sex, although acting, singing, or dancing may have an erotic dimension absent from the typical goods one finds in *The Wealth of Nations*. Prostitution, rather, is invoked to name a theoretically perverse economy, a diversion from what Smith conceives as the basic laws governing the economy. Smith may have used the term to dismiss an aberration that need not occupy the thought of sober political economists. Nonetheless, he is accurate in pointing out the stakes in this dismissal. First, what Smith denotes as "public prostitution" represents an expansion of the scope of economy. Singing, dancing, and acting are goods entangled with social and cultural life, in contrast to Smith's focus on need-satisfying goods. His prototypical goods—bread, meat, and beer—can be conceptualized in relation to an isolated individual, whose relation to them, unlike in the case of singing, acting, and dancing, does not imply others. It is this focus on simple asocial goods which allowed Smith, and the canonical tradition after him, to entertain the theoretically absurd distinction between economy and society. The sexual metaphor he uses clarifies that the expansion in the scope of economy is not neutral: the social supplement inverts the laws of "ordinary" economy. Second, this subversion of economic laws is reflected in a unique conceptualization of money. Smith unwittingly achieves a remarkable theoretical innovation: *an accurate economic definition of money as an obscene object*. In the realm designated by "public prostitution" money is not a neutral means of exchange. It is entangled with ethical prohibitions—there are things that money cannot or should not buy—and more importantly it is also the means to *overcome* these prohibitions (these things can be bought with *more* money). Denoting professional singing and dancing as "public prostitution," Smith formulates the strange concept of exchange we have encountered in association with prostitution: an exchange where one pays for paying. It is not the case where people pay more for a good because it is legally or morally sanctioned, as, for example, in buying drugs. The sanction in this case results from the fact of payment. Singing and dancing are, in themselves, beautiful and admirable talents. It is the involvement of money that renders the admirable despicable, which subsequently demands a further payment.

In Benjamin and MacKinnon, the purchase of sex brings about the special economy marked by paying for paying. Smith formulates the inverse connection: an obscenity inherent in money eroticizes certain aspects of economic life. Paying for paying underlies the metaphorical nature of money: a double relation it sustains with goods, both exchanged for them and changing their nature. Smith highlights thus the guiding principle of this book in exploring the sexual economy of capitalism: the way the economy of sex is articulated beyond its limits in a broader eroticized economy.

Smith's conceptualization of money as an obscene object should be taken in the most literal sense. Its obscenity is economically objective. That is to say, it is not a mere "cultural" fact associated with money, in distinction from its objective economic roles (in general, it is doubtful whether such a distinction could be coherently maintained). It should be included in its economic conceptualization (or rather serve as a basis for it) because it marks a particular form of exchange where money is present on both sides. One cannot underestimate the significance of this concept of obscene money. It should have been an axis of an overall transformation in the understanding of capitalist economy. Focusing on asocial, need-satisfying goods, one can conceive of money as a neutral medium, a universal equalizer commensurating all goods, making possible comprehensive calculation of interests. This idea, in turn, is central to how the notion of balance has become an organizing principle of the mainstream economic outlook. The idea of balance permeates mainstream economics at all levels of analysis and has persisted through the paradigm shift from classical to neoclassical economics. In the classical framework, the notion of balance is manifested in the view of exchange as involving equivalent values, in the idea that prices gravitate to their natural level, and, of course, in Smith's "invisible hand." In neoclassical economics balance is embedded in the idea that prices equalize the marginal utility across all consumption of individuals, and on a higher level in the concept of market equilibrium. What should be stressed is that the concept of money as a universal equalizer is disintegrated by Smith in the very act of pointing out exceptions to it. It is meaningless to argue that money is a universal equalizer *except* in cases where it is not. Moreover, as an obscene object, the effects of money are diametrically opposed to the functions economics traditionally attributes to it. "Paying for paying" disrupts equivalence. The presence of money on both sides of exchange precludes its possibility to serve as an abstract measure and a means of calculation. Rather than supporting a view of the economy informed by notions of balance, the concept of obscene money gestures at a notion of economy composed of skewed calculation and disrupted equivalence. It is, rather, an economy *thrown off balance* by money.

Smith's argument is bound to appear to us outdated. Once economics jettisoned—too quickly maybe—the classical concept of value, the question that bothered Smith lost its meaning. Once price is understood as reflecting the pleasure of consumers rather than the labor of producers, there is no longer any mystery in the "exorbitant rewards" paid to singers and dancers. Yet it is not Smith's question that is of interest here but the alternative configuration of money, goods, and exchange that surfaces in it and the fact that it is designated by a sexual metaphor. We can easily find contemporary examples that demonstrate the relevance of this configuration today. The notion of paying for paying, though theoretically perverse, is in fact ubiquitous. It lies at the root of various forms of luxury consumption and even more so in the contemporary blurring of the *distinction* between luxuries and necessities. It seems like the proper economic formulation of the marketing idea of the "shopping experience," where customers pay more for goods to finance the staging of an atmosphere where payment is fun. It is in fact ingrained in marketing as whole. Veblen (1908) grouped marketing together with financial interests, and in contrast to productive capital, as forms of economic activity which create profit at the price of social waste. His rationale is simple but today has disappeared from our sight due to the ubiquity of marketing: the constantly increasing expenditures of firms on marketing are eventually funded by customers, who pay for the labor invested in selling them things.

As in Smith's original example, paying for paying is especially evident in the entanglements of economy and social life. A hilarious advertising parody by the group CollegeHumor demonstrates this most clearly. It is a mock commercial for a brand called "Second Cheapest Wine." The wine is pictured in several social scenes: a man orders it on a date in a restaurant;

a woman chooses it at a wine store for a party and then later gives it to the male host. A luscious faux-luxury-commercial voice-over spells out the obscene economic logic of the brand, a logic that in real life takes effect only by its remaining implicit: "You don't know much about wine, but you do know that you shouldn't get the cheapest. That's why we make it easy for you to get the second cheapest. Second Cheapest Wine is fermented only from the second cheapest grapes. We'd elaborate but you'd have no idea what we're talking about. Second Cheapest Wine is in the front of all wine stores, so you don't have to search while the clerks obviously judge you." The economic principle that the parody demonstrates applies to many social circumstances. Viewed in economic terms, various social circumstances require a form of minimal waste. One can of course waste more than the minimum with an aim of winning the respect of others, but what is more important is that a minimal gesture of waste is essential if only to avoid embarrassment. The parody is clever because it formalizes this social practice in economic terms: it is not the quality of the wine that is at stake, but its price as its basic social quality. In economic terms that is a precise example of paying for paying. The luscious voice-over is crucial. The scenes themselves are not very erotic. The couple at a date seem embarrassed and somewhat bored rather than thrilled when approached by a waiter asking whether they would like wine. As in Smith's argument, eroticism is more of an effect of the form of perverted exchange than a cause of it.

Neoclassical economics has forgone most of the assumptions of the classical framework. It has, however, accentuated the individualistic outlook ingrained in Smith's focus on need-satisfying goods and rejection of social ones. When value, reflecting social production, was replaced by utility or pleasure as the basic theoretical concept, goods have become encapsulated within solipsistic subjectivities. For all theoretical purposes goods are represented by their utility, which is a purely subjective magnitude, unreachable to anyone but the hedonistic subject itself. Smith's delineation of economy, the distinction between "normal" and "aberrant," is replayed at the margins of the discipline. We can see it in Joseph Stiglitz's approach to the question of inequality, unpopular among economists. Stiglitz lists a host of mechanisms that interfere in markets and thus increase inequality. One of the major mechanisms is lobbying conducted by rent-seeking corporations to ensure their disproportional profits. More than 3.2 billion dollars were spent on such lobbying in 2011 alone. The question is what type of fact this is. Two different conceptions of economy ensue from categorizing it as either a political fact or an economic fact. Viewing lobbying as primarily a political fact reconciles it with notions of equilibrium and basic fairness of markets. Markets are fair, and external political interventions distort them. An obvious shortcoming of this categorization is the systematic form of lobbyism: it is not a matter of political contingency that rich monopolies hire skilled lobbyists to keep their profits flowing, but a basic economic reality. Categorizing lobbyism as an economic activity, however, necessitates a comprehensive revision of the concept of economy: of both the scope of economy and its mechanisms. In this alternative conceptualization, economy includes what is external to the market, such as politics and social life, and in parallel it acknowledges the fact that money can make money. More importantly, this difference in delineation is reflected in the fundamentals of the economic worldview. Stiglitz summarizes well the grounds for the belief in the fairness of markets: "Those with higher productivities earned higher incomes that reflected their greater contribution to society. . . . If someone has a scarce and valuable skill, the market will reward him amply, because of his greater contribution to output. If he has no skills, his income will be low" (2012, 30). What in principle escapes this simple and alluring framework is the skill of making money. Such a skill cannot be conceived within the framework of contribution and reward. It is meaningless to say that one is "rewarded" for one's skill of making money—that person simply makes money. And that is precisely the skill that lobbyists lend to rent-seeking corporations, the skill of increasing profits regardless of contribution to output or society. The categorization of lobbyism as external to the core of economics thus combines moral and theoretical grounds (a combination which should not come as a surprise: the canonical tradition of economic thought has always had a moralizing undertone). In this sense it replicates the pattern of Smith's argument, which morally dismisses a theoretical inconveniency. Smith's metaphor of "public prostitution" strictly applies to lobbyism: the work of settings laws and regulations for the management of public affairs is an admirable talent, but it becomes despicable when laws are made for the sake of gain (and professional lobbyism is, of course, a classic case of the modern use of the economic metaphor of prostitution).

Smith's use of the metaphor of public prostitution plays an ambivalent role: it brackets off some part of the economy in order to sustain the harmonic view of the market as inherently balanced, and at the same time it hints that eroticized economy may be the key to understanding this bracketed supplement. Marx's approach is the opposite. At the root of his thought is an insistence not only to include this supplement but to present it as the distinguishing feature of capitalism. As is well known, Marx's critique of his contemporary economists is not grounded on a rejection of the concept of value but rather on pursuing it to its full logical consequences. Marx accepts the supposition that value reflects the amount of social labor required for the production of commodities. He simply insists on the requisite question: if exchange, as a rule, involves equivalent values, then how can it be that value is accumulated in the form of capital? His answer does not rely on an exception to the law of value but rather on its *totalization*. Surplus value can be accounted for when *everything* is included within the sphere of exchange of equivalent values, that is, everything including the special commodity that workers sell to capitalists in the form of their labor power. In this sense Marx follows through the path that Smith dismisses. Smith maintains a notion of economy grounded on equivalence by excluding social life from its scope. By totalizing the notion of exchange of equivalents Marx shows how the system as a whole is thrown off balance. Everything is exchanged according to its value, yet in the total accounting things do not add up: capital accumulates, and some people live off the labor of others.

In the deliberation that leads to his solution, Marx invokes a topology, similar to the one introduced in this chapter: "Capital cannot therefore arise from circulation, and it is equally impossible for it to arise apart from circulation. It must have its origin both in circulation and not in circulation" (1976, 268). Capital cannot originate within circulation where only equivalent values are exchanged. Deviations from the law of value, as when a merchant sells commodities above their value, can explain changes in the distribution of values but not their total increase. Yet, neither can the origin of capital be outside circulation, because here "the commodity-owner only stands in a relation to his own commodity." He can produce values by his own work but not capital in the form of "values which can valorize themselves" (268). The work he has invested in his product creates value in an equivalent amount but not surplus value. The creation of surplus value is situated therefore both inside and outside of the sphere of circulation, or the market. It results from a short circuit, a point of contact between the inside and the outside. In "economistic" terms, it results from the fact that when it becomes a commodity, labor power produces surplus: the value it can produce is greater than its own value, when measured according to the same law of value, that is, by the value invested in reproducing the laborers themselves from one workday to the next. I call this an "economistic" explanation not because it is wrong, but because it blurs the fact that a new type of subject matter has entered economic thought with the concept of surplus value. As Marx notes, "In contrast . . . with the case of other commodities, the determination of the value of labour-power contains a historical and moral element" (275). Surplus value results from the inclusion of a certain outside within the economy: the inclusion in calculation of workers' way of life, their needs, the level of civilization in their country, their habits, and their expectations. The value of commodities, in theory, can be strictly calculated according to labor time. The value of labor, the measure of calculating, cannot itself be calculated in the same way. It refers to the incalculable—habits, expectations, ways of life, and more. Totalizing the economic perspective subverts equivalence from within by including the incalculable within the economy. Sex and the family also belong in this external inside. They emerge from a macro perspective, where the wages of workers need to maintain them not only as individuals but as a population: "The seller of labour-power must perpetuate himself 'in the way that every living individual perpetuates himself, by procreation.' . . . the sum of means of subsistence necessary for the production of labour-power must include the means necessary for the worker's replacements, i.e. his children, in order that this race of peculiar commodity-owners may perpetuate its presence on the market" (275).

Smith and Marx refer to quite different things when they invoke sexuality. Smith's invocation is metaphorical in nature and brings to the fore an obscene undertone that accompanies some sorts of civilized consumption.

Marx's reference is literal and lacks any sign of eroticism: a clinical view of sex designed to include it among the means and conditions of production. The map they outline, however, is similar. The inclusion of sex reconfigures the concept of economy, from one based on notions of balance and harmony to one articulating their systematic disruption. This reconfiguration is reflected in different conceptualizations of the basic components of economic thought: money, goods, and exchange. In the standard view, exchange is grounded on equivalence, and money sustains a web of all-inclusive commensurability and calculability. All-inclusive, that is, on the condition that one omits from it a special domain, the domain of social life that Smith denotes by things that money should not buy, and Marx qualifies as containing a historical and ethical element. Once this domain is included as an external inside, the role of money in this configuration changes: rather than a tool for measuring and calculating, money emerges, paradoxically, as a medium that circumvents the possibility of measurement and calculation. How can we account for the recurrence of this map in such different contexts? Benjamin's idea to seek in culture "the expression" of economy is a possible answer, provided that as expression we include culture, as a special domain, in the economy. In terms introduced in this chapter, Marx's literal and clinical reference to procreation and perpetuation belongs strictly speaking to the economy of sex. Smith's obscene and metaphorical invocation of prostitution shows how the economy of sex is expressed in an eroticized economy. Money of skewed calculation emerges in both domains: capital, money that makes money, on the one side, and obscene money as a form of pure waste, on the other.

TWO

Sex in Economic Thought

WHAT WOULD HAVE ECONOMICS LOOKED LIKE if instead of artisans, workers, and shopkeepers it modeled its theories on prostitutes, lovers, husbands, and wives? What it would have looked like if in addition to shoemakers exchanging goods with bakers it included in its scope courting, marriage life, and desires as they are entangled with economic activity and economic objects? The funny thing is that this question is far from hypothetical. The beginning of modern economic thought in the eighteenth century is marked precisely by this dilemma, drawn over the shift between two seminal texts: Bernard Mandeville's scandalous *Fable of the Bees* and its prudish rewriting in Adam Smith's *Wealth of Nations*. While many of the ideas in these two books may seem at first glance quite similar, their arguments are set in utterly different human environments. For Smith, the generic figure of an economic agent is represented by three characters: the baker, the brewer, and the butcher, recurrently invoked to demonstrate general principles, such as the nature of exchange or the function of money. Mandeville's world is much more vivid and populated, alongside traders and craftsmen, with husbands and wives, prostitutes, and mistresses.[1] Just as Smith is not particularly interested in bread, meat, and beer, it is not sex itself that interests Mandeville. He sometimes refers to prostitutes even in relation to subject matter that is not explicitly sexual. One can dismiss this as a penchant for provocation. This chapter argues otherwise: the suffusion of an erotic atmosphere in Mandeville reflects an alternative theoretical ground for economic thought. A parallel reading of Smith and Mandeville shows how the inclusion of sex is expressed in an alternative economic ontology: alternative conceptions of goods, money, exchange, and more. This chapter thus presents the encounter between them as a scene of primal repression, which shaped the fundamentals of the mainstream economic worldview. Paradoxically, the theoretical implications of this repression became most evident once economics tried to reincorporate sex into its scope, with the rise of economic imperialism, beginning with the work of Gary Becker in the 1970s. As the second part of this chapter shows, it is one thing to bring sex into the scope of economic inquiry after the notion of a genderless generic economic subject has been firmly established, and a completely different thing to establish economic thought on sex and gender to begin with. The reentrance of sex into the economic worldview is in fact the completion of the primary repression of sex: it represents an insistence that nothing differentiates sex from bread, meat, and beer.

Primal Repression

Obscenity as a Theoretical Choice

Thomas Horne described Mandeville's provocative book as "a silent reference point for much of the social thought of the eighteenth century" (1981, 559), and many have pointed out the unacknowledged influence it had on Smith. Both texts revolve around a similar idea, which later became known as the self-regulating market. Both were fascinated by the idea that in the modern market, the self-seeking conduct of individuals propels collective prosperity. Both viewed the economy as a vast impersonal system, where acts of individuals aggregate to bring about unintended consequences. Nevertheless, the differences between their respective elaborations of these ideas are crucial. Albert Hirschman describes the difference in terms of taming or refinement. Mandeville wrote of passions and vices that propel economic activity, and Smith replaced these with the ethically neutral, even if unpleasant, notions of interests and advantage (Hirschman 1977,

19). This substitution no doubt explains the fates of the texts and the ideological roles they eventually assumed.

Smith's formulation of the beneficial effects of self-seeking activity is the celebrated notion of "the invisible hand." Not much else has survived from his thought, after the rise of neoclassical economics in the last third of the nineteenth century. Yet the invisible hand is still invoked, mainly as an ideological trope. Smith provided with it the most efficient justification for the free market and for selfish economic conduct in it. When individuals seek their own benefit, the idea says, they contribute to collective prosperity more than they would have had they intended to. Mandeville's text could not perform this ideological task, not because he opposed the free market, but because he embraced it too enthusiastically. His own familiar phrase, "private vices, public benefits," refers to the necessity of excesses for a thriving market. To quote from the ending of the rhymed parable that opens *The Fable of the Bees*: "Fraud, Luxury and Pride must live, / While we the Benefits receive" (Mandeville 1962, 38). Obviously, this could not have become a hymn of praise for the market. The parable, "The Grumbling Hive: or, Knaves turn'd Honest," which was published separately in 1705, describes through the story of a fabled beehive the contribution of all kinds of sins (including six of the seven deadly sins—lust, pride, gluttony, avarice, sloth, and envy) to a prosperous economy. When honesty descends on the flourishing beehive, its economy collapses. When thieves stop stealing, there is no more need for locksmiths and lawyers. People stop attending taverns, and women are satisfied with one good outfit the whole year. In a self-perpetuating process the economy spirals into a deep recession until finally, "to avoid Extravagance," it "flew into a hollow Tree, / Blest with Content and Honesty" (38). Mandeville's enthusiastic justification of the free market could not be as easily converted as Smith's into an ideological trope. It reverberates in popular culture outlooks on capitalist economy. An example that immediately comes to mind is the figure of Gordon Gekko from Oliver Stone's *Wall Street*, which Amin Samman presents as an example of the way proper names are woven into history, circulating beyond their origin and serving as models for action and for understanding. In the dissemination of Gekko's name beyond the movie, Samman sees a medium through which history "feeds upon itself." While in economics greed is typically presented as a pathology, Gekko's embrace of it serves as a practical model, a diagram of financial activity, "a manipulative drive to differential acquisition, premised on the treatment of psychology as natural, finance as magical, and the law as artificial" (Samman 2019, 126). Gekko spells out explicitly what economics disavows: "Greed, for lack of a better word, is good. Greed is right. Greed works. Greed clarifies, cuts through, and captures the essence of the evolutionary spirit." The difference between the two paths of justification of the market suggests that an inseparably ideological and moralistic drive is embedded within the theoretical foundations of the mainstream in economics. Purging Mandeville's obscene vocabulary, Smith also changed the landscape of economy, the objects and persons populating it. His benign worldview could not withstand any notion of a necessary evil.

The preliminary theoretical difference between Mandeville and Smith concerns the delineation of economy: the scope of economy and of the types of questions applied to it. Smith's choice of baker, brewer, and butcher as generic agents reflects the focus of his economic inquiry on the social organization of production: the division of labor in society and the way labor products are distributed through the market between workers, rentiers, and owners of capital. The husbands, wives, and prostitutes in Mandeville's text reflect, first of all, the inclusion of consumption, alongside production, in the scope of economy. The crucial point is that consumption in Mandeville is also thoroughly social, although in different terms than production. It is social as comparative and competitive, ridden with vices and passions like pride, envy, vanity, and shame. While for Smith economy begins at the doorstep of the family home, for Mandeville the family home is the abode of its own economy, different yet entangled with the economy of production.

Mandeville's is a more open-ended concept of economy, which aims to integrate various levels of inquiry. In the remarks he appended to the fable after its initial success, one finds conventional economic questions, such as whether luxury imports are harmful to the economy, alongside provocative arguments that revolve around a certain type of a moral economy, where vices are inherently entangled with virtues. Thus, for example, prostitution is necessary to "preserve the Hounor of our Wives and Daughters"

(Mandeville 1962, 71), and vice versa, virtuous women unknowingly increase the demand for prostitution (71). Mandeville's remarks also include psychological inquiries about the nature of shame, pride, and other affects. Why do virgins blush at the sound of obscene words? Because they imagine that others guess that they understand them. Such arguments may seem to bear little relevance to any familiar notion of economy. Keeping in mind that they were formulated before the establishing of the classical concept of economy, the challenge is to figure out to which concept they do belong. The blushing virgins attest that it is the mirror image of the mainstream concept, founded on the image of the autonomous subject, who has become known as the *homo economicus*. Mandeville developed an economic theory grounded on *porous subjects*, haunted by their imaginings of others' imagining of them. His economy is both internal and external to the psyche, marked by the constant crossing of the border between them.

Smith does not refer to Mandeville in *The Wealth of Nations*, but in his *Theory of Moral Sentiments* he disparages him as a vulgar writer whose "lively and humorous, though coarse and rustic eloquence" may impress "unskillful" readers ([1759] 1984, 308). Obscene vocabulary, however, is not just a matter of style. For Mandeville, economic knowledge is inherently obscene, because it requires acknowledging a disavowed aspect of social life. Obscenity reflects an economy situated at the crossing of borders: between the home and the market, production and consumption, the external and the psychic. Production and the market are explicit and obvious economic issues. Consumption supplements them, yet there is something obscene in pointing out an economy that permeates it, specifically in its connection to the family home. The crucial point, however, is to consider how this concept of obscene economy is expressed in the context of concrete theoretical questions in an alternative view of economic fundamentals, such as money, exchange, and goods, and in an alternative understanding of the economic system as a whole.

Exchange: People, Objects, and Passions

Both Smith and Mandeville view exchange as beneficial to all parties involved and thus to society as a whole. This is how Smith explains: "It is not from the benevolence of the butcher, the brewer, or the baker that we expect our dinner, but from their regard to their own interest. We address ourselves, not to their humanity, but to their self-love, and never talk to them of our own necessities, but of their advantages" ([1776] 2007, 10). Further on, in a discussion of the role of money, we meet again the baker and the butcher: "The butcher has more meat in his shop than he himself can consume, and the brewer and the baker would each of them be willing to purchase a part of it" (15). That is a powerful scheme for understanding exchange between selfish individuals. So powerful that it seems that mainstream economics has never stepped outside its limits. What is this scheme? X has something that he doesn't need but Y wants and vice versa, so they exchange. That is simple enough, but the crucial point is that so many other entanglements of things, people, and desires are excluded from this scheme: I want what he has, I want what others want, I want others to want what I have, I want him *not* to have what he has. These excluded entanglements of things, people, and desires are the very substance of economy in Mandeville. They are the economic definitions of envy, vanity, and pride that propel a thriving economy and distinguish it from a righteous but stagnating one: "Envy it self, and Vanity / Were Ministers of Industry" (Mandeville 1962, 32).

That is why Hirschman's presentation of the difference between Smith and Mandeville in psychological or anthropological terms is partial. It is not the futile question of "human nature" (whether humans are motivated by interest or by passions) that separates them. What makes a return to them so enlightening is that their different conceptions of the human subject are mapped onto different understandings of economic objects. In Smith, goods mark the clear boundaries of subjects. They are the counterpart of the complete interiority of human desire, of its independence of and externality to others' desires: "Y wants what X has but does not need." That is the significance of Smith's choice of bread, meat, and beer as paradigmatic goods. One's desires for them can be easily imagined as purely internal, having nothing to do with others' desires (and for that reason, it is better to see them as objects of needs rather than desire). Bread, meat, and beer imply a conceptualization of the economic subject as autonomous and asocial.

Mandeville, by contrast, demonstrates the beneficial effects of exchange and self-seeking conduct with an intentionally vulgar example. "A Highwayman having met with a considerable Booty, gives a poor common Harlot, he fancies, Ten Pounds to new-rig her from Top to Toe; is there a spruce Mercer so conscientious that he will refuse to sell her a Thread Sattin, tho' he knew who she was?" (Mandeville 1962, 65–66) The claim encompasses a theft, a gift, and an exchange in one sentence. What joins them together is the trivial insight that money keeps on rolling throughout the economy. The money that the harlot pays for shoes, stockings, and gloves flows to a hundred different tradesmen before the month is over. Mandeville could have demonstrated this principle with bakers, brewers, and butchers like Smith. His choice of obscene subject matter entangles this principle with a different understanding of economic objects. Objects do not stand for the independence of passions but for their interpenetration. Rather than tracing the boundaries of autonomous subjects, objects are interlaced with interpersonal passions. In this economy, objects move together with passions and further stir passions. The highwayman gives money to the harlot to win her affection, and she buys with it a thread satin, an object to be looked at and to arouse others' desires. This view of goods is associated with a view of money as an obscene object. Money is impersonal and uniform. It carries no traces of its past—it "has no smell." Yet it is the complete opposite of the economists' neutral money. Because of its uniformity and impersonality money is the vehicle of passions, making possible the movement of illicit passions across decent society. Money's lack of memory is the secret of the fundamental economic lesson of Mandeville, the transformation of private vices into public benefits. Who contribute to public prosperity? They are certainly not of the virtuous type:

> It is the sensual Courtier that sets no Limits to his Luxury; the Fickle Strumpet that invents new Fashions every Week; the haughty Dutchess that in Equipage, Entertainments, and all her Behaviour would imitate a Princess; the profuse Rake and lavish Heir, that scatter about their Money without Wit or Judgment, buy every thing they see, and either destroy or give it away the next Day; the Covetous and perjur'd Villain that squeez'd an immense Treasure from the Tears of Widows and Orphans, and left the Prodigals the Money to spend. (Mandeville 1962, 178)

The claim is not about the necessity of vice for a healthy society, as some commentators have proposed. It is strictly about money. Without money the provocative list loses coherence. It is only money that can transubstantiate evils to virtues, vices to benefits.

Rather than satisfying solipsistic needs, objects in Mandeville embody intersubjective desires. They are thus the obverse of the porous nature of economic subjects. At one point Mandeville answers a possible objection to his description of the economy as suffused with passions. Some people, he writes, may wear rich clothes simply out of custom, "with all the Indifferency imaginable," contributing nonetheless to the movement of trade. His reply to this objection is brilliant, foretelling Žižek's ([1989] 2008, 31–33) idea that objects can embody subjective qualities which subjects do not experience as such: "It is impossible, that those who trouble their Heads so little with their Dress, could ever have wore those rich Clothes, if both the Stuffs and Fashions had not been first invented to gratify the Vanity of others, who took greater delight in fine Apparel, than they" (Mandeville 1962, 91). Vanity is part of the substance of economy precisely because it takes effect even when subjects do not experience it as a subjective affect. Passions are objectively embedded in goods, regardless of whether their owners indeed experience them. People may wear others' passions. Notice how this insight of Mandeville is crucial for understanding the excesses of consumption in late capitalism. When we hear that someone bought an excessively expensive car, we may think that he did so to impress others. That is, we think he is an idiot: spending tens of thousands of dollars to impress other drivers and passersby whom he will never even meet. Truth be told, he is indeed an idiot, but not of *that* kind. Mandeville's argument provides the ground for a better form of explanation: that person bought the car for whatever subjective reasons he has, yet the car is *objectively* designed to impress other drivers and passersby.

Luxury

The ontological question about the status of objects translates into a clearly defined theoretical dilemma regarding the place of luxury in the economy. Economic common sense, from Smith onward, attributes a marginal status to luxury. This may seem indeed a reasonable presupposition: people, so we are accustomed to think, first satisfy their needs, and if they have enough to spare, may spend their money on luxuries. In a closer look, this line of reasoning is a reflection of the ahistorical nature of the economic mindset, of its inherent blindness to history. Any historical perspective on capitalism must acknowledge the ongoing process of luxuries becoming necessities, to be replaced by new forms of luxury—a process that *in principle* characterizes any economy in constant growth. A historical perspective on capitalism must attribute a primary theoretical role to luxury.

The telling point is that both Smith and Mandeville are somehow aware of this fact, but whereas the latter turns it into a fundamental principle, the former represses it while acknowledging it. If luxury, Mandeville writes, is everything "that is not immediately necessary to make Man subsist as he is a living Creature, there is nothing else to be found in the World" (1962, 77). Smith, fascinated with the immense growth facilitated by the division of labor, makes a similar point in the celebratory conclusion of the first chapter of *The Wealth of Nations*: the personal effects of a day laborer appear to us as extremely simple and coarse, yet "the accommodation of an European prince does not always so much exceed that of an industrious and frugal peasant, as the accommodation of the latter exceeds that of many an African king, the absolute masters of the lives and liberties of ten thousand naked savages" (Smith [1776] 2007, 8). It is hard to see that even the peasant's humble accommodation is in some sense of the term a luxury. One needs to invoke for that purpose an external perspective, a comparison with an African king. That is exactly what draws Smith's attention to this example. It is a luxury which lacks the social quality of luxury, namely, its visual conspicuousness and competitive nature. When it comes to conspicuous luxury, luxury *within* an economy, Smith associates it with barrenness: "Luxury, in the fair sex, while it inflames, perhaps, the passion for enjoyment, seems always to weaken, and frequently to destroy altogether, the powers of generation" (52). It is precisely the social aspect of luxury that bothers Smith: its entanglement with envy and imitation. He spells this out explicitly in listing luxury consumption as the ultimate economic damage of monopolies. Monopoly profits destroy the natural parsimony of merchants and encourage them to consume expensive luxury.

What is worse is that their servants and employees tend to follow their example. As a result, the capital of the country, "instead of increasing, gradually dwindles away, and the quantity of productive labour maintained in it grows every day less and less" (396). Here, again, a moralistic tendency is inseparably embedded in the theoretical framework that Smith bequeathed to mainstream economics. An acknowledgment of the inherently social nature of consumption is expressed in the context of both a moral scandal (luxury and its effects on the desires of subjects) and a theoretical exception (monopoly). Luxury is discarded on moral grounds to create a theoretical framework consisting of asocial goods.

Mandeville, by contrast, renders luxury a primary category of the economy. Paradoxically, it is important because there is no way to define it, at least not it in terms of things and their qualities: either everything or nothing is luxury. In some sense, every product of human labor is luxury, but if we depart from the strict definition of the concept as all that is "not absolutely necessary to keep man alive" then "there is no Luxury at all." The point is that luxury sorts people as it sorts things. That a thing appears to one as luxury characterizes that person rather than the thing. Thus, "neither the World nor the Skill of Man can produce any thing so curious or extravagant, but some most Gracious Sovereign or other, if it either eases or diverts him, will reckon it among the Necessaries of Life." Everyone wants "to keep themselves sweet and clean," but what they mean by this are completely different things that reflect their habits and ways of life, rather than the qualities of objects. "People may go to Church together, and be all of one Mind," but "when they pray for their daily Bread, the Bishop includes several things in that Petition which the Sexton does not think on." Religion unites a community while underneath economy circumvents the possibility of unification. Luxury introduces a fundamental fissure into the economy.

To be sure, in both Smith and Mandeville the concept of economy involves a totalizing outlook, in the sense of viewing it as all-encompassing system governed by laws unique to its own. Yet their forms of totalization are completely different. Smith's disavowal of luxury and his parallel focus on needs gestures at a totalization of the economy as a homogeneous field, populated by selfsame individuals, motivated by more or less the same needs. In Mandeville, by contrast, it is precisely luxury that makes totalization possible: "Luxury employ'd a Million of the Poor, and odious Pride a Million more" (1962, 32). This form of totalization rests on the basic principle that every purchase is a sale. Luxury is ridden with vices such as pride and envy and is constantly suspected of moral corruption, yet its purchase is transformed by the flow of money to the basic needs of the poor. In this version, a social antagonism is the obverse of totalization. Totalization takes effect through ineradicable heterogeneity. In Mandeville's framework, in other words, excesses belong to the very substance of economy.

Today no one would be surprised to learn that what one person considers a necessity is a luxury for another. This insight is embedded in the foundations of neoclassical economics. The principle of diminishing marginal utility stipulates that the more things one has, the less is his enjoyment from any further thing. What is trivial to the rich is luxury to the poor. This economistic formulation, however, circumvents the social aspect of luxury, its entanglement with envy and pride. Commenting about the economic significance of the spending habits of the rich, Thomas Sowell takes care to clarify: "To me, antiques are just old furniture and a stamp that won't get my letter where it is going is just a little piece of paper with some glue on it" (2002, 24). It is no accident that for an economist the spending habits of the rich can only appear bizarre. His mindset cannot account for envy or pride. Strange as it may seem, the imagined economic subject is too selfish for envy, which marks an intense intimate relation to others. As Jon Elster puts it, envy does not mean merely "I want to have what he has" but "I want him not to have what he has, because it makes me feel that I am less" (1991, 49). This slippage between having and being lies at the root of Mandeville's concept of luxury: what people consider luxury reflects who they are. His theory has the simple advantage that it incorporates envy, this fundamental aspect of the lived experience of economy evident to anyone but avowed economists, and accounts for it *as an economic phenomenon*. Envy is necessarily produced by, and fuels, an economy as totalized heterogeneity. Its incorporation in economic thought is made possible by a different articulation of the relation between subjects and objects, or in a conception of the object as a medium of intersecting subjective passions.

Balanced Systems and Systematic Imbalance

Smith and Mandeville are both fascinated by the idea that the economy is a system, a totality governed by its own unique laws. Yet two completely different meanings of the notion of system follow their theoretical choices. Smith inaugurated the idea that a system entails some sort of internal balance. From his perspective, the market economy can be seen as a system *because* it manifests an internal balance. This basic meaning of "system" precedes theorizing. It is a preliminary guide of the theoretical investigation. That is why it persisted through the comprehensive paradigm shift between classical and neoclassical economics, where the notion of balance informs the concept of market equilibrium. Mandeville developed a different idea of system: an inherently imbalanced system, one that reproduces itself through its imbalance.

Smith's fascination with balance is apparent in his arguments that prices of goods gravitate toward their "real" price, measured in labor, and that wages, profits, and rents gravitate toward their natural rates in a given economy. It is worth recalling the mechanism of these arguments. They rely on abstraction, which is another way of saying that they bracket both things and money, putting them outside the kernel of the economic outlook. Money price, for Smith, is only a nominal price because the value of things is defined by the labor invested in their production. Mechanisms of supply and demand constantly push nominal prices toward real prices or values. They similarly push wages, profits, and rents to common respective rates across different branches of production (Smith calls them "natural rates" although he knows that they reflect historical conditions of economies—one more symptom of a disavowal of history). The question of the validity of these arguments is irrelevant for our purposes. What is important is the way a notion of a balanced system is maintained by bracketing both things and money outside theory. Goods are perceived as stand-ins for the labor invested in their production, and their specific thingness becomes irrelevant for economic understanding. One more layer of the conjunction of moralistic and theoretical considerations behind the rejection of luxury surfaces here: luxury is too much of thing for its thingness to be abstracted away.

The most famous notion of balance that Smith develops is the invisible hand that guarantees that when people worry solely for their own benefit, they unintentionally promote the benefit of society. It is important to recall it again, because in a closer look it essentially means that the economy is *not* a system or is such only in a weak sense of the term. What it means is that individuals are not affected by their being in the economy. They go on minding their own business as if the system were not there, and the impersonal system guarantees that everybody's efforts work for the good of society. This is not a system if by that term we mean something that also affects the units that compose it.

That is precisely the meaning of system in Mandeville. Economy is a system because it puts individuals *off balance*. The stuff of economic life—goods entangled with envy, shame, pride, vanity, and lust—is for Mandeville a way of being in a market economy. Because objects mediate *imagined* social relations, they affect being in a market economy marked by a paradoxical synthesis of distance and intimacy: relations to others are both too distant (mediated, uncertain, impersonal) and too close, under one's skin, so to speak (imagined and thus affecting one's view of oneself as belonging to society). This porousness of individuals has a concrete economic significance that gestures at a notion of market economy as a system of inherent imbalance. Mandeville sketches it as a constantly moving social ladder where everyone strives to imitate those above him and distance himself from those below. The poorest laborer's wife in the parish will "half starve herself and her Husband to purchase a secondhand Gown and Petticoat." Shopkeepers imitate merchants. The merchant's wife, "who cannot bear the Assurance of those Mechanicks, flies for refuge to the other End of the Town." At the court, the women of quality are aghast: "This Impudence of the City, they cry, is intolerable." The chain that begins with the laborer's wife's desire for a petticoat escalates until "at last the Prince's great Favourites . . . are forc'd to lay out vast Estates in pompous Equipages, magnificent Furniture, sumptuous Gardens and princely Palaces." While style moves upward, money flows downward, when the construction of those palaces "sets the Poor to Work" (Mandeville 1962, 90–91).

The theatricality of this scenario might be used to dismiss it as whimsical in comparison with Smith's more "theoretical" work, marked by his untiring return to the abstract figures of the baker, the brewer, and the butcher. In truth, the theoretical force of this scenario lies precisely in its theatricality. The concreteness and vividness of Mandeville's depiction reflects a theory that focuses on what Smith intentionally omits from his theory: money and things. It focuses its gaze on the thingness of things and the nothingness of money. It encompasses all too visible things stirring social passions on the one hand, and invisible movements of money, on the other. This economy is indeed a system in this view, but one which is inherently imbalanced. Better yet: it is a system insofar as it is imbalanced. Market economy, when it comprises also what is outside the market—the family home, social life, trends—is a system powered and replicated by the constant imbalances it produces.

Smith's perspective on the economy is essentially static. There are processes in it, but they are invoked to explain how things—wages, interest, profits—return to their natural state. Mandeville's is ineradicably temporal. Growth is not a secondary feature of the economy but its mode of existence. It must grow in order to be what it is. Excesses and passions are the traces of this temporal perspective in any synchronic view of the economy, at any of the moments that comprise its temporal sequence. Maybe because of these unpleasant consequences, the positioning of growth as a first principle was kept out of view in later developments of the discipline. Paul Krugman writes that the question of growth—why it takes place at different rates at different times—is one of the only two great mysteries of economics (1994, 24). It is doubtful whether Mandeville could help him solve the mystery. But maybe the question was bound to become so mysterious after the eradication of the scandalous possibility of inscribing growth in the foundations of economic thought.

The Financial Soul and the Pleasures of Imagination

The primacy of luxury and growth is closely related to a further accepted hierarchy that Mandeville inverts: that between real and financial economy. In Smith, real is the opposite of nominal, a conceptual opposition informing also the contemporary one between financial and real economy. In ordinary language usage, however, *real* is the antonym of *imaginary*.

Mandeville's thought is distinguished in crossing this latter opposition: the good and evil of honor and dishonor are imaginary, "yet there is a Reality in Shame, as it signifies a Passion, that has its proper Symptoms, over-rules our Reason, and requires as much Labour and Self-denial to be subdued, as any of the rest" (1962, 51). The imaginary has real symptoms, some of them economic: movements of goods and money stirred by social passions. Interestingly, Mandeville also situates a notion of finance at a foundational level, inscribed on the human psyche. It informs his central psychological concept of self-love, which should be strictly distinguished from simple egoism. While egoism is associated with an individualistic view of society, self-love is irreducibly social, as it is includes the wish to be honored by real or imaginary others. It grounds a view of social life as inherently hypocritical. It is also founded on a financial metaphor. "The Man of Manners," Mandeville writes, picks for himself the worst part of the dish. His explanation for this invokes the concept of interest: "The Pleasure he receives in reflecting on the Applause which he knows is secretly given him, is to a Proud Man more than an Equivalent for his former Self-denial, and overpays to Self-love with Interest, the loss it sustain'd in his Complaisance to others" (1962, 62).

Mandeville does not really refer here to finance, but this makes it all the more significant that he foretells what became the standard economic explanation of financial interest. More than a century later Alfred Marshall explained: "Human nature being what it is, we are justified in speaking of the interest on capital as the reward of the sacrifice involved in the waiting for the enjoyment of material resources" ([1890] 2013, 193). In both formulations, abstinence is rewarded with interest. What sets them apart is the pleasure of imagining and its unique reality. Marshall's view eradicates both the social and the imaginary from the formula. His explanation is oriented to the real: to reconcile the fact of interest with "the enjoyment of material resources," which the neoclassical theory has rendered the sole substance of economy. One sacrifices enjoyment today to get tomorrow the same type of enjoyment only to a greater measure. In this formula financial interest is a secondary effect laid over the foundational level of real economy: solipsistic subjects and their immediate pleasures of real things. The formula ostensibly introduces a temporal dimension to the hedonistic framework of economics, but in truth it explains away time itself. This formula, in truth, is complete nonsense. It rests on the allegedly commonsensical yet totally absurd idea that one apple today can be compared with two apples tomorrow. Tomorrow's apples are incomparable with today's because they are imaginary. Notice how much more is involved with the familiar hierarchy between real and financial economy: a negation of the reality of imagination, of the social, and of time.

That is the key to the way Mandeville inscribes a financial metaphor on the psychic economy of the individual. Abstinence entails a pleasure of imagining. It is the imagination itself that is pleasurable. It is an inherently social pleasure, springing from "reflecting on the Applause" one knows "is secretly given him." More importantly, the imaginary pleasure is bigger not in magnitude, but because it belongs to a different order. It is bigger *as* social and imaginary rather individualistic and real. One sacrifices real enjoyment for imaginary, and thus *incomparably*, bigger enjoyment.

The standard economic opposition between real and financial masks another opposition, between real and imaginary. The disavowal of the imaginary is the flipside of the view of the financial as secondary to the real. Mandeville's use of a notion of psychic interest does not purport to explain financial interest. Can he nonetheless teach us something about finance? His idea of a surplus pleasure of imagination gestures at an alternative understanding of finance. In the standard view, an investor forgoes the use of money to have more money in the future. Following Mandeville, maybe the correct formulation is that the financier is not simply after more money but after more *than* money (or, in other words, after what money cannot buy). That is the spirit of Gordon Gekko's justification of greed: "Greed, in all of its forms—greed for life, for money, for love, knowledge—has marked the upward surge of mankind." A more theoretical account of this is Weber's argument about the origin of the capitalist spirit in the Protestant ethic. At the heart of Weber's argument is the insight that a ceaseless pursuit of profit can be motivated only by what absolutely transcends the horizon of the economy, namely salvation. Keeping in mind that the immediate background of Luther's schism from Catholicism was a protest against the selling of indulgences by the Church, it is precisely when salvation emerges literally as what cannot be bought that it accompanies an unconditional drive for profit.

Sexual Economy

Beyond apparent similarities, Smith and Mandeville laid down completely different foundations for economic thought. Smith's economy consists of autonomous subjects and need-satisfying objects moving in harmony in an internally balanced system. Mandeville's is organized around various notions of excess: it consists of luxuries alongside necessities, which mark economic subjects as porous, thrown off balance by their imaginings of others. In parallel, these two economies are distinguished by their relation to sex and whether or not it is included in the economy. What is the theoretical relation between sex and the economy suggested by this map? What theoretical place does sex play in Mandeville's thought? These questions are complicated by the variety of ways Mandeville alludes to sex. In some of the examples cited, the family is the locus of a unique economy. Such is the description of the play of imitation and social distancing that begins with the laborer's wife's desire for a secondhand petticoat and ends with "sumptuous Gardens and princely Palaces." In other places it seems that sex is invoked for the sake of provocation, such as in Mandeville's claims that prostitution preserves the honor of wives and that chaste women increase the demand for prostitutes. In still other cases sexual content might seem an arbitrary choice of subject matter: why is it specifically a harlot that the highwayman fancies?

To understand the theoretical role of sex in Mandeville one should begin by taking his provocative style seriously. More precisely, provocation is not just a matter of style, but inherently related to a certain concept of economy and to a way of studying it. Provocation is the result of the act of tracing the economy, of unearthing an economy whose workings rely upon its remaining hidden from sight. Smith's is a righteous theory, harmoniously combining moral and theoretical outlooks, because it limits its view to the "proper realm" of economy, namely the social organization of production. The trouble is that production is inherently tied to consumption. Identifying an economy informing consumption is the root of Mandeville's provocation. It expands the scope of economy to an improper realm: the household. The conjunction of two heterogeneous realms brings about an economic outlook focused on how illicit passions and motivations are woven into the fabric of decent society. Sexual themes and tropes express the nature of this economy as a form of *sublimation*.

In one of his vulgar arguments Mandeville identifies economy with sublimation: "If a Man should tell a Woman, that he could like no body so well to propagate his Species upon, as her self, and that he found a violent Desire that Moment to go about it," he would be called a brute and never be admitted into civil company. That does not mean that he should not conquer his passion. Instead, he can approach the lady's father, "demonstrate his ability splendidly to maintain his daughter," and court her. After their wedding "he obtains what he wanted without having ever ask'd for it," and the next day they receive visitors, and "nobody speaks a word about what they have been doing." Manners and their inherent hypocrisy are economically productive: "By being well bred, we suffer no Abridgement in our sensual Pleasures, but only labour for our mutual Happiness, and assist each other in the luxurious Enjoyment of all worldly Comforts" (Mandeville 1962, 57–58). This vulgar kernel informs household consumption and the way it is eroticized and gendered. "I can make it evident, that with or without Prostitutes, nothing could make amends for the Detriment Trade would sustain, if all those of that Sex, who enjoy the happy State of Matrimony, should act and behave themselves as a sober wise Man could wish them" (143).

A thriving economy requires that women subvert the codes of modesty and complicity formally expected from them. If they do abide by them, the effects would be worse than a plague. Consumption would be diminished by at least a fourth, so that "the Death of half a Million of People could not cause a tenth Part of the Disturbance to the Kingdom, that the same Number of Poor unemploy'd would certainly create" (Mandeville 1962, 143).

An ambivalent message is addressed at women: they are expected to be chaste, obedient, and modest, but it is a grave misfortune if they fulfill these expectations. We are familiar with such messages today and see them as part of the way a patriarchal order is inscribed on the very notions of femininity. The protagonist of Candace Bushnell and Katie Cotugno's *Rules for Being a Girl* protests against this in her school's newspaper:

> Put a little color on your face. Shave your legs. Don't wear too much makeup. Don't wear short skirts ... Don't be a doormat, but God, don't be bossy. Be chill. Be easygoing. Act like one of the guys. Don't *actually* act like one of the guys ... Don't be easy. Don't give it up. Don't be a prude. Don't be cold ... Don't give him the wrong idea. Don't blame him for trying. (Bushnell and Cotugno 2021, 80–81)

In Mandeville the ambivalent message is a specific kind of an economic law, reflecting the place of the family as the point of articulation of the two interlocking and heterogeneous economic orders of production and consumption.

What is sublimated in wives' extravagant consumption, however, is the notion of marriage as ownership. The eroticization of female consumption attests that Mandeville refers to the capitalist version of patriarchy. This becomes clear in his further argument which turns to the husbands and explains why men succumb to their wives' desires for luxury. "Some few Men have a real Passion for their Wives, and are fond of them without reserve," he explains. Others that don't care "love out of Vanity": "They take Delight in a handsome Wife, as a Coxcomb does in a fine Horse, not for the use he makes of it, but because it is His: The Pleasure lies in the consciousness of an uncontrolable Possession, and what follows from it, the Reflexion on the mighty Thoughts he imagines others to have of his Happiness" (Mandeville 1962, 144).

The analogy between wives and horses resonates with perverse eroticism. The telling point, however, is that it expresses a theoretical perversity, an impossible pleasure, unthinkable in standard economic terms. It is the idea that there is a pleasure in ownership as such, apart from the pleasures of use of one's property. The *Oxford Dictionary of Finance and Banking* defines ownership as "rights over property, including rights of possession, exclusive enjoyment, destruction etc." The peculiar phrase "exclusive enjoyment" discloses the problem that ownership poses to economics. The dirty connotations that surround it are important. They reflect the fact that from a standard economic perspective ownership cannot be pleasurable.

People can enjoy their possessions, but enjoyment of ownership itself is an "exclusive enjoyment" in the literal sense: enjoyment of the fact that others *cannot* enjoy one's possessions. The dirty connotations of the phrase attest that some repressed content insists on returning. Economics keeps wishing to reduce ownership to a conceptual couple: a person and a thing. Exclusive enjoyment brings back the irreducibly social nature of ownership. Mandeville's analogy between beautiful wives and fine horses is a form of "exclusive enjoyment" as a pleasure in the imaginings of others' imagining.

More importantly, the analogy between wives and horses is a failed analogy. Its failure designates both an impossibility of ownership and its eroticization. The coxcomb has an "uncontrolable possession" over his horse which the husband does not have. The latter's possession of his wife is manifested rather by succumbing to her demands. In the difference between them, each side of the analogy becomes the secret code of the other. A horse can be fully owned, but it is only a horse. A woman cannot be fully owned, and that is what makes her the ultimate object of ownership. Impossibility fuels the eroticization of ownership, which is then expressed in a perverted economy, where the household, rather than being the abode of thrift and calculation, becomes the locus of excessive consumption. Eroticized ownership is oriented toward an unreachable end: the pleasure of owning a fine horse is oriented toward owning much more than a horse; marriage is eroticized by the unreachable end of complete ownership of a wife. Eroticization renders things as stages in an ongoing process, where full ownership is impossible and thus demands constant display.

Good evidence that Mandeville touches here a key issue of capitalist economy is that Smith also acknowledges the imaginary pleasure of ownership in a way which offsets his economic outlook. It is indicative that he refers to it in *The Theory of Moral Sentiments* rather than in *The Wealth of Nations*, apropos the question of why people pursue wealth beyond the practical use they can make of it. What the rich really want, Smith explains, is "to be observed, to be attended to, to be taken notice of with sympathy, complacency, and approbation" ([1759] 1984, 23). Reading further we learn that this aim of accumulation cannot in truth be realized. Rather, it is substituted with a psychological mechanism, where, as in Mandeville, objects are the medium of imagining others' imaginings. The result is a somewhat pornographic depiction of property which could not have possibly entered Smith's economic work:

> The rich man glories in his riches, because he feels that they naturally draw upon him the attention of the world, and that mankind are disposed to go along with him in all those agreeable emotions with which the advantages of his situation so readily inspire him. At the thought of this, his heart seems to swell and dilate itself within him, and he is fonder of his wealth, upon this account, than for all the other advantages it procures him. The poor man, on the contrary, is ashamed of his poverty. (Smith [1759] 1984, 23)

The pleasure of ownership renders things surfaces on which one imagines the imaginings that others have of oneself. This view of ownership, however, inscribes the logic of capital on property. Like Marx's concept of financial capital as a "value greater than itself" (1976, 257), the pleasure of ownership exceeds the uses that property affords with an imaginary social surplus. The poor man's property expresses the logic of capital in reverse: it is a value smaller than itself. Smith's argument may seem all too familiar to us, a version of the colloquial wisdom that what the rich *really* want is honor or social status. That may well be the case, yet what should be noted is that this trivial observation already diverges from the mainstream economic outlook. It speaks of a benefit from property acquired neither by use nor by exchange, but simply by possessing. Situated beyond both use and exchange, the imaginary pleasure of ownership is one form in which what money cannot buy is articulated in the economy. It refers to what money acquires without buying.

Taken together, these arguments of Smith and Mandeville gesture at a far-reaching theoretical possibility, namely, that goods and property have a uniquely capitalist form, a form that inscribes the logic of capital on everyday things. Both suggest that capitalism may be understood not only as a social system of production of things but is articulated in the nature of the things it produces. The advantage of this view is best demonstrated against the backdrop of Karl Polanyi's ([1944] 2001) influential thesis that market economy emerged through a process that disembedded economy from society. In traditional economies, according to Polanyi, production, consumption, and distribution of goods is inseparable from the fabric of social life. Such economies may *have* markets, in the form of localized, and often monitored institutions, but they are not wholly *organized* as markets. The emergence of the free market as a comprehensive organizing principle of the economy during the first half of the nineteenth century severed the economy from the fabric of social life, wreaking havoc on it until a social reaction set in place defense mechanisms against the lethal effects of blind economic forces. The free market in this view is an effective fiction. It can assume a form of an automatic, self-regulating mechanism on the condition that everything within the confines of economic activity becomes a commodity. For the market to subsume the whole economy, labor, land, and money were made into "fictitious commodities." They are inherently at odds with the nature of commodity, but when they are managed as if they were commodities, the free market can indeed emerge as an overarching autonomous mechanism, operating according to the laws of economics. Polanyi's thesis resonated so forcefully in critical discourse because it seems to capture the antisocial, dehumanizing tendencies attributed to capitalist economy: the utilitarian attitude we assume of our fellow human beings under the guise of economic conduct, our powerlessness vis-à-vis economic considerations and economic forces. Here lies also the conceptual error ingrained deeply in Polanyi's view. Strictly speaking, there cannot be anything "antisocial" in a capitalist economy or for that matter in any human reality. An opposition between social relations and market or economic relations is at bottom untenable. So-called economic relations are but one type of social relations, which cannot be defined in strictly negative terms.

Polanyi's idea of "disembedding," however, can be reformulated in positive terms. One need only substitute "fictitious" with "imaginary" to see this. Calling things "fictitious," Polanyi emphasized an unreal nature of the new commodities that constituted the market. By contrast, the term "imaginary," as Mandeville has understood, refers to a unique mode of reality. For that reason, "imaginary" does not allude to a detachment of the economy from social life. It is a specific mode of sociality of objects, characterized by both the remoteness and closeness of others to oneself. In some senses it is an intensified sociality. Mandeville throughout his writing, and Smith in his exceptional argument about the pleasure of ownership, characterize market economy precisely in this positive sense of disembedding. Goods may be severed from their entanglement with interpersonal relations. But this disembedding marks a form of introjection, a folding of a social aspect into objects, regardless of their involvement in interpersonal relations. This introjection can be understood in complementary subjective and objective senses. In a subjective sense it is signaled by the need of both Smith and Mandeville to insert a psychological mechanism into the relation of ownership: the imagining of others' imaginings of oneself through objects. Whether or not this psychological mechanism follows the crude description of Smith is less important. In a more general formulation, what he alludes to is the way objects mediate one's imagined way of belonging to society when they are severed from interpersonal relations. This also marks the objective sense of disembedding as introjection: objects are oriented to ends they cannot fulfill. In this, everyday objects resonate the endless movement of capital.

The Erotic Disavowal of Sex

In the last third of the nineteenth century a new theoretical framework emerged in economic thought. The neoclassical theory sought to explain the prices of goods as reflecting the enjoyment of satisfaction of consumers from them rather than the labor invested in their production. The new theory, which eventually came to dominate the discipline, has also changed its name, from "political economy" to the more scientific sounding "economics." During its crystallization, Francis Ysidro Edgeworth presented a wild fantasy: an imaginary apparatus he called "hedonimeter." He imagined it as a "psychophysical machine" that registers the precise measure of pleasure experienced by an individual. Wild as it is, this fantasy captures the kernel of the new paradigm which sought to found economic theory on a single principle: the view of the human as a pleasure maximizing organism. It is also a fantasy about economics as a science, freed from the political vestiges of its classical past (the imaginary machine, Edgeworth writes, would grant "the science of pleasure" a similar status to that of "the science of energy"). It is a fantasy about the human being as a measurable scientific object. Let me quote Edgeworth's description in full, its length being a key issue:

From moment to moment the hedonimeter varies; the delicate index now flickering with the flutter of the passions, now steadied by intellectual activity, low sunk whole hours in the neighbourhood of zero, or momentarily springing up towards infinity. The continually indicated height is registered by photographic or other frictionless apparatus upon a uniformly moving vertical plane. Then the quantity of happiness between two epochs is represented by the area contained between the zero-line, perpendiculars thereto at the points corresponding to the epochs, and the curve traced by the index; . . . The integration must be extended from the present to the infinitely future time to constitute the end of pure egoism. (Edgeworth 1881, 101)

Clearly, there is an orgasm in the text. The content explicitly refers to it, describing "the delicate index . . . momentarily springing up towards infinity." More importantly, it is also echoed in the form of the text. The abundance of utterly superfluous details—the movements of the delicate index, the frictionless apparatus, the curve sketched over the vertical plane—disclose an unmistakable pleasure in imagining. The rhythmic change of phrases mimics the up and down movements of the index—"now flickering with the flutter of the passions, now steadied by intellectual activity, low sunk whole hours in the neighbourhood of zero"—leading to a climax.

The hedonimeter, of course, was never built. The crucial step forward of the neoclassical theory was to show that we don't need to build it because we already have it: money can be conceptualized as a perfect hedonimeter. The price we are willing to pay for something measures its marginal utility and equalizes it to the marginal utility of any other good we buy. Nonetheless, Edgeworth's wild fantasy is important because it discloses the distinct features of the anthropology underlying the new theory: pleasure can be reduced to a uniform quantity, and the view from pleasure renders the individual a solipsistic consciousness, seamlessly interfaced with a machine. The hedonimeter, in this respect, is a forerunner of the gruesome "brain in a vat," a favorite theme of some analytic philosophers.

Read as a fantasy—an imaginary scenario that causes immense pleasure—Edgeworth's text undermines the assumptions it is meant to demonstrate. How can pleasure be measured if the idea of its total measurement is itself so pleasurable? Edgeworth aims at a comprehensive pleasure measurement, but what he unwittingly expresses is the structure of surplus pleasure, a pleasure that by definition escapes measurement.[2] The content of the fantasy speaks of a totalization of pleasure as a homogeneous quantity, but its form gestures at another type of pleasure which disrupts measurement. In this it echoes the way Marx delineates surplus value against the backdrop of classical political economy's concept of value. The totalization of value to the point where everything, including labor power, is exchanged according to a law of equivalence, leads to surplus value which disrupts equivalence. In both cases, money has to do with the disruption of equivalence. In Marx, when money assumes the role of the exclusive representation of value, it also becomes the first form of appearance of capital which accumulates surplus. As for Edgeworth, keeping in mind that money is the practical hedonimeter, what disrupts the possibility of measurement is a pleasure of money.

The eroticism of the machine expresses both the desire for a total measurement and its disruption. Sex denotes the pleasure that escapes measuring, but also the pleasure of total measurement. The hedonimeter, in other words, is an erotic disavowal of sex: an eroticized drive to include even sex within a homogeneous space. This might sound like a too sweeping conclusion, but as we shall see, that is exactly what came to the fore about a hundred years later, with the rise of economic imperialism. Its presumption to encompass the whole spectrum of human behavior within the principle of pleasure maximization was consummated in its approach to sex, and it is there that it displayed its most idiotic nature. This presumption, however, is embedded in the philosophical foundations of this paradigm.

The rise of neoclassical economics is the most significant paradigm shift in the history of modern economics. During the twentieth century, neoclassical theory assumed a dominant status in the discipline to the extent that many economics students today no longer know it by its name: they simply call it microeconomics. It is not the exclusive theoretical framework in the discipline—most notably, Keynesian macroeconomics, at least in its original formulation, diverged from the neoclassical assumptions. Yet the neoclassical framework dominates the economic worldview, or economics insofar as it fosters a coherent philosophy, grounded on its definitive answer to the question of what the human being is.

The contours of this theoretical transformation are familiar to anyone interested in the history of economics. The concept of utility (the euphemistic terminology for pleasure) was substituted for the classical concept of value as the organizing principle of the economic outlook. In place of the classical objective basis of prices—labor invested in production—neoclassical economics established a subjective basis in utility. The turn to a subjective basis paradoxically fulfilled the "scientific" aspirations of economists: it allowed the new theory to elaborate a complete mechanism of price formation which the classical framework lacked. By introducing a subjective quantity, which can never be observed other than by its effects in prices, the theory could claim to possess an accurate explanation of prices. One should just keep in mind that "accurate" is not synonymous with "true."

The paradigm shift, however, looks smaller when viewed from outside the canonical tradition. What persists through the transformation is what is left out of the mainstream as repressed or disavowed theoretical possibilities. Sexual economy is one vantage point which reveals a dimension of continuity between classical and neoclassical economic thought. Adam Smith reformulated a theoretical ground that circumvented the provocative ideas which Mandeville articulated in a terminology that entangled economy with passions, the family, sex, and gender relations. Neoclassical theory developed a different economic ontology: different conceptualizations of the field of inquiry, of the human being, of goods, money, and prices. Yet in a closer inspection, these alternative conceptualizations share with classical thought the disavowal of similar scandalous possibilities.

Objectless Theory

Edgeworth's hedonimeter resonates with the basic ontological premise of neoclassical economics, as an objectless theory: a theory where objects are fully substituted by their subjective reflections. In *Principles of Economics*, the founding text of the new paradigm, Alfred Marshall formulates this most explicitly: "Man cannot create material things. In the mental and moral world indeed he may produce new ideas; but when he is said to produce material things, he really only produces utilities" ([1890] 2013, 53). The theoretical upshot of this ontology is the fabrication of a fully homogenized economic sphere, comprising one single magnitude: consumption is pleasure and labor is displeasure or negative pleasure. All labor activities are now viewed as utterly equivalent, various forms of "arrangement of matter to adapt it better for the satisfaction of wants" (53). Making a log of wood into a table is no different in this respect from taking fish out of the depth of the sea or from putting each of them in a store for sale. This bold statement ostensibly marks a significant difference from classical political economy's emphasis on production. For the sake of comparison, consider Smith's fascination with the pin factory in the opening paragraphs of the *Wealth of Nations*, where labor is divided into eighteen different skills. From a different perspective, however, the objectless world of Marshall expands on a basic premise of classical thought. Beginning with Smith, as we saw, political economy viewed objects as placeholders for values. For the sake of theory, they are conceived as embodiments of abstract values—abstracted, that is, from their very thingness. The difference, therefore, is that neoclassical economics ontologizes what for political economy might have been only a theoretical step, a move beyond the manifest reality of the material world into the abstract economic laws governing it.

More importantly, the banishment of objects from economic theory, their substitution with subjective utility, is also the culmination of the distinction between economy and society implicit in Smith. Objects are something else that exists besides our consciousness. They are objects insofar they are not reducible to our perceptions of them. Human-made objects stand also for the presence of other human beings. Hannah Arendt explicated it in a simple formulation: "To live together in the world means essentially that a world of things is between those who have it in common, as a table is located between those who sit around it; the world, like every in-between, relates and separates men at the same time" ([1958] 1998, 53). The banishment of objects from economics is also the banishment of society. This becomes most apparent in neoclassical economics' suspicion of luxury.

Luxury II

"The world would go much better if everyone would buy fewer and simpler things, and would take trouble in selecting them for their real beauty" (Marshall [1890] 2013, 113). Well, thank you for the advice, Alfred! This insertion of a moral reprehension addressed at "everyone" cannot but reflect a theoretical difficulty. Its true meaning is that the world would go much better if it adhered to the beautiful laws of economic theory. As in Smith the theoretical difficulty lies in the excessive thingness of the luxury object and the way it inseparably entangles economy and society. Marshall laments the misuse of wealth in all ranks of society, the "unwholesome desire for wealth as a means of display" (113). Display may be morally wrong, but its greater fault is theoretical: it relies on objects that entail others, infringing the premise of an objectless world. Following the cross-reading of Smith and Mandeville, we should of course invert the order: economic theory was configured in advance to circumvent a moral scandal.

A clear echo of Mandeville indeed surfaces in Marshall's dismissal of luxury, resounding in the fear of vanity and envy: "There are indeed true and worthy pleasures to be got from wisely ordered magnificence: but they are at their best when free from any taint of personal vanity on the one side and envy on the other; as they are when they centre round public buildings, public parks, public collections of the fine arts, and public games and amusements" ([1890] 2013, 113). The conceptual map could not be more clearly drawn. Luxury, as inherently social, should be confined to public things, and its infiltration into free market economy is a moral hazard: "It would be a gain if the moral sentiment of the community could induce people to avoid all sorts of display of individual wealth" (113).[3]

Disavowal of Desire

The moralistic imperative is deeply engrained in the theoretical foundations of neoclassical economics. This becomes evident with respect to the intersection of its view of objects with its conceptualization of the economic subject. The banishment of objects from theory is accompanied by the eradication of desire, as distinct from needs, pleasures, and utilities.

This is stated most clearly in an allegedly technical assumption that Marshall makes: "[People] may have desires and aspirations which are not consciously set for any satisfaction: but for the present we are concerned chiefly with those which do so aim; and we assume that the resulting satisfaction corresponds in general fairly well to that which was anticipated when the purchase was made" ([1890] 2013, 78).

That is a truly astounding moment: satisfaction from goods corresponds to the anticipated satisfaction from them. On the one hand, it is an absolutely necessary assumption for the theoretical edifice. For objects to be replaced by a subjective quality, this quality must be uniform. It does not matter whether one calls it pleasure, need, utility, or even desire, so long it is indeed one quality and thus susceptible, at least in principle, to quantification. But on the other hand, this necessary assumption is both meaningless and wrong. It is meaningless because it quantitatively equates two subjective qualities that belong to different orders: satisfaction and anticipated satisfaction. There is no sense in claiming that actual satisfaction from an object corresponds to the satisfaction anticipated at the time of purchase, because the former belongs to the order of enjoyment, while the latter, "anticipated satisfaction," belongs to the order of imagination, desire, or fantasy. Despite being senseless, from a certain perspective the assumption is also wrong. It is wrong according to conceptions of desire, which define it as both excessive and incomparable to needs: excessive precisely because it is incomparable. Lacan puts this explicitly, but so is the whole tradition of thought which sees desire as insatiable: the things it is after are always frustrating once acquired.

That is not a hair-splitting remark after Marshall. On the side of economic reality, the whole of consumer culture becomes invisible for an outlook that disregards the gap between enjoyments and desires. It is blinded to the whole play of seduction and exaggerated expectations that permeate advertising, marketing, and shopping spaces. On the side of economic theory, the whole edifice of neoclassical economics relies on the possibility of viewing the human being as a simple mechanism driven by one principle. Here lies one more dimension of continuity between classical and neoclassical economic thought. Recoiling from the moral scandal of Mandeville, Smith replaced his inherently conflictual notion of self-love, composed of irreducibly contrasting drives, and associated with a view of society as essentially hypocritical, with the unitary notion of self-interest. The neoclassical concept of utility consummates the moralistic motivation of this replacement.

Economic Imperialism: Final Repression

Economics eventually reincorporated sex and the family in its scope, but in a closer look this was a completion of the process of repression of sex. Gary Becker, the pioneer of "economic imperialism," applied economic tools for things like relationships between parents and children, crime, addictions, marriage, and more. His work is a sad example of a victory of philosophy. It is doubtful whether it made a real contribution to our understanding of the family or crime. Its significance lies elsewhere, in the way it fortified the coherence of the economic outlook. Economic imperialism is in truth a logical consequence of the assumptions of neoclassical economics. That is how Becker explains his method: "The heart of my argument is that human behavior is not compartmentalized, sometimes based on maximizing, sometimes not, sometimes motivated by stable preferences, sometimes by volatile ones . . . Rather, all human behavior can be viewed as involving participants who maximize their utility from a stable set of preferences (1976, 14).

The argument is in truth tautological. It does rest on any knowledge of human nature, but on a conceptual analysis of the idea of "maximization." There is simply no sense in the idea of maximizing "sometimes." For maximization to have any meaning it must assume a totalized, homogeneous space of choice. To give a concrete example: economics invested tremendous intellectual efforts in showing how all economy is reducible to a person's autonomous decision to buy commodity X rather than commodity Y. But these efforts would prove useless if they did not include in these pleasure calculations also the possibility of stealing X or Y, risking the displeasure of getting caught. The significance of economic imperialism for the coherence of the economic outlook means that it actually has little interest in the various types of human behavior it studies. The consistency of theory is its true interest.

Becker's outlook on marriage demonstrates this. It consummates mainstream economics' ignorance of sex.

> According to the economic approach, a person decides to marry when the utility expected from marriage exceeds that expected from remaining single or from additional search for a more suitable mate. Similarly, a married person terminates his (or her) marriage when the utility anticipated from becoming single or marrying someone else exceeds the loss in utility from separation, including losses due to physical separation from one's children, division of joint assets, legal fees and so forth. Since many persons are looking for mates, a *market* in marriages can be said to exist. (1976, 10)

Romantics may protest that this argument ignores love and its role in marriage. This may be true, but it does not necessarily pose a theoretical challenge to Becker. Since the economic concept of utility is infinitely flexible, Becker would explain that it includes the pleasures of being with someone we love. Psychologists would further doubt whether this hedonistic framework can indeed be applied to love as an essentially intersubjective emotion, often accompanied by agonies and frustrations rather than utilities. This dialogue of the deaf could probably go on endlessly, as characteristic of the hermetic worldview of contemporary economics, so let us leave it at that. There is a bigger theoretical problem with Becker's argument, namely that it cancels the distinction between marriage and prostitution. Within the framework that Becker sets, both are to be located along the same spectrum, prostitution being the extreme pole where a man expects no further utility other than momentary sexual pleasure from a relation with a woman. In this sense, the economic point of view may seem to verge on a long-standing feminist theme that conjoins marriage and prostitution. Simone de Beauvoir wrote that "marriage is directly correlated with prostitution, [which is] like a dark shadow over the family." Quoting Antonio Marro she explains that, from the standpoint of economics, for both prostitutes and married women "the sexual act is a service; the one is hired for life by one man; the other has several clients who pay her by the piece" (1956, 529). A sharp difference, however, separates the feminist and the economic coupling of marriage and prostitution. What economics cannot incorporate is the notion of "a dark shadow" that de Beauvoir summons.

Its world, so to speak, is too thoroughly illuminated to allow for shadows. The critical force of de Beauvoir's statement stems from the fact that prostitution is not at all like marriage, and for that reason can serve as a hidden key to understanding some aspects of marriage. De Beauvoir invoked a topology, where the anathema of bourgeois society is akin to its decent foundation. Her statement draws its efficacy from the scandalous power of an obscene subtext. Becker's argument, by contrast, can be described as vulgar rather than obscene, vulgarity being a byproduct of unawareness of subtextual obscenity. In this sense, the imperialist expansion of economics into the realms of sex and the family represents the final form of repression of them.

Richard Posner, Becker's ally in the field of law and economics, makes this clear. What drives the sudden interest of economics in sex is the vested interest of the discipline in rationality, or more precisely in its own narrow version of the concept (which, taken to its logical conclusion, applies also to the movement of an amoeba toward light). Posner's aim in his *Sex and Reason* is to show "how the type and frequency of different sexual practices ... can be interpreted as rational responses to opportunities and constraints" (1992, 111). The somewhat cringey feeling that this claim inspires results from the fact that sex does not really interest Posner. Sex is enlisted in the service of economic theory. Posner's aim is to show that *even* sex can be explained with the same tools that economic thought developed to explain how we rationalize our clothes and food consumption. Economic rationality itself becomes a quasi-erotic aim, fueled by the insistence that there is nothing special in sex. This insistence is the only path open to mainstream economics to approach the subject because it was founded on a radical homogenization of the field of economy. Thus, Posner explains, sexual passion may belong to the domain of the irrational, but this should not preclude an economic investigation of it: "One does not will sexual appetite—but one does not will hunger either. The former fact no more excludes the possibility of an economics of sexuality than the latter excludes the possibility of an economics of agriculture" (5).

The unpleasant resonance of male chauvinist analogies between sex and eating is not coincidental. It is an inevitable result of the orthodox economic worldview, grounded on the conviction that a human being is a simple mechanism activated by one principle that commensurates all possible pleasures, including sex and eating. That is not to say that Posner is a chauvinist. To the contrary, when a male chauvinist refers to a woman as "a piece of meat," his pleasure is derived from his awareness of the mismatch of the pejorative, from his knowledge that she is *not* a piece of meat. It is the act of objectifying that arouses him rather than its alleged result. He objectifies women as part of a fantasy of complete domination, of dominating women as if they were objects, which would lose all its sense if they were indeed objects. He wallows in the obscenity of the analogy, which the economic mind cannot discern after two and a half centuries of systematic denial of the possibility of obscene economy. From the solipsistic perspective of economics, the pleasures that objects afford us are strictly indistinguishable from the pleasures that human beings afford us. From this perspective, other people are indeed enjoyable objects, and there is no need to objectify them.

Sex, of course, is not at all like eating. For one thing, it necessarily involves other people (or fantasies of them). However, the course that led economics to equate them raises the suspicion that it misconstrues not only sex, but also ordinary goods. Food is a good example for this, as suggested by the use of the term *food porn* with reference to the endless stream of seductive photographs of dishes on Instagram, on cooking shows, and in advertising. Freud could have easily explained why we call these images food porn. In some cases, the pleasure principle can be understood as a nirvana principle, aiming to reduce mental tensions due to various stimuli. Hunger is a perfect example: we eat in order to decrease the feeling of hunger. But in "The Economic Problem of Masochism" Freud admits that this early understanding of pleasure was misguided. There are cases where stimuli are themselves pleasurable. That is the case with sex: "The state of sexual excitation is the most striking example of a pleasurable increase of stimulus" (Freud [1924] 1961, 160). Food porn is an appropriate term because it refers to an enjoyment proper to excitation, enjoyment from an endless foreplay with food, from the deferral of eating for the sake of the pleasure of seeing. In this sense, food porn marks a real dimension of the eroticization of food.

The notion of sexual economy is important because it designates a diversion from the flat world of mainstream economics. It is not simply that sex designates a special realm of economy different from that of food. The difference rather splits the whole of economy from within. It splits economic subjects between irreducibly heterogeneous drives, which are then inscribed on the sphere of economic objects. Food is for both eating and seeing, but it follows different economic laws in relation to each role. Food for eating belongs to the economy of stability, of eradication of stimuli and excitations. Freud and Mandeville would have agreed on that. The nirvana principle works in the service of the death drive, conducting "the restlessness of life into the stability of the inorganic state," (Freud [1924] 1961, 160) just as the fabled beehive, after eradicating all excesses "flew into a hollow Tree,/ Blest with Content and Honesty." Food for seeing is another matter. It belongs to the economy of excess and endless deferral. It is more than itself (promising pleasures beyond mere satisfaction of hunger), but its pleasure is never consummated. It is capital in the form of a spectacle of food.

THREE

Love and Marriage

LOVE DESIGNATES THE UNIQUENESS OF THE SEXUAL ECONOMY of capitalism in its difference from precapitalist economies. Once it became the sole legitimate motivation for marriage, in what Coontz (2006) calls "the love revolution," the family explicitly assumed the place of an external inside of the economy: internal to the economy yet external to the market. From another perspective, following some key feminist thinkers, love is the form of persistence through change of patriarchy: it disavows the patriarchal notion of monogamy as a regime of ownership, while giving it a new and implicit form.

What, therefore, is the economy of love? One of its clearest manifestations is the American engagement ring ritual. A Google search of the question "How much should I spend on an engagement ring?" brings about more than 47 million results. A common myth points out three times your salary as a rule of thumb, but experts say that it is an outdated rule (Donovan 2023). That there is no explicit rule may intensify the unsettling nature of the question. One finds various "engagement ring calculators" online, some of them use only basic financial input (salary, debts) while others probe into the nature of the relationship (ages, is it a first marriage?). In a recurring scene in romantic comedies, the fiancée shows the ring to her friends, whose vocal admiration may conceal a shred of envy. The crucial economic significance of this scene is that we can wholeheartedly believe the young women when they admire the beauty of the ring, while maintaining that "it's so beautiful!" in this context is practically synonymous with "it's so expensive!" In this sense, the engagement ring is aestheticized money. Its beauty both expresses and disavows its monetary nature. To give money in these circumstances would be disgraceful: an insinuation of purchase and ownership. It would bring to the surface the patriarchal tradition, which love has made obsolete. The engagement ring as aestheticized money encapsulates the broad historical transformation where marriage as ownership of women was replaced by love and romance, while maintaining some of its economic meaning encoded in monogamy. The engagement ring is a money equivalent which lacks exchangeability. In economic terms it fills only one of the functions of money, being a store of value but not a means of exchange (a paradoxical economic entity: a store of value which ideally is utterly illiquid). The engagement ring is the sublime double of Adam Smith's metaphor of "public prostitution" discussed in chapter 1. Yet its economy is the same: there are things that money should not buy, and therefore they are expensive. The engagement ring is qualitatively expensive regardless of its price, expensive even when cheap. Its beauty expresses expensiveness, and it is expensive, or wasteful, as a store of value lacking exchangeability.

One can find the same economy in Viviana Zelizer's (2005) studies of engagement practices in the first decades of the twentieth century. Etiquette manuals of the time dwelled on the question of what gifts are appropriate for a young bride to receive from her fiancé. Their answer was that they must not contain any element of sustenance: "He may give her a fur scarf, but not a fur coat," as one of the guides advised. Both are luxurious, but the coat, in contrast to the scarf, is also practical. A proper gift should be pure luxury. A wrong gift would cast the bride "in a category with women of another class," meaning prostitutes and kept women. The economy of love subverts the accepted hierarchy between luxuries and necessities. This subversion is expressed in a strange role of money: one pays *more* in order to repudiate any notion of payment.[1]

The practice Zelizer describes seems to belong to a unique moment in the history of love and marriage. At that time, after marriage a wife would typically be maintained by her husband, but until that moment she had to avoid accepting anything that suggested sustenance. The need to distinguish the period of courtship and engagement from marriage suggests that a tension still haunted at this stage the association of love and marriage. It was still a unification of opposites, marked by different economies: that of luxury and waste, on the one hand, and that of sustenance, on the other. The economy of love, manifested at this stage in a pure form, so to speak, subverts the standard economic outlook in that it renders luxury a necessity.

Luxury and Capitalism

To explore the opposition between the economy of love and that of traditional patriarchal marriage it is worthwhile to return to a neglected genealogy of capitalism. In *Luxury and Capitalism* Werner Sombart develops a provocative argument tracing the origin of capitalism to "a transformation in the relations between the sexes" (1967, 42). To put it in a nutshell, Sombart argues that the secularization of love in the Renaissance brought about the emergence of a semiformal class of concubines and courtesans. This new class of women triggered the demand for luxury gifts, and as it spread by imitation to the broader circles of high society, it gave rise to a luxury industry that drove the economy from its traditional stable organization into an emergent capitalist form. As the last sentence of the book summarizes: "Luxury, then, itself a legitimate child of illicit love, gave rise to capitalism" (171). The book can be easily dismissed as a misogynist fantasy, attributing the rise of capitalism to the desire of women for luxuries. The misogynist undertone results from Sombart's presumption to point out a *cause* of the rise of capitalism and is highlighted by a relation of mechanical causality he applies to the link between love, luxury, and economy. What his book lacks, in other words, is precisely a notion of sexual economy grounded on a more complex notion of overdetermination, where love is not simply a cause of new forms of consumption but is also expressed in new economic practices and objects.

Sombart begins his historical narrative with the secularization of love from the eleventh century onward. The minnesingers and troubadours mark the beginning of a separation of sexual love from the religious cosmic order to which it was subordinated during the Middle Ages. Their poetry expressed a cult of sensual, earthly love—initial steps toward "the emancipation of the flesh" in Sombart's terms, brought to maturity in thirteenth-century Italy, and culminating in a "refinement which approaches perversion" in eighteenth-century France (1967, 47–48).

Running through this grand narrative is an opposition between love and marriage. "What free love ... could never become reconciled to was the institutionalization of love by marriage" (Sombart 1967, 48). The tension is clearly expressed in Boccaccio's and Montaigne's view of love and marriage as mutually exclusive. "Love loathes anything which deals with other matters and shuns every relation contracted for other reasons, such as marriage, where connections and wealth are at least as important as charm and beauty" (49). This opposition, however, has its own history, where love which emerged as opposed to the institution of marriage becomes itself an *informal* institution. Sombart notes how in Petrarch's days it became "good form for a young man to seduce a married woman" and how princes ceased to be embarrassed about their illegitimate offspring and began to boast about them. He further notes the growing numbers of prostitutes in the big cities at the close of the Middle Ages (51). The most important aspect of this history was the emergence of a new class of women, between respectable women and prostitutes, known by many names: *courtisane*, concubine, *maîtresse, grande cocotte*, and more. With these women, Sombart claims, love itself became semi-institutionalized. After being first freed from religion, it became an "art of love," that "emerges again from the dilettantism of the preceding centuries," with its own female masters "devoting their whole life to its practice" (51). It is a strange form of institutionalization, giving shape to something that remains illicit. Before going into details, one can see in this view of love an erotic parallel to the idea that capitalism entails a constant revolutionizing of society. As Marx and Engels describe it in the *Manifesto*: "All fixed, fast-frozen relations, with their train of ancient and venerable prejudices and opinions, are swept away, all new-formed ones become antiquated before they can ossify. All that is solid melts into air, all that is holy is profaned" (Marx and Engels 1965, 35).

The linchpin of Sombart's argument connects love and economy. He argues that the institutionalization of illicit love has fueled a growing demand for luxury goods. Financial records of European courts, beginning with the fifteenth century, indeed show an increase in the expenditure on luxury goods which Sombart attributes to the "endless pursuit of love of women" by kings, the most famous example of which is the Versailles palace that Louis XIV built in the seventeenth century for his mistress, Louise de la Vallière. The desire for luxury spread from the court to the nobility and high society. Sombart recounts in this context the influence that women such as Madame de Pompadour exerted in shaping the tastes and fashions of society. A contemporary witness observed that "we live now only by Mme de Pompadour; coaches are à la Pompadour, the color of dresses is à la Pompadour; we eat meat stews à la Pompadour, and in our houses we have mantelpieces, mirrors, tables, sofas, chairs, fans, boxes, and even toothpicks à la Pompadour" (Sombart 1967, 73). From the aristocracy the desire for luxury spread by imitation to the nouveaux riches and the bourgeoisie.

The increasing demand for luxury, according to Sombart, contributed to the rise of capitalist economy. His argument rests on a relatively thin definition of capitalism, as consisting of enterprises that require "a minimum outlet of exchange values." This increase in commerce can be attributed either to quantitative expansion in the production of ordinary goods or to a more limited sale of high-priced goods. The former possibility, Sombart argues, is disproved by the early history of capitalism: during the Middle Ages and the next few centuries thereafter the demand for ordinary goods remained essentially unchanged. The demand for consumption goods by the masses, as well as for instruments of labor, was met by traditional local patterns of production at home and by artisans. An increase in the demand for luxury, which required greater investment of labor, could have been the cause for increase in output characterizing capitalist production.

Sombart presents his argument as a historical observation supported by some detailed accounts of consumption in the courts and of culture and commerce in European cities in the eighteenth and nineteenth centuries. The argument is important, however, because it encapsulates a conceptual, ostensibly tautological, kernel. The distinction between "ordinary goods" and luxuries cannot be grounded on objective differences. It is, rather, a distinction between different social temporalities embedded in objects. Ordinary goods are inherently related to tradition. They are ordinary insofar as they are embedded in traditional ways of life, and for that reason the demand for them *by definition* tends to be stable. Luxuries entail a different temporality: they are always novel objects, more or less soon to become habituated, ordinary. In this sense, luxury is conceptually related to capitalism insofar as we conceive of it as a constantly developing economy. The distinction between ordinary goods and luxuries is a reflection of the distinction between traditional and capitalist economy. Traditional economy consists of ordinary goods, while capitalist economy must include luxuries of constantly changing forms. In its contemporary phase, it is doubtful whether capitalism encompasses such things as "ordinary goods." This conceptual aspect hidden within Sombart's historical observation is not invoked to dismiss his argument. It rather highlights the paradoxical nature of the transformation he aims to explain. It is not simply a change from one form of economy to another, but a change from an unchanging economy to a constantly changing one. To return to the *Manifesto*, that is precisely how Marx and Engels characterize the uniqueness of capitalist economy. While for all earlier industrial classes "conservation of the old modes of production in unaltered form, was . . . the first condition of existence," the bourgeoisie "cannot exist without constantly revolutionizing the instruments of production, and thereby the relations of production, and with them the whole relations of society" (Marx and Engels 1965, 34).

Sombart's search for a historical cause for the emergence of capitalism may explain why his thesis is not often taken seriously as well as its misogynistic undertone. A notion of mechanistic causality informs his outlook, apparent, among other things, in the connection he makes between sexuality and luxury: "Indubitably the primary cause of the development of any kind of luxury is most often to be sought in consciously or unconsciously operative sex impulses" (Sombart 1967, 60–61). This causal framework translates into some absurd claims about the role of women in promoting capitalism. One section is titled, no irony intended, "The Triumph of Woman." Sombart presents there some axes of change in the typical forms of luxury from the seventeenth century onward. Though insightful in themselves, they are all presented as driven by female desires. Whereas in the Middle Ages luxury was largely public, in the seventeenth century women began to draw it into the domestic sphere. Women also stimulated the *objectification* of luxury: a change of its typical forms from social practices such as feasts and entertainments to luxury objects. Women "could derive only scant satisfaction from the display of a resplendent retinue. Rich dresses, comfortable houses, precious jewels were more tangible" (95). Women also fueled the tendency of sensualization and refinement of luxury which also had significant economic effects, necessitating greater expenditure of labor, and insofar as it demands rare materials, intensifying international capitalist commerce.

These claims clearly echo the eighteenth-century anxiety over the effeminizing effects of luxury (Breckman 1991). Rather than dismissing them as misogynistic fantasies, however, it is more fertile to reframe them. It is obviously ridiculous to claim that women by their nature desire jewels and rich dresses. It may be significant, however, to note that at some historical point, a certain form of femininity is expressed with jewels and dresses. That is precisely the point where a framework of sexual economy can salvage Sombart's outrageous speculation. Once the causal terminology is put aside, we can see that Sombart's thesis unearths a connection between new economic practices and a new erotic regime. This erotic regime encompasses illicit love relations between men and women, a certain form of seductive femininity, female desire to be seen in a certain way, and a parallel male desire to display the objects of their love. All these are articulated in the economic practice of the luxury gift. The significance of this practice is immense. It expresses the opposition between two sexual economies: that of traditional marriage, on the one hand, and of illicit love, on the other. Marriage, oriented toward the stability and prosperity of the household, subsumes sex within an economy of utilitarian calculation. The luxury gift expresses in economic terms the opposition of illicit love to marriage. It subverts the utilitarian economic framework of marriage, and it does so in a *double sense*. It subverts it in the form of the transaction, as a gift that demands no return, at least not explicitly. This subversion is then reflected in the nature of the gift as a luxury good, a superfluous thing embodying waste.

Sombart attributes a causal role to the growing demand for luxury in enhancing production and sales necessary for the move toward capitalist economy. This causal connection may be part of the historical fabric that characterized the rise of capitalism. Alongside it, luxury gives an erotic *expression* to a new economy. It articulates a new form of ownership of women. It is an uncertain form, marked by the volatility of love and economically expressed in the replacement of exchange as a paradigm for gender relations with that of the gift. It also expresses erotically the movement of capital. The capitalist, in contrast to the hoarder, must throw his capital back to the market in order to receive back more. Similarly, the luxury gift is given for the absolute "more" it cannot guarantee, namely love.

That is the key to a charitable rereading of Sombart: replacing the framework of causality with a notion of overdetermination. In place of seeking the cause of capitalism in new patterns of sexual relations, this shift of focus entails inquiring how capitalist economy is entangled with sexual relations, and how new economic practices and objects express new forms of gender relations. That is what Sombart practically achieves beyond his intention to present a causal explanation. His accounts can be read as describing an eroticization of economic life that runs through different levels of commerce: new goods and production enterprises, new types of shops and commercial spaces, new marketing methods, a new social atmosphere. Sombart dwells, for example on the rapid growth in specialized retail trade in London in the early eighteenth century. As part of this process, shops selling ready-made clothes replaced shops of fabric for home production of clothes. On a purely economic level, these specialized shops required a greater variety of goods and thus greater inventory and capital—hence their connection to capitalism. Their commercial logic also dictated a new aesthetics of display and seduction, as testified by contemporary witnesses: "They look more like palaces and their stocks are of exceeding great value" (Sombart 1967, 134). It also entailed new marketing methods and a new social atmosphere. Sombart cites from Daniel Defoe a story about a merchant who for two hours presented to a certain lady merchandise worth £3,000 without her buying anything (135). In *The Fable of the Bees*, Mandeville also refers to such scenes, highlighting how wooing accompanied the selling of merchandise to women. The crucial point in this context is the interlocking of effects on economic, social, and erotic levels. A new commercial logic is embodied in a new type of shop, which entail new marketing methods, new social relations, and a new figure of the consumer. The diverse inventory is supplemented by the persona of the customer as a connoisseur. A repertoire of female figures is implied by economic practices and a logic of investment: a woman who knows exactly what she wants, a woman who need to be wooed, a whimsical woman.

A specific type of these retail stores, trinkets and novelties shops, encapsulates Sombart's association between luxury and sexuality. "These shops," he writes, "became the meeting places for the world of fashion, particularly the gentlemen who came to select presents for their lady-loves." He also quotes a contemporary observer, Louis Sebastien Mercier, who claims that these gifts "were presented to respectable women who would not accept cash money" (Sombart 1967, 133). Of course, even if we accept these observations as purely factual, as Sombart seems to do, they provide but little support to the for the claim of a causal connection between sexuality, luxury, and capitalism. Yet, shifting the focus from causality to expression, they are no less important even if read as partly imaginary. As such they show how commodities and money carry sexual meanings and fantasies, articulated in a unique economy: gifts to women as a disavowal of exchange. They do not show that consumption is motivated by sexual impulses, but they show how commodities and money are eroticized.

Sex and the Department Store

Sexual economy is probably the most prominent theme of nineteenth-century realist literature, obsessed with interplays between wealth, status, love, desire, and marriage. Their economic infrastructure scarcely requires interpretative efforts to be exposed. They are, in fact, textbooks of sexual economy in narrative form. Emile Zola's *Ladies' Paradise* is a comprehensive literary counterpart to Sombart's thesis, interweaving business models, commerce, sexuality, and marriage. The plot is set against the backdrop of an economic transformation: the collapse of traditional shops brought about by the arrival of a new department store, *Au Bonheur des Dames*, founded by the young widower Octave Mouret, which Zola modeled on the real department stores *Bon Marché* and *Louvre*. Mouret's success rests on a simple business principle: to increase inventory turnover as much as possible using a sophisticated commissions system for sales personnel. As Mouret explains to the literary figuration of Baron Haussmann: "The whole system lies in this. It is very simple, but it had to be found out. We don't have a very large working capital; our sole effort is to get rid of our stock as quickly as possible to replace it by another . . . . In this way we can content ourselves with a very small profit" (Zola 2013, 70). Across the street, in the soon to be relinquished traditional shop The Old Elbeuf, the draper Baudu believes that "the art was not to sell a large quantity, but to sell dear" (25).

The new business model, however, entails a new social experience of shopping. The frequent giant sales must be extravagant, and the design of the department store radiates with seductive power which makes the traditional shops look stale. Even the hostile shopkeepers cannot take their eyes off its glittering windows and lustrous displays. Shopping also becomes an experience of the crowd, mostly a feminine crowd, which Zola depicts in erotic terms:

> The ladies, seized by the current, could not now go back. As streams attract to themselves the fugitive waters of a valley, so it seemed that the wave of customers, flowing into the vestibule, was absorbing the passers-by, drinking in the population from the four corners of Paris. They advanced but slowly, squeezed almost to death, kept upright by the shoulders and bellies around them, of which they felt the close heat; and their satisfied desire enjoyed the painful entrance which incited still further their curiosity. (2013, 220).

This depiction is in truth a reflection of Mouret's business model. Complementing his idea of quick turnover through extravagant sales is a libidinal economic model, propelled by and propelling female desires: "Mouret's unique passion was to conquer woman. He wished her to be queen in his house, and he had built this temple to get her completely at his mercy. His sole aim was to intoxicate her with gallant attentions, and traffic on her desires, work on her fever" (Zola 2013, 215). This strategy of desire is manifested in different forms of promiscuity that envelop the department store: the male clerks' flirtatious service to female customers, their liberal leisure habits, the rumors they spread, and their conversations about love affairs among themselves and between Mouret and some female workers. Mouret himself is a notorious womanizer, and he combines his business conduct with a constant flirtatious courting of high-society women. Moreover, he believes that his promiscuous reputation is one of the secrets of his store's success. This provides the backdrop to the main plotline of the novel: Mouret's falling in love with Denise, Baudu's orphaned niece, who starts working in the department store due to the economic hardship of her uncle's shop. Mouret refuses to acknowledge his awakening love to Denise due to his belief in the powers of promiscuity.

Two love plots run through the novel, reflecting the clash between traditional economy and the new ways of business. In Baudu's decaying shop, the clerk Colomban is engaged to be married to Baudu's daughter, Genevieve. In marrying her he will inherit the business, just as Baudu himself inherited it from his own father-in-law. But the long-planned wedding is postponed because of the shop's deteriorating state. Baudu, who wants to deliver the business to his son-in-law in good shape, keeps hoping that it will recover. Throughout its inevitable collapse we learn that Colomban is secretly in love with Clara, a promiscuous salesgirl in the department store across the street. Genevieve suspects this and falls ill in parallel to her father's economic demise. On her deathbed Colomban abandons Baudu's house, after having spent several nights with Clara. The end of respectable, old-fashioned commerce is also the collapse of traditional sexual economy, the cornerstone of which is marriage as a form of exchange. Its substance is the stuff of tradition: business practices habituated through apprenticeship and property transferred through marriage. It is traditional not simply in the sense that it precedes fully fledged capitalism. The way it entangles business practices, property, and marriage confers temporal stability on all three. Family lineage is solidified by property transfer, and a social property regime is solidified by marriage.

In the department store across the street, love and promiscuity derail the traditional figuration. Mouret the womanizer gradually falls in love with Denise. He promotes her and seeks her advice on every matter. That is why, though she is secretly in love with him too, she is forced to quit the store: rumors start to spread regarding the secret of his special relation to her. At the plot's denouement, Mouret invites Denise to his office, and in a last attempt to convince her to stay, forgoes his belief in the power of a promiscuous reputation and proposes to marry her. A million francs intake from the big sale—the most he has ever made—is lying on the table between them, but the lovesick businessman has lost all interest in money. The money on the table does not signal exchange but its repudiation. It marks love as what money cannot buy. In the context of commerce, it marks love as derailing the traditional sexual economy figuration. Denise is at first reluctant but eventually confesses that she loved him all along and throws herself on his neck. There is, however, a final obstacle to be overcome. Announcing the marriage will confirm the rumors that surrounded the relationship between the two. It will confer on it a form of obscene exchange, where Denise achieved the big prize: marriage rather than a passing romance. Mouret comes up with the most artificial solution. The last sentence of the novel reads: "He did not quit Denise, but clasped her in a desperate embrace, telling her that she could now go, that she could spend a month at Valognes, which would silence everybody, and that he would then go and fetch her himself, and bring her back, all-powerful, as his wedded wife" (Zola 2013, 391–92). The artificial nature of this solution is not coincidental. It points at what Sombart characterized as an opposition between love and marriage that persists even when love becomes the motivation for marriage. On a theoretical level it points at an inherent tension in capitalist sexual economy. Marriage remains the cornerstone of the social regime of property. It cannot escape its status as an economic arrangement. Its uniqueness is that it cannot be conceived as an exchange, and the insinuation that it is confers on it an obscene nature. Furthermore, the obscene is materially articulated in the new economy centered on luxury and its seducing powers. The big sales, the display of abundance, the popularized luxury: all provide a material grammar for love and promiscuity.

Macroeconomics of Morals

To fully appreciate the potential of Sombart's ideas we should pay attention to the stark contrast between his thesis and a more familiar genealogy of capitalism, originating from the same intellectual circle: that of his friend and colleague Max Weber. In two significant aspects Weber's *The Protestant Ethic and the Spirit of Capitalism* appears diametrically opposed to *Luxury and Capitalism*:

- *Secularization versus sacralization.* While Sombart focuses on the liberation of love from the religious significance it traditionally held in the context of marriage, Weber traces the origin of capitalism to a religious dogma that extended itself into formerly profane spheres of life. The germ of the capitalist spirit lies, according to Weber, in the Lutheran idea of work as a vocation. The dogma which attributed religious significance to the totality of human earthly activity paved the way to an economic conduct of a systematic pursuit of profits for their own sake.
- *Hedonism versus asceticism.* While Sombart saw the sensual pleasures of illicit love as propelling economic change, Weber emphasized "this-worldly asceticism" in generating capital. The combination of work as a vocation with strict avoidance of enjoying the fruits of labor resulted in the initial formation of capital.

If we keep in mind, however, their different perspectives on capitalism, Sombart and Weber may actually complement each other. Weber conceives of capitalism primarily as a regime of production and profit making whereas Sombart proposes to view it in terms of unique forms of consumption and money spending. Their views can be combined due to the basic economic fact that every purchase is a sale and that what is consumed was produced beforehand. This simple fact is the ground for macroeconomic arithmetic. Adjoining Weber to Sombart gestures at a wider notion of macroeconomics, encompassing not only neutral magnitudes such as investment and savings, but also mores, ways of life and desires. To read them together means that what was produced in ascetic devotion was consumed in promiscuous sin.

If this suggestion seems far-fetched, notice that ascetic production and promiscuous consumption are not mental attitudes floating somehow in the air. They are articulated in relations between money and luxury and are thus materially interlaced with each other. The Weberian entrepreneur features "an attitude that seeks profit rationally and systematically"

(Weber [1930] 1992, 27). He prefers money over the things that it can buy. For him, in other words, all goods are suspected of being luxury, as clearly expressed in the quotes from Benjamin Franklin that open Weber's essay (keeping exact account of all expenses "you will discover how wonderfully small, trifling expenses mount up to large sums" [16]). Obviously, this capitalist spirit cannot apply to the whole of society. When everybody prefers money over goods the result is a recession. Weber's claim about early entrepreneurs amassing capital through hard work, calculation, and thrift could have its measure of truth to the extent that they entail their opposite, agents who reject the calculating spirit and prefer things over money. These are precisely Sombart's courtiers and gentlemen. Like Weber's entrepreneurs, they also had a money-centered ethic, but it was grounded on its despicable nature: "Money, and all that was associated with money, was looked upon with contempt. To be concerned with money matters, to balance expenses and income, was considered vulgar and left to the care of stewards . . . . The steward receives his instructions. It is then up to him to worry about from where the money is to come. Whether or not the steward pays the merchant is not a gentleman's concern" (Sombart 1967, 87). An economic attitude combining money as means of calculation and an ascetic rejection of pleasure is mirrored by, and materially entailed with, a hedonistic attitude grounded on abhorrence of the vulgar, calculating spirit embedded in money.

In contrast to Franklin, Daniel Defoe knew that these two attitudes were in truth interwoven in the eighteenth-century commercial life. His business manual to aspiring retailers, *The Complete English Tradesman*, echoes Franklin's austere spirit. "Pleasures rob the tradesman . . . They are downright thieves" ([1839] 1987, 75) "The most innocent diversion becomes criminal, when it breaks in upon that which is the due and just employment of the man's life" (75). A tradesman that does not relate to his business as "a calling" would better forgo it from the outset. However, in contrast to Franklin, Defoe is also aware of the fact that the temptations threatening to destroy the tradesman are themselves products of flourishing commerce. The present age, he writes, offers new pleasure "which no age before this have been in danger of": "The present age is a time of gallantry and gaiety; nothing of the present pride and vanity was known, or but very little of it, in former times: the baits which are every where laid for the corruption of youth, and for the ruin of their fortunes, were never so many and so mischievous as they are now" (78).

The symmetry between the different ethics involved with consumption and production seems to characterize a specific historical phase of early capitalism. It marks the process of drainage of wealth from the dwindling aristocracy to the rising bourgeoisie. The two ethical positions are two different manifestations of the relation of capitalist money to what money cannot buy. In Weber's thesis it is manifested in the role that the Protestant understanding of salvation played in the emergence of the capitalist spirit. The doctrine of predestination made the question of salvation unnegotiable by humans, detaching people's fate in the next world from their earthly conduct. This detachment is echoed in the capitalist spirit of seeking profits regardless of enjoyments and satisfactions such profits can acquire, which practically means seeking profits for their own sake. This capitalist spirit, however, can be described in more material and less "spiritual" terms if we keep in mind its direct entanglement with money. The immediate cause of Luther's schism was the practice of selling indulgences by the Catholic church, denounced at length in his *Ninety-Five Theses*. A monetary event, the sanction on selling indulgences, occupied a key role in the Protestant Reformation. It cannot be thought of as other than a pivotal event in the history of money. Though they are ostensibly the same, money that can buy salvation and money that cannot are completely different economic objects. The capitalist spirit and the Protestant ethic are material elaborations of this difference, and of the presence of what money cannot buy in economic life. What money cannot buy can be articulated in a limitless search of profit. In Sombart, the category of what money cannot buy finds a parallel hedonistic expression. Love is a clichéd example to the claim that there are things that money cannot buy. The cliché, however, situates love as utterly external to the economy. Sombart goes beyond this when he sketches an economy involved with the institutionalization of illicit love. What he shows, in other words, is an economic articulation of what money cannot buy. Its paradigmatic form is the luxury gift to the concubine: its luxuriousness is a material form of disavowal of the possibility of an economic transaction, a purchase, between a man and a woman.

The symmetry between puritan capitalists and spendthrift aristocrats obviously no longer applies to contemporary capitalism. There is no economically significant aristocratic class anymore and not many puritan capitalists either. Billionaires compete among themselves in the sizes of their monstrous yachts and in conspicuous consumption that borders on the fantastic, such as a recreational trip to outer space. Yet the category of what money cannot buy still applies to economic life, and we shall get back to some of its contemporary forms later on, mainly in the fifth chapter. The crucial point for now is that its entanglement with what it cannot or should not buy renders money an ethical substance and that the ethics embedded in it are indistinguishable from its economic function. In orthodox economics money is ethically neutral because it is conceived as external to the circle of commodities. Its externality makes it a perfect means: for calculation, commensuration, balancing accounts, and setting preferences. This picture is subverted by the primacy of luxury in economic life, as an object of either desire or phobia, in Weber's and Sombart's theses. In luxury, money is not external to the circle of goods, due to a double relation to them. Money is a means of purchase for luxury, as for any other good, but in the case of luxury the opposite means-ends relation also holds true because luxury is the means to display wealth or to produce a concrete experience of wealth. As an object of either phobia or desire, luxury marks an economy where money is not an external means of balancing and calculating real needs and preferences but is interwoven into desires and avoidances. In parallel, luxury is also related to the ethical substance of money. Luxury, as a rule, belongs to the ethical domain as captured by the advertising formula "you deserve this." Weber and Sombart suggest from different perspectives that luxury expresses the ethical substance of money, engrained in its relation to what it cannot buy (salvation, love). In both cases, the ethical substance of money maintains a notion of economy organized around excess rather than balance.

Money as Ethical Substance

"Ethics embedded in money" is a possible short definition of capitalism. Money is capital insofar as it implies ethics. Marx describes the capitalist as an agent who follows an impersonal imperative to accumulate capital. This imperative is objectively enfolded in the definition of capital as a form of circulation M-C-M' which can take place insofar as its sole aim is limitless increase. This is an objective definition of capital in the sense that it consists solely of objects—money and commodities. It can only take effect, however, to the extent that human agents activate it and, therefore, to the extent that it entails a subjective supplement. The definition of the capitalist is accordingly a subject that behaves *as if* the imperative to accumulate capital is objective, embedded in objects. The capitalist, in other words, is the person who derives ethics from objects. One may object that it is a false derivation—objects cannot exert ethical imperatives. That is a too quick objection. The derivation is performative, circumventing the distinction between true and false. Capital is an objective reality to the extent that economic agents perform the ethical imperative as if it emanates from money.

Here lies a point of convergence between Marx and Weber, despite the latter's critique of materialist approaches to history. The quotations from Franklin that Weber uses to define the capitalist spirit form a systematic exploration of ethics embedded in money. Franklin's advice mixes simple rules for prudent business conduct with self-discipline techniques. In a closer reading, however, these are somehow derived as answers to the question "What is money?" "Remember, that *time* is money" (Weber [1930] 1992, 14): spending time idly is a loss not only of expenses during that time, but also the profits that could have been made. The question "What is money?" brings about an answer in the form an ethical imperative once money is understood in terms of potentiality, which is ethical to begin with. Money is not identical to the inert object that plays the role of money. What it is consists also of potentials, of what can be done and could have been done. Franklin ostensibly bridges the gap between "is" and "ought" because as a potential, money is closer to begin with to the realm of "ought." The abstract and colorless nature of money confer an ascetic, unconditional form on the ethic embedded in it. One cannot argue with monetary calculations, characterized by a disproportion between deeds and consequences. Six pounds a year, considered as a loan interest, allows one to use one hundred pounds. For that reason, "He that spends a groat a day idly, spends idly above six pounds a year, which is the price for the use of one hundred pounds" (16).

Money was ethically suspicious before capitalism. As is well known, the Catholic Church condemned usury. Jacques Le Goff notes that this injunction singles out a unique status of money in medieval economic thought and practice. Interest in kind, on loans of tools or land, was acceptable, yet money interest was considered a loathsome sin (1990, 18–19). The medieval doctrine, however, underscores the specificity of the relation between capitalist money and ethics. The condemnation of usury spells out an ethical *relation* to money, which means that ethics is not yet embedded in money. Money was an object that required special ethical care, but it was still considered an inert object, not in itself an ethical substance. The medieval justifications for the condemnation of usury make this clear. The more familiar justification was that money, unlike land or cattle, is barren and cannot beget money. In other words, money is but an inert object, and it is a moral duty of people not to treat it as if it is a living being. Thus, Dante placed usurers in hell together with sodomites: both commit sins against nature, which is worse than the sin of greed (50–51). Le Goff, however, cites a more sophisticated, and economically nuanced, reasoning for the condemnation of usury. What the usurer sells to his debtors is time: they pay for the time lapse between a loan and its settlement. Usury is a grave sin because only God can own time (33–46). What should be noted is that with the rise of capitalism this reasoning became, in reverse form, the *explanation* of interest. Neoclassical economics spells this out explicitly. To quote Marshall again: "Human nature being what it is, we are justified in speaking of the interest on capital as the reward of the sacrifice involved in the waiting for the enjoyment of material resources" ([1890] 2013, 193). The crucial point, however, is that this reasoning no longer belongs to the ethical realm but wears a factual form. Monetary interest results from an alleged fact about human nature. The moral status of usury did not simply change from condemnation to approval. It is a more complex transformation, through which an ethical dimension has *folded into* money. It entails a disappearance from sight of the ethical dimension in the guise of objectivity. In this sense, money changes from an object that demands special ethical attention to an ethical object, an object whose very existence is entangled with ethics. Simply put: money has become an ethical substance once we have lost the way to ask whether usury is moral.

Further advice from Franklin: "Remember, that *credit* is money." Here, too, ethics is derived from an ontological revelation about money. It consists of harsh, almost paranoid rules of conduct for maintaining one's good reputation ("The most trifling actions that affect a man's credit are to be regarded. The sound of your hammer at five in the morning . . . makes [your creditor] easy six months longer" [Weber 1992, 14–15]). For us there is something perplexing about this far-reaching derivation. This is because for us credit and money are indistinguishable. Franklin derives an ethic from the identity because he still considers credit and money as two different things. The question of whether or not they were indeed different things at his time cannot be unequivocally answered. Read in retrospect, Franklin's advice characterizes a transition phase in the process of birth of modern money. The credit theory of money holds that money originates in debt. Setting aside the question of whether it applies to all forms of money, capitalist money is distinguished by the institutional form of its creation from debt. Geoffrey Ingham (2013) traces its origin to debt bills of merchants, which assumed the role of money when they began to circulate and themselves serve as means of payment. Capitalist money assumes its modern form when the debt becomes impersonal when issued by private banks and later central banks. If indeed money is created from debt, it is obviously an ethical substance: an object whose very existence relies on an obligation. Unlike Franklin, we no longer notice its ethical dimension because credit has become synonymous with money. We no longer have money objects such as gold coins to induce the belief that some forms of money belong to the ethically neutral realm of the strictly factual. We no longer see the ethics underlying money because we call it economics.

It is somewhat of a misfortune that Marx adhered to the concept of commodity money. The commodity theory of money was popular among early modern economists. The idea that money is a commodity that through blind economic forces assumes the role of a universal means of exchange fitted their ideological motivation to portray the economy as an autonomous, self-regulating realm of human activity. Responsible historical accounts of modern money, however, usually explain its emergence with some fusion of state theory and credit theory of money. Claiming that money is created by the state and created as a debt embed the economy in political and institutional contexts to begin with. The distinction between commodity theory and credit theory of money, however, is not a simple opposition between truth and error. The commodity theory of money may indeed be a myth, but for a very long time it was a necessary illusion. Debt bills of merchants could circulate as means of exchange because they referred to "real money," different from themselves. In a broader historical perspective, it took humanity a long time to get rid of the illusion that a commodity confers value on paper bills—not until the final dissolution of the gold standard in the 1970s. Even today, one may conjecture, money functions insofar as it appears as an object, although the credit theory of money presents it in terms of a social relation. Marx's version of the commodity theory of money, however, is different from that of economists and can be adapted to a credit theory. As noted in chapter 1, Marx described the emergence of money in terms of an "exclusion" of one object from the sphere of commodities: "The social action of all other commodities, therefore, sets apart the particular commodity in which they all represent their values" (1976, 180). This notion of exclusion makes Marx's unique version of commodity money more reconcilable with the credit theory of money. If a commodity assumes the role of money by an effacement of use value, then the endless deferral of redemption of debt bills can be seen as furthering this logic, a further stage of the exclusion of money from the ranks of commodities.

In the partly illusory distinction between credit and real money one finds an expression not only of the ethical dimension of capitalist money, but also of its relation to eroticism.

Sex and Credit

A two-way metaphor characterizes the relation between credit and illicit love. In economic literature, such as Defoe's *The Complete English Tradesman*, erotic metaphors describe the distinction between money and credit. In nineteenth-century novels, such as *Madame Bovary* and *The Way We Live Now*, one finds the inverse relation where credit and finance are metaphors for eroticism and love in their opposition to traditional marriage. There must be some real kernel to this two-way connection.

Like Franklin, Defoe still considers money and credit as two different things and thus can use the difference between them as a vantage point for an economic ontological inquiry. Defoe shares with Franklin the ascetic ethic derived from the notion of credit. There are only two things required to maintain good credit, he writes: industry and honesty ([1839] 1987, 239). This similarity makes it all the more interesting that Defoe describes the relation between money and credit also in erotic terms: "Credit is, or ought to be, the tradesman's *mistress*" (233). Credit must be wooed in a certain way. One must play "hard to get" to acquire it: "If you court her, she is gone; if you manage so wisely as to make her believe you really do not want her, she follows and courts you." Why is credit like a mistress? An unspoken analogy may confer meaning on this metaphor: credit is like a mistress insofar as money is like a wife. In another text Defoe calls credit a "substantial Non-Entity," and describes it as "a distinct Essence from all the Phenomena in Nature," and as "the lightest and most volatile Body in the World" (quoted in Hartley 2008, 45). "Real" money is analogous to marriage as the solid foundation of economic life, fortified by tradition. The entanglement of marriage and property relations confers on both a solid nature, of that which persists through time. Together they form the substance of traditional economy, as an economy ostensibly comprised of solid entities. Credit is analogous to love and concubinage due to its ephemerality. Like love it is always on the verge of collapsing and requires constant maintenance to exist. It may be associated with volatile elements of economic life, as in luxury and its play of seduction and appearance.

For Defoe, credit is a supplement to money. If one has money, or successfully pretends he does, one can easily acquire credit. Yet it is a strange form of supplement, cannibalizing that to which it is appended. Successful merchants conduct their business on credit only. Upon their death they leave no cash, yet they are rich if one takes into account the stocks and the debt bills they hold. Credit involves a make-believe: to have it, one must pretend one does not need it. This recognition seems to run in contrast to Defoe's emphasis on the importance of honesty. It is reconciled with it due to the ontological distinction he draws between money and credit.

Credit, as a "substantial Non-entity," is performative. Honesty is part of this performativity. What's important is that one would appear honest. Performativity in its strict sense as defined by John Austin also lies at the basis of credit money, as apparent in its beginning in debt bills of merchants. It is created when the words "I owe you," phonetically represented in IOU, become things. This performative aspect subverts the logic of supplement that Defoe invokes. It makes credit a supplement that can substitute for that to which it is appended. If one can get credit by sheer make-believe, it would be pure waste to conduct business in cash money.

In other places in the book Defoe refers to love and marriage in the lives of tradesmen. In these cases, the analogy between love and credit is reversed. A certain notion of credit emerges as an internal principle of love. One chapter warns aspiring tradesmen from the dangers of marrying too soon, out of love or passion. This, Defoe writes, has brought many aspiring tradesmen to ruin. Premature marriage shares the temporality of credit in a reverse form. With credit, one can pay with future money (e.g., with debt bills). In love marriage, the young tradesman finances his wife by foreclosing future profits. The leverage afforded by credit works in this case in reverse to bring devastating results. A young tradesman received from his father £2,000 to set him up. The father strained himself to the utmost to secure the funds, not knowing that his son had secretly married the servant-maid of the house where he lodged. £600 of his stock were wasted before he got into a partnership with another young man, who had brought to their business £2,000. The poor tradesman was obliged to make a private article to accept only a third of the trade. Afterward "the beggar-wife proving more expensive, by far, than the partner's wife (who married afterwards, and doubled his fortune), the first young man was obliged to quit the trade . . . he sank gradually, and then broke, and died poor" (Defoe [1839] 1987, 000).

Another story shows how the performative nature of credit inserts itself into the daily life of the household. Defoe quotes a long conversation between a tradesman and his loving wife. Taking pains to discover the reason for his mood, the wife eventually discovers that their expenses are too high. She immediately suggests lending a hand to the efforts of saving: she will dismiss three maids, she will keep no visiting days, and she will forgo treats and entertainments. The husband is skeptical. This might make things worse: "They will say I am going to break upon your doing thus, and that's the way to make it so" (103). The wise wife eventually comes up with a solution: she will spend the summer with her aunt in Bedfordshire, far enough so that their acquaintances will not come to visit. The performative nature of credit expands beyond strictly commercial relations into the household, where it colors lifestyles. To maintain credit in business one must keep the appearance of a certain measure of luxury consumption at home. The paradoxical economic principle again revealed here is the necessity of luxury. As noted, Defoe goes to great lengths to demonstrate the dangers of luxury consumption in the habits of the tradesman himself, yet luxury becomes obligatory in the context of the household, a duty bestowed on the wife. Zelizer (2005) pointed out the necessity of luxury in courting practices at the beginning of the twentieth century. In her example, so it seems, love generates a unique economy, a sort of an enclave distinguished by an inversion of the ordinary economic hierarchy between luxury and sustenance. Defoe demonstrates an opposite movement, where the exceptional economy of love permeates ordinary economy: an exception to the economy which is nonetheless crucial for the normal functioning of commerce. In terms of this book, Zelizer focuses on the capitalist economy of sex: the unique economic expression of erotic relations between men and women. Defoe shows how the economy of sex is reflected in the broader context of eroticized economy. The theoretical lesson enfolded in his anecdotal example is that the concept of economy morphs depending on whether one includes marriage within its compass. Identifying economy with the market, as separate from the household, one can ascribe to the familiar notion of economy as grounded on calculation, thrift, and profit maximization. Including the household within its compass shows how the economy of calculation and profits is inherently entangled with its opposite, an economy of waste and luxury as a material expression of love.

Psychoanalysis provides a way to consider the erotic metaphors for credit. In a sense, credit is indeed eroticized money. Defoe's view of credit is grounded on an ontological distinction between money as a thing and credit as no-thing, a "substantial Non-entity." According to Alenka Zupančič, the philosophical challenge ingrained in psychoanalysis is its approach to sex as ontological negativity. Sex comprises an ontology of the human world grounded on negativity. Sex itself is "a substantial Nonentity": human sexuality is something created from nothing, from a foundational absence. We are accustomed to think that culture shapes and restrains the expressions of sexuality. This common insight may seem to imply that there is a precultural form of human sexuality which is then restrained and shaped. What psychoanalysis teaches, however, is that shaping and restraining are themselves the basic forms of human sexuality. Norms that impose forms on sexual relations (such as reproductive coupling) do not simply hide or repress "something else (for instance, a perverse debauchery, or pure self-perpetuating enjoyment), but rather the *something which is not there* (something missing)" (2017, 16–17). Credit can be conceived in erotic terms—"the tradesman's mistress"—because it embodies what Zupančič describes as the ontology of sex. It is something created from a foundational lack: debt that becomes a thing, a means of payment.

Turning to Freud, one finds a more robust way to understand the eroticization of money in credit. In some places, Freud presents sexuality as characterized by a detachment from purpose. Things are sexualized when they are repeated beyond their purpose. The perfect example is thumbsucking by infants, which Freud presents as the model for infantile sexuality. "Thumbsucking, which manifests itself in the nursing baby and which may be continued till maturity or throughout life, consists in a rhythmic repetition of sucking contact with the mouth (the lips), wherein the purpose of taking nourishment is excluded" ([1905] 1981, 179–80). Thumbsucking is sexual insofar as it originates in nourishment but is repeated independently of the purpose of nourishment. That is a good description of the process through which credit money is instituted. Debt bills are originally aimed to be redeemed by real money. They become money when their purpose is excluded: when they begin to circulate, postponing indefinitely their original purpose.

Love and Credit

Eva Illouz remarks that "it is not sexuality that is the unconscious of consumer culture, but consumer culture that has become the unconscious drive structuring sexuality" (2019, 52). An ironic reversal is at work here.

The tirelessly repeated cliché that "sex sells" suggests that our sexual desires are harnessed and manipulated to persuade us to buy things. Maybe they are. But at the same time, things, commodities, assume the role of a material grammar for expressing sexuality. To realize the full potential of this insight, however, we need to note that it predates the twentieth-century visual media industry to which Illouz mainly refers. Commodities as structuring sexuality pose a challenge to economics because they accompany the history of capitalism. To expand on the erotic nature of credit and luxury, we can turn from Defoe's financial advice to literature.

Immersed in imaginings of aristocratic lifestyle, Emma Bovary "confused in her desire the sensualities of luxury with the delights of the heart, elegance of manners with delicacy of sentiment" (Flaubert 2004, 57). After spending one night at a ball in the Marquis d'Andervilliers's chateau, her marriage to the country doctor Charles Bovary seems to her coarse and confining. She is captivated by romantic fantasies of high society life in Paris. Reading ladies' journals, she devours all accounts of "first nights, races and soirees." She even buys a map of Paris and strolls with the tip of her finger up the boulevards. Luxury appears to her as synonymous with romance.

Emma's confusion of luxury and love does not remain on the imaginary level. She embarks on a love affair with Rodolphe, a local landowner, who cruelly abandons her, and then with the clerk Leon Dupuis. She runs the affair on credit. The sly fancy-goods merchant Monsieur Lheureux tempts her to buy fashion items on credit and lends her money to finance her love travels to Rouen. She keeps rolling her growing debt, which Lheureux passes to other merchants, until payment is demanded, and the couple's property is foreclosed and auctioned. Desperate, she turns to ask for Rodolphe's help. He welcomes her passionately, ready to resume their love affair, but quickly becomes estranged upon learning that she came to ask for money: "A demand for money being, of all the winds that blow upon love, the coldest and most destructive" (Flaubert 2004, 326). The economy of love: love is wasteful; it costs money, but money must not be mentioned in its context (which is another way of saying it is wasteful).

Credit expresses the folly of love. Love can flourish so long as Emma can keep rolling her debt. She is oblivious of the basic economic fact that debts eventually demand redeeming. Through her oblivion, money becomes not only a literary device to depict the folly of love, its rejection of a calculating spirit. Money becomes an active agent, a nonhuman literary character alongside the human ones, leading Emma to her tragic death. Yet Emma's conduct is not simply an economic folly. Debt bills that keep rolling indefinitely are the condition of possibility of her love but also the form of credit-based money. Her erotic life mirrors the emergence of credit-based money or expresses the eroticism engrained in it.

Trollope's *The Way We Live Now* does more detailed work in situating credit at the juncture between traditional and capitalist sexual economies. "Love is like any other luxury. You have no right to it unless you can afford it" ([1875] 2012, 731). That is what Lady Carbury says about her daughter's, Hetta, desire to marry the penniless Paul Montague rather than her financially stable cousin Roger Carbury. Love is a luxury, an unnecessary supplement, from the traditional perspective on marriage as oriented at economic stability. But throughout the novel a certain form of love is related to luxury in the ordinary economic meaning of the term, in plays of seduction and falling in love that take place at extravagant balls hosted by the financier Mr. Melmotte. The novel combines a financial plot with some love stories. As Anat Rosenberg has shown, the financial aspect of the novel revolves around the relation between words and money, signs and value (2017, 65–73). What should be emphasized is that a similar relation informs the love plots: the relation between words and love. In the financial plot, Mr. Melmotte, a swindler with a shady past, climbs the social ladder in London by his extravagant parties and by a sort of a pyramid scheme revolving around a fantastic plan of constructing a railway from Salt Lake City to Vera Cruz. He is coarse and vulgar, and nobody likes him, yet impoverished aristocrats seek his company in the hope of getting a piece of the promised fortune or of marrying his daughter Marie, an unattractive and socially secluded young girl ("Everybody goes there," Hetta excuses her going to Melmotte's party to her honest cousin Roger, and he answers, "Yes, that is the excuse which everybody makes" [Trollope (1875) 2012, 64]). Melmotte has no intention of building the railway. There is no reason for him to do it when he can raise money with brilliantly printed programs, gorgeous maps, and "beautiful little pictures of trains running into tunnels beneath snowy mountains and coming out of them on the margin of sunlit lakes" (71). Melmotte makes money from words, thus financing his lavish lifestyle, which feeds back on his ability to make money from words. Melmotte makes money by speaking about money. His words are money: "Money was the very breath of Melmotte's nostrils, and therefore his breath was taken for money" (298).

Paralleling Melmotte's scheme is a seduction scheme of Felix, Hetta's handsome and unscrupulous brother, to marry Melmotte's daughter. He has no estate and his title is too low, so Melmotte scornfully dismisses the match, but Felix has a handsome face and knows how to dance and talk, so he uses his looks and skills to approach the daughter directly. His financial goal in seducing Marie taps into the form of his wooing. It does not consist of him confessing his love for her, but in convincing her she already knows he loves her. After their dance at the ball Felix tells her:

> "I'll tell you what you would like best in all the world."
> "What is that?"
> "Somebody that liked you best in all the world."
> "Ah,—yes; if one knew who?"
> "How can you know, Miss Melmotte, but by believing?" (Trollope [1875] 2012, 35)

Credit and finance bridge the gap between knowing and believing. Believing that something has value makes its valuable. The same goes with the play of seduction. When they depart Felix whispers, "You know who it is, likes you better than any one else in the world." And when she protests, "Nobody does;—don't, Sir Felix," he answers "I do," and holds her hand.

The financial spirit of seduction is highlighted by its counterpart in the novel, the authentic and honest love of Roger Carbury for Hetta. Roger represents traditional, precapitalist wealth. He could have lived comfortably from the profits of his estate, but he prefers to manage it himself instead of putting it in the hands of an agent. He "lived on his own land among his own people, as all the Carburys before him had done, and was poor because he was surrounded by rich neighbours" (Trollope [1875] 2012, 44). His unflinching honesty is marked by a rejection of the logic of credit. Hetta explains to Paul why everybody respects Roger: he always says what he thinks, and "if he spent a thousand pounds, everybody would know that he'd got it to spend" (331). Roger loves Hetta desperately, but his predicament is that his love is also honest, alien to notions of deception or masquerade. "The man had no poetry about him. He did not even care for romance. All the outside belongings of love which are so pleasant to many men and which to many women afford the one sweetness in life which they really relish, were nothing to him." He can conceive of love as an extension of friendship. He is already the dearest friend of Hetta, and in his confession to her he suggests that "it is quite possible you might come to love me" (169). It is also naturally set in a continuum with property relations: "I am sure,—quite sure that you are the only possible mistress of this house during my tenure of it" (168). Hetta respects Roger and sees him as her closest friend. In a sense she even loves him dearly. Yet his practical approach to love circumvents the possibility of her *falling in love* with him. She almost yields to his pleas, and the narrator adds: "Had he seized her in his arms and kissed her then, I think she would have yielded." Obviously, he could not have kissed her. Not simply because that would have been a breach of his respectful conduct, but it would have also been a financial form of love, alien to his persona: getting what you aim at by pretending that you have already achieved it.

Trollope's approach to money is anachronistic. Melmotte's financial scam eventually fails, and he commits suicide. The failure, however, resonates a moral suspicion of words that turn into money, which is a suspicion of credit as such, as distinguished from "real" money. Trollope's ironic narrator discloses his moral position, as well as his misunderstanding of money: "As for many years past we have exchanged paper instead of actual money for our commodities, so now it seemed that, under the new Melmotte régime, an exchange of words was to suffice" (Trollope [1875] 2012, 387). It is a misplaced irony: paper, as becomes clear in retrospect, is as real as any other form of money. Yet in the domain of love, Trollope is forward looking. He already knows there is no possibility of sustaining a parallel notion of "real" love as distinguished from the romantic pattern suffused with seduction and the play of appearances and colored by credit and finance. Such is the honest love that Roger offers to Hetta, free from make-believe and entangled with friendship and inherited property, but the literary form itself seems to preclude the possibility that Hetta will accept the offer.

How can money, this dull object, play a dramatic role in literature? The question seems specifically relevant to the tradition of nineteenth-century realist novels. To risk a generalization, during the twentieth century literature lost much of its insight about money. Money can still be central to narratives, but typically it no longer wears the form of an active agent. In both Flaubert and Trollope the insight of literature springs from a misunderstanding: a distinction between credit and "real" money. It is a constitutive misunderstanding, a necessary illusion accompanying the emergence of the capitalist form of money created by debt. For a long time, debts could circulate as means of payment on the condition that they referred to something else, a real object that can ultimately settle accounts. In the illusory distinction between money and credit, the former is an inert object (like Roger Carbury, it "has no poetry about it") while the latter is inherently related to imagining and seduction. The distinction opened a space for both love and literature, a space of free imagination limited by a cruel reality principle.

In Flaubert and Trollope three oppositions outlined the terrain of sexual economy: credit and money, love and marriage, and luxuries and traditional ways of life. Each opposition could serve as an interpretative key to the others. Twentieth-century literature lost clear sight of sexual economy because in reality these oppositions became blurred: credit is money, love became subsumed in marriage, and even the economic distinction between luxuries and necessities is no longer clearly marked—not because there are no luxuries anymore, of course, but because even the simplest goods can contain an element of luxury. The blurring of these distinctions does not necessarily entail a disappearance of the sexual economy that was so clearly visible to nineteenth-century writers. It may signal, rather, a more comprehensive eroticization of the economy.

Separate Spheres

Nineteenth-century novels entangle money with love and marriage. In various ways the history of money is practically entangled with the history of the family. The Victorian version of patriarchal ideology revolved around the doctrine of separate spheres, which stipulated that the different natures of men and women allot different social roles to both. While men should act in the public sphere of politics and economy, women belong in the private sphere of the household and family care. Coontz (2006) shows how this doctrine is articulated in relation to money. The spread in the use of money diminished the part of local barter exchange and household production in the economy. As late as 1797 one Bostonian woman could still complain, "There is no way of living in this town without cash" (Coontz 2006, 154). This growing dependence on money was articulated in gender roles. In an economy that included household production and barter exchange alongside money, women's home-keeping was naturally considered a form of labor. The growing dependence on money rendered women's work noneconomic. In parallel, Dabhoiwala (2013) notes a deep transformation in the conception of femininity during the eighteenth century. The long-lived conception of women as sinful, promiscuous, and seductive gave way to their conception as pure and morally innocent. These two transformations supported the distinction between the private and the public sphere: a feminine sphere of intimacy, tenderness, authenticity, and moral integrity set as a shelter from the masculine sphere of work and business. What should be emphasized is that these new conceptions of femininity and the family home are reflected in the status of money. They express in gendered terms a cynical attitude entangled with capitalist money. That women are morally pure and at the same time confined to the family home and excluded from the economy of money is another way of saying that money as masculine allows one to suspend moral considerations. That the family home is associated with authenticity means that money allows one to suspend his perception of self and adopt a cynical attitude. This moral suspicion of money is reflected in phobias that revolve around its crossing the gender barrier. Jackson Lears (1995) notes that a recurrent theme in American popular culture in the nineteenth century referred to traveling vendors seducing housewives to purchase seductive superfluous goods. Dabhoiwala (2013) notes the moral panic in nineteenth-century England around the notion of "mercenary marriage." Lists of eligible women noting their estimated fortune and place of residence allegedly served gentlemen in finding a target for seduction. The panic, of course, did not arise from the intermingling of marriage and property, a long-standing norm in the propertied classes. It resulted from the infiltration of love and seduction to the marriage and property nexus, whose corollary is a monetized outlook on the marriage deal. The shift from traditional property to a monetary outlook is evident in the notion of mercenary marriage as well as in the monetized estimates of fortunes of women.

The sexual revolutions of the twentieth century make the nineteenth-century entanglements of money, love, and marriage seem obsolete. As love gradually became the dominant motivation for marriage, it no longer articulated the difference between traditional and capitalist sexual economies. The question is whether the sexual economy so clearly portrayed in nineteenth-century literature lost its hold on gender relations, or whether it disappeared from sight because it came to cover the whole of them. The latter possibility will be demonstrated in chapters 5 and 6, which present, respectively, the eroticization of consumption and the infiltration of financial logic into eroticism. For now, a quick look at the early stages of the sexual revolution can show how the detachment of eroticism from marriage is expressed in the way credit and finance inform new rituals of love and courting, even as they lead to marriage.

A Willard Waller's (1937) classic study of dating in American colleges in the 1930s was one of the first explorations of the rise of erotic culture independent of marriage. The intriguing point is that the detachment of erotic activity from the traditional locus of sexual economy resulted in a new economy, structured around notions of credit and finance. Waller contrasts dating to traditional forms of courtship, still customary at the time. The difference has to do with the status of words and signals. In traditional courting every step in the process "has a customary meaning and constitutes a powerful pressure toward taking the next step—is in fact a sort of implied commitment to take the next step" (Waller 1937, 728). In traditional courting, signals have a "cash value" leading to the goal of marriage. Dating, by contrast, is an erotic activity, in Bataille's sense of the term, as detached from the biological function of sex in reproduction. In Waller's words, it is a "thrill-seeking" activity conducted for its own sake, in a whole range of new legitimate practices: dancing, petting, necking, the automobile, the amusement park, and more. In parallel, the status of signals in dating is different. It is governed by performative signs taking part in a play of seduction: dancing well, having "a good line." The detachment of dating from the goal of marriage, however, does not entail its liberation from economy. Rather, it marks a new form of economy, embodied in differential erotic values of respective dates. For men, these erotic values are more or less objectively constituted. Whether a young man is an "A class" date is determined by the status of his fraternity, his clothes, his supply of spending money, his access to a car, and more. The erotic value of women, by contrast, follows the logic of credit. The most important factor determining a young woman's erotic value is her popularity as a date, the perception that everybody wants to date her. Like credit, she has erotic value insofar as she is perceived as someone to whom everybody attributes erotic value. This perception can be intentionally cultivated but might also be undermined by mistakes. To cultivate reputation, a female student should not date the same student too often. Girls "must be seen when they go out, and therefore must go to the popular (and expensive) meeting places" (730). Mistakes such as accepting last-minute invitations might, on the other hand, impair a girl's reputation and diminish her erotic value. The erotic value of female students as distinct from that of men follows the pattern of capital: "Here as nowhere else nothing succeeds like success" (730). The immediate parallel is the notion of financial capital which appears as money that begets money. The erotic value of women recapitulates Marx's definition of financial capital as "money which is worth more money, value which is greater than itself" (1976, 257).

The parallel to finance is underscored in cases where dating eventually leads to marriage. In contrast to traditional courting, dating as a new form of courting involves "falling in love," a process which typically occurs "with a certain unwillingness." Like traditional courtship, falling in love is driven by reciprocal signs, but their nature is different. They are inflated signs belonging to the realm of make-believe. The young man tries to convince the young woman that he has already fallen seriously in love with her, "a sort of exaggeration, sometimes a burlesque, of coquetry" (Waller 1937, 733). Just as financial values are affected by expectations, and as promises of future value can materialize in the present, falling in love involves sentiments that are formed through pretending: "Each encourages the other to fall in love by pretending that he has already done so" (733). As in financial assets, the slippage between expectations and reality is prone to crisis. Waller's description of the process resonates with the notions of financial bubbles and business cycles: in some cases, falling in love is facilitated by a series of "periodic crises" which redefine the relationship on deeper levels of involvement. Lovers' quarrels are fueled by the ambivalent status of speech in the context of dating. A form of erotic technique is involved. Waller stresses the role of "the conventionalized 'line'" in dating, noting how this form of erotic speech facilitates a sort of "pluralistic ignorance" because it obscures the real state of mind of the interlocuters. It gives rise to the suspicion that one's partner does not experience a growth of feeling parallel to one's own. The process as a whole displays a dynamic of self-inflating values and detachment from reality:

> A idealises B, and presents to her that side of his personality which is consistent with his idealised conception of her; B idealises A, and governs her behaviour toward him in accordance with her false notions of his nature; the process of idealisation is mutually re-enforced in such a way that it must necessarily lead to an increasing divorce from reality . . . one falls in love when he reaches the point where sentiment-formation overcomes objectivity. (Waller 1937, 734)

While signals in traditional courting imply solid commitments, falling in love is governed by signs of the nature of masquerade. They perform something which is not there yet but can sometimes materialize through its signaling.

Today, not only traditional courting but also dating seem almost obsolete. Writing in the second decade of the twenty-first century, Emily Witt describes a sexual domain that has allegedly lost all coherence. The words once used to describe relationships no longer seem appropriate. Maybe the heritage they carry of a time before the awakening of gender consciousness makes them awkward for use. "One friend," she writes, "referred to a 'non-ex' with whom he had carried on a 'nonrelationship' for a year" (Witt 2017, 5). After a long and somewhat melancholic expedition into the world of alternative sexualities, however, Witt recalls that within this hazy field of erotic relationships one word remained stable: "*Marriage* was the one word in our era of sexual freedom that has not lost its specificity. In contrast to the linguistic murk of *dating* we still knew what *marriage* meant" (155). Although people in her social circle, herself included, find it harder to marry, marriage itself displays an institutional persistence. As Witt puts it: "To be married in life was in perfect congruence with what it meant to be married on one's tax form" (155). There are no proper names for sex outside marriage. Marriage is the only name, and it too is inappropriate, alluding to tax forms rather than sex. That is a characteristic of the strange dominating position that marriage still holds over the domain of sexuality. Marriage holds this position as a relic, a blind institutional persistence. Love plays an ambivalent role in this persistence. Marriage in Witt's social circle "had to be an expression of the purest love and show a deliberate break with history" (156). Love is a break with history and at the same time a form of institutional persistence. It repudiates the stale institutional heritage of marriage while justifying one more iteration of it. Witt calls these "neo-marriages." A sign of their ambivalent relation to history, as both its disavowal and its persistence, is the need to celebrate them in new forms. Some of these weddings are more celebratory ("I went to weddings in rural Vermont, New Orleans, Los Angeles, and Quebec. I went to weddings in Lisbon, Chicago, Brooklyn, and upstate New York"). In some of them, ceremonies serve as an aesthetic adornment ("I went to Catholic weddings, Jewish weddings, and Hindu weddings"), while others discard ceremonies. They all seem, in a sense, a ritualistic distancing from traditional ritual. Spending may also have played a role in marking the celebration of pure love: "Most of my travel and spending money," Witt writes, "went toward weddings" (155).

From a different angle, polyamory demonstrates the resilience of monogamy, which can survive even the loss of its most solid traditional ground of sexual exclusivity. Polyamory is grounded on contempt of centuries of sexual shame and hypocrisy and a belief in sex as a natural, healthy, and pleasurable appetite. That it is not necessarily an emancipation of sex from centuries of institutional coercion is evidenced by a proliferation of rules, boundaries, and self-discipline mechanisms recommended in polyamory guides. The skills that Hardy and Easton's best-selling guide *The Ethical*

Slut (2017) lists as essential for polyamory sometimes remind one of the skills demanded in high-tech firms: "Get yourself a group calendar and use it: some of the online calendars, where everyone can enter appointments and see what other appointments others have made, work well for this" (88). Successful polyamory demands communication skills, planning, limit setting, honesty. It is set against monogamous sexuality but can buttress monogamous marriage with an inflation of disciplinary tools. Maybe polyamory is the monogamy of the information age. Just as property and commodities are increasingly dematerialized, the exclusivity of monogamy is maintained in abstract terms.

FOUR

Prostitution and Finance

THE SEXUAL ECONOMY OF CAPITALISM IS CHARACTERIZED by the conceptual triad of marriage, love, and prostitution. When marriage is conceived in terms of an expression of love, rather than as an exchange, practical considerations in spouse selection cast on marriage a suspicion of prostitution in disguise. This chapter explores the economy revolving around this third aspect of the triad. Its first part addresses the moral controversy about prostitution. It does not add new arguments to this controversy but focuses instead on the conceptualizations of economy underlying it. Arguments about legalization or criminalization of sex work imply notions of the economy and the market, of what they are and what they should be. Some critics claim that feminism should strive to eradicate the stigma of prostitution rather than sex work itself. The chapter avoids this question to addresses the stigma as a fact, a basic *economic* fact which pertains in specific ways to capitalism. The selling of sex is socially abhorred, and this fact tells us something significant not only about sex and femininity but also about money. The second part of the chapter turns to fantasies about prostitution. Popular culture recurrently associates prostitution with finance. The chapter shows the economic logic at the root of this association.

Money

Sex worker Jo Weldon notes a strange absence of the question of money from contemporary discourse about prostitution. She has been interviewed often by researchers, but while every one of them asked her whether she was sexually abused as a child, no one ever asked her a single question about her financial mindset (Ditmore, Levy, and Willman 2013, 147–48). This absence of the question of money from the discourse on sex work attests that prostitution provides a unique vantage point on money in capitalism. We can get a glance at it through the familiar cliché that in capitalism everything has its price. In a naïve reading, this cliché only recapitulates the idiotic economic conception of money as a neutral means, a measure of value which sustains a web of universal equivalence between all possible goods. This reading obviously misses the obscene and real meaning of the cliché. Saying that everything has its price refers primarily to things that *should not* be bought—it implies that these too are sometimes bought, or suspected as being bought, or indirectly bought, or that one can buy a substitute of them. Prostitution embodies this cliché. The economic meaning of prostitution is that *even* sex can be bought (and in the cases of the "girlfriend experience" and sugar daddies *even* a semblance of love can be bought). In prostitution men buy sex as an equivalent of this "everything" that money can buy. That is why prostitution is symptomatic of capitalism: it is an exception to the world of commodities which stands for this world as a whole.

The omission of the question of money from the discourse on prostitution is echoed in the controversy over the term *sex work*. Sex workers and activists Juno Mac and Molly Smith, authors of *Revolting Prostitutes*, show how the circumvention of the question of money frames the controversy between pro and anti-prostitution feminists in a way which blinds them to the real interests of many women in prostitution. They divide the controversy between "Happy Hookers" (or "Erotic Professionals"), who defend the right to engage in sex work, and "Exited Women" and "carceral feminists" who push for its criminalization. Strangely enough, both sides share a common perspective: they both conceive of prostitution primarily as kind of sex rather than a kind of work. On the one hand, the opponents of prostitution see the term *sex work* as a euphemistic attempt to normalize it. They consequently insist on seeing it as a degrading sexual practice rather than a degrading form of work. Mac and Smith report on a meeting with a Scottish government minister, interested in hearing the experience of a small group of sex workers: "She observed that we all seemed to have started selling sex in order to *get money*, in a tone suggesting not only that she was slightly incredulous. But that selling sex in order to earn an income seemed terribly mercenary to her" (2018, 46). The minister invoked in response the familiar stories of sex workers who use drugs, ignoring the obvious fact that they too are in prostitution for economic reasons: to buy drugs. On the other hand, for some proponents of prostitution it is not enough to present it as a form of work. Advocates, especially from within the sex economy, are pushed to bestow on it a mission of liberating society from age-old sexual prejudice. Some of them go so far as to present it as fulfilling and empowering, and position themselves as "answering a vocational 'calling' that seems to have barely anything to do with being paid" (31). What is omitted between these two positions is the experience of the "unhappy sex workers," who choose to remain in prostitution "as a rational survival strategy in an often shitty world" (49). They oppose criminalization which would destroy their livelihood, without glorifying sex work. They may experience prostitution as horrible yet better than other occupations open for unskilled women, like factory work or cleaning.

The omission of the question of work from the discourse on prostitution reflects ways of construing the economy and the market. What do the opponents of prostitution say when they deny its status as work? Kajsa Ekis Ekman portrays the public campaigns defending sex work in the 1970s and 1980s, beginning with COYOTE's "Hookers' Balls," as an orchestrated effort, driven partly by brothel owners, to normalize prostitution. The impact of such campaigns was "that people began to speak regularly of prostitution in terms of 'work'" (2013, 59). What is the meaning of her protest, granted that in some basic sense of the term, prostitution is obviously a form of work? It is how some women make a living and take part in the economy. One might think that what Ekis Ekman really means is that prostitution is not a *legitimate* form of work. Such a claim implies a general ethical outlook on market economy, on what can legitimately be included in it and what cannot. An implicit economic theory is entangled with the resistance to the term *sex work*. It also brings about a theoretical economic question: what is economy if prostitution, as an exception, is factually included in it? Ekis Ekman, however, does not confuse "is" and "ought" in her argument. She supports her claim with a factual distinction: in prostitution, in contrast to other occupations, women sell *themselves*. This only highlights the question of prostitution as an exception to the market. How do we conceptualize the market that factually includes prostitution? What is the relation between prostitution and legitimate occupations? The resistance to "sex work" precludes the possibility of viewing prostitution as a symptom: a point of exception to the market, which is nonetheless included in it, and for that reason provides a unique perspective of it.

This possibility arises from the perspective of some sex work activists. The familiar idea that prostitutes "sell themselves" enrages some of them. Melissa Gira Grant, an author and a former sex worker, argues that this cliché mistakes representation with reality, overlooking the skills that sex workers apply in complying with their clients' fantasies and desires. Feminist critique is haunted by notions of objectification and female submissiveness involved in prostitution, but to present them as meaning that prostitutes sell themselves is to ignore the way these notions are consciously performed. "Acting as if we share our customers' desire is the work of sex work" (Gira Grant 2014, 86). That does not mean that sex work is like any other work, but it allows Grant to present the boundary between prostitution and legitimate occupations as sketched across a continuum. This aspect is underlined in a process that has reshaped in recent decades both the formal economy and the sex economy, bringing them closer to each other: the growing share of service work in post-Fordist economies on the one hand, and the gentrification and mainstreaming of sex work on the other. The rise of the service economy increasingly involves workers in the need to fabricate consumers' experiences—what Joseph Pine and James Gilmore (1999) termed "the experience economy." Some service workers—like a bartender or a hairstylist—are even expected to create a semblance of intimacy, which Arlie Hochschild (1983) termed "emotional labor." Against this background, Gira Grant (2014) argues, parallel changes in the sex work disclose a sense of its convergence with the formal economy.

The sex economy in the last few decades went through a process of gentrification. Its raunchy manifestations, such as red-light districts in urban centers, were curtailed. As the internet took their place, it adopted some expressions which align with the language of the service economy, such as "girlfriend experience" and "sugar daddies." This convergence highlights the symptomatic status of prostitution in relation to capitalist economy. Prostitutes do not sell themselves to customers, but they explicitly stage the fantasy of selling themselves. And this fantasy is implicit in the move toward the experience economy, where many service workers are increasingly ordered to stage similar fantasies of offering intimacy to customers.

The theoretical economic stakes of the question of sex work become most evident in the context of the connection between sexual abuse in childhood and prostitution. The claim that many sex workers are former victims of sexual abuse in childhood plays a central role in the arguments against prostitution (Ekis Ekman 2013, 69–70). There are, however, two ways to interpret the claim. In their use of the claim, anti-prostitution activists allude to a psychological causality leading from sexual abuse to sex work. Sexual abuse in childhood inflicts grave harm on the formation of selfhood and self-esteem, putting young girls in a condition that makes it possible for them to see themselves in the abhorrent image of the prostitute. It imprisons the girl in a cycle of repeating the abuse. This psychological explanation implies again an exclusion of the prostitute from the sphere of economy. Bound to repeat the traumatic abuse, she is deprived of the basic capability qualifying the economic agent in the ideological conception of the market, namely free choice. Mac and Smith, by contrast, propose a simple economic causality connecting sexual abuse in childhood with prostitution. Victims of sexual abuse within the family are obviously more likely to lack an economic safety net later in life, which severely limits the scope of their free choice. It is not only that the economic explanation is more plausible than the psychological one. The latter appears as a vestige of vulgar approaches to psychology. In any other case one would hesitate to take seriously psychological explanations applied to whole populations. We could not seriously accept today a psychological explanation for why people become lawyers or economists. More importantly, although the sexual abuse argument springs from feminist circles, it recapitulates nineteenth-century allegedly scientific studies of prostitution, by authors such as Cesare Lombroso and Alexandre Parent-Duchâtelet, who under the guise of objectivity and moral neutrality tried to diagnose prostitutes through their character and physiological distinctions from normal women. Their motivations and worldview are far removed from contemporary anti-prostitution feminists, but the latter retain the framework which explains prostitution by viewing the prostitute as a special type of person. Innate qualities no longer make up the figure of the prostitute, but the sexual abuse argument still portrays her as a distinct figure. That is the theoretical economic question encapsulated in the sex work debate: the ideological conception of the market as the sphere of free choice and mutually beneficial exchanges relies on rendering the prostitute a special persona, excluded from this sphere. The rest of the chapter addresses the question of what view of economy results from including sex work in it, not just as one more type of work, but as an exception whose inclusion changes the view of the field from which it is excluded.

A famous chauvinist anecdote attributed to George Bernard Shaw gestures at the theoretical economic meaning of prostitution. It is said that Shaw once told a woman at a party that people will do anything for money. The woman refused to believe this, so Shaw asked her, "Would you sleep with a man for a million pounds?" The woman answered that maybe she would. "Would you do it for five pounds?" asked Shaw. "Certainly not!" said the woman. "What do you take me for? A prostitute?" "We've established that already," said Shaw. "We're just trying to fix the price." The story expresses the misogynist idea that every woman is potentially a whore. It thus captures the unique status of the whore stigma. The pejorative "whore" is allegedly addressed at *some* women, yet because it has to do with femininity as such, it looms over every woman. But there is an economic underside to it. Paying for sex is equivalent to *everything* that money can buy, and thus prostitution consummates a characteristic of money. Doing so, the story questions the economic concept of price. When sex is involved, there is no correct price. This is suggested by the extreme volatility of possible prices, fluctuating between five and a million pounds. Moreover, there is no correct price, because the price changes the status of what it buys. Having sex for five pounds clearly makes the woman a prostitute. Doing it for a million, she is a prostitute in disguise, a diffusion of the prostitute metaphor into decent economy and society.

A real counterpart of the story is found in a paradoxical feature of the sex economy. As Mac and Smith point out, the sex workers who disavow the monetary motivation in their occupation are also those that make more money. The "erotic professionals," who cultivate the impression that they love their work, are at the economic high end of the industry. Mac and Smith quote an interview with an escort: "A prostitute will do everything for money. Not me . . . I try to forget about the money . . . I don't even think about [payment] until the very end. I don't demand payment up front, because the guys I go with are always good people . . . I also adore sex. I wouldn't be in this profession if I didn't like it" (2018, 31). That is a very strange economy, where the price goes up when the seller insists that she is not interested in money. This anomaly reflects two forms of articulation of what money cannot buy in sex work. Prostitutes who "will do everything for money" reflect the obscene meaning of the category: money can buy everything including what it should not. The escort who doesn't "even think" about money embodies the sublime meaning of the same category: the impression of passion is entangled with a denunciation of the monetary aspect of the act. She gives a further demonstration of Adam Smith's claim that there are things that should not be exchanged for money and for that reason are expensive.

The Fantasy of the Market

Amia Srinivasan (2022) sees the carceral tendency in feminism as a retreat from the revolutionary demand to change society that characterized the feminist movement of the 1970s. It is a part of a broad shift "away from the transformation of socio-economic life towards securing women's equality in the pre-existing structures of capitalism" (Srinivasan 2022, 163). Some versions of the discourse of sex work, though opposed to carceral feminism, share its embrace of the market. While carceral feminism consecrates the market with the demand to legally exclude disruptive subject matter from it, the discourse on sex work can embrace it with the demand to include even sex in the market. It expresses an erotic infatuation with the market.

Ekis Ekman provides some examples of this erotic embrace of the market by the media. The COYOTE's "Hookers' Balls," she writes, were promoted with a promise "to rub elbows with 'real whores'" (2013, 49–50). Stories about establishing sex workers' trade unions gave newspapers ample opportunities for sordid headlines, which can be read as sublimated ways of "rubbing elbows" with whores: "Hookers Arise!"; "Hookers of the World Unite"; "Love's Laborers Organize"; and "Organizing the Oldest Profession" (49–50). Writing about a sex workers' conference, the newspapers give in to an erotic fantasy. What kind of fantasy is it? As a sexual fantasy, an organization of prostitutes alludes to a harem. It is the fantasy of possessing all women. At the same time, it is also a fantasy about economy and organizations. It is a fantasy about the permeation of prostitution into decent society and about an all-encompassing market, subsuming even prostitution within its purview. It is an erotic embrace of the market. This explains why even neoliberal writers, as Ekis Ekman notes, enthusiastically embraced the idea of trade unions for prostitutes (60).

The erotic embrace of the market finds a sober articulation in Martha Nussbaum's defense of prostitution. "All of us . . . take money for the use of our body" (Nussbaum 1998, 693), she argues, and goes on to a deliberately naïve comparison between the bodily services provided by women in prostitution and those provided by factory workers, domestic servants, nightclub singers, professors of philosophy, and masseuses. She cannot find any quality that inherently distinguishes the services that prostitutes sell from those of the other occupations. Some of them involve intimate touch; others involve things that are considered intimately associated with self-hood. The framework that makes the comparison possible is the economic conception of money as a neutral medium that sets for everything its correct price. It is this framework that is the true subject matter of Nussbaum's deliberation. Its fantasmatic nature surfaces in a cringey invention that for some reason she finds it necessary to add to the list of professions: the occupation of a "colonoscopy artist," who "gets paid for having her colon examined with the latest instruments, in order to test out their range and capability" (701). Money not only buys everything, but it makes it possible to imagine anything. Unable to find in the occupation itself the reason for the stigma of prostitution, Nussbaum finds refuge in the garbage bin of all weak arguments, namely, in *culture*. It is a vestige of age-old prejudice regarding female sexuality. It "boils down to the view that women are essentially immoral and dangerous . . . The prostitute, being seen as the uncontrolled and sexually free woman, is in this picture seen as particularly dangerous, both necessary to society and in need of constant subjugation" (709). There is an unmistakable anachronism in this claim. Popular culture is flooded with images of uncontrolled, sexually free femininity, presented as models of admiration rather than shame. To say that her argument is anachronistic, however, is not to say that it is simply wrong. The stigma of prostitution is no doubt an inheritor of age-old phobias of female sexuality and is still a powerful tool of oppression of women. The point that escapes Nussbaum is that this stigma has gone through a transformation and is today inextricably entangled with money. The stigma is not about sex but about its exchange for money. Such an obvious point necessarily escapes Nussbaum because of the liberal conception of the market that underlies her deliberation. From this perspective she can only try in vain to inquire what is it in sex that distinguishes it from other occupations, making its exchange for money stigmatized. Her failure underlines the way prostitution is a symptomatic exception to the liberal concepts of money and the market. Money is not just paid to a prostitute for a service she provides. It makes her a prostitute.

From what vantage point in the capitalist economy can prostitution be seen as an exception to the liberal conception of the market? One way to see it is by suspending for a moment the otherwise justified dictum to listen to the authentic voices of sex workers themselves. Mac and Smith protest the tendency to view sex workers as helpless victims, selling their bodies and foregoing control over their selves. "One of the key ideas used to treat prostitution as 'not work' is the idea that we are simply holes: that we are offering up *purchased consent*" (2018, 43). Some feminists critics get carried away by the rhetoric about men paying prostitutes to do whatever they like with their bodies. This perspective, Mac and Smith argue, is blind to the lived experience of sex workers who constantly draw boundaries to what they agree or do not agree to do. These boundaries are prevalent in the sex industry to the extent that there are common abbreviations familiar to clients to signify them in adverts. Mac and Smith, however, know perfectly well where this rhetoric of control comes from: "We live in a culture where it is assumed that to penetrate someone sexually is intrinsically an act of dominance and to be sexually penetrated is to be made subservient" (45). In other words, while *factually* sex workers do not turn over control over their selves to clients, that may be precisely the fantasy that fuels the sex industry. The boundaries declared by sex workers enable male clients to stage their personal fantasies of domination. While sex workers do not really sell themselves, what clients are after is the fantasy of dominating a woman.

Here lies another way to formulate a distinguishing feature of prostitution that escapes Nussbaum. In prostitution, men pay for domination over women, expressed in sexual terms. In this context, Nussbaum's strategy of deliberate naivete may in fact be fruitful. We need only to reformulate her naïve reservation, and center it around the concept of domination rather than exchange. "All of us . . . take money for the use of our body" (1998, 693) means also that all of us give others the right to dominate us. Waged workers forfeit their autonomy and accept some measure of domination by others. Wage laborers are typically not hired for a predetermined task but for performing things demanded from them during working hours. For economists this fact emerged at some point as a puzzle. It is indeed a mundane reality, but it diverges from the economic view of the market as composed of autonomous individuals buying and selling goods and services. Ronald Coase presented the puzzle explicitly in "The Nature of the Firm" by pointing out that relationships within firms diverge from the model of the market economy: "If a workman moves from department Y to department X, he does not go because of a change in relative prices, but because he is ordered to do so" (1937, 387). Unlike Nussbaum's analogy between prostitutes and professors of philosophy, this one actually highlights the unique economic status of sex work. We all take money for the right to dominate us, but in an ordinary economy this domination is supposed to serve an external purpose, while in prostitution it is an end in itself. When a boss orders an employee to do something, he is not supposed to *enjoy* his power of command (well, maybe he does, but then there is something very wrong in the situation, at least for the official language of the economy).

The unsettling notion of pleasure in domination marks both an exceptional status of prostitution within capitalist economy and a dimension of continuum between it and the formal economy. It suggests that domination may be the ulterior principle of economy, which in capitalism becomes disguised within the market form. In other words, the pleasure of domination expresses how the economy is still fundamentally *political*, concerned with differential power relations between people rather than with people having more things or less things. Slavoj Žižek's ([1989] 2008) interpretation of commodity fetishism points precisely at this. Marx's commodity fetishism, he argues, explains both the break and the continuity between feudalism and capitalism. In feudalism, economic exploitation was organized through direct relations of domination, between lords and vassals or artisans and apprentices. In capitalism political relations between people are strictly egalitarian, yet exploitation persists as it is mediated through commodities. Feudal relations of domination are disavowed but persist in a new form mediated by objects (18–22). Prostitution, in this framework, expresses this disavowed kernel of capitalist economy. In this sense, prostitution is the real of capitalist economy, as attested by the lack of proper words to describe it in the terminology of exchange. What does the sex worker "sell" for money? All options appear as either euphemistic (prostitutes sell sex, they provide a sexual service) or as taking part in the degradation of prostitutes (they sell themselves, they sell their bodies).

Men, Women, and Money

The sexual revolution of the twentieth century is at the backdrop of contemporary debates about prostitution. For proponents of sex work, normalizing prostitution is a consummation of sexual liberation. Their opponents see the invocation of sexual liberation in this context as one more form of false ideological justification of prostitution. The obscene kernel of money and sex nexus, however, reveals a strange mode of resilience throughout the sexual revolution, a mode of persistence through change. Literature provides a clear view of it through the broader theme of illicit money transfers from men to women. To begin with, it is a telling fact that a money transfer from a man to a woman can be a key event in a literary plot. Two novels, from the beginning and the end of the twentieth century, manifest a transformation of the theme while preserving its obscene kernel. Accepting a money gift from a man is the original sin of Lily Bart, the protagonist pf Edith Wharton's *The House of Mirth* from 1905, as well as of Janey Wilcox, the protagonist of Candace Bushnell's *Trading Up* from 2003, which in many respects appears as a reworking of Wharton's novel. Both women become social outcasts once rumors and stories about the money gift start to circulate. The two manifestations of scandal, however, show an inversion of roles between money and sex.

In Wharton's novel the rumors about Lily receiving money from Gus Trenor, the husband of one of her best friends, give rise to insinuations as to what she must have given in return. Her social circle banishes her, and because she lacks financial resources, her position deteriorates until she has no option but to work for her living, a task for which she is utterly incompatible. She slowly sinks into a numb existence and eventually dies. Such a plot, typical of the Victorian era obsession with the purity of women, appears outdated today. It is Bushnell's literary achievement that she succeeded in producing a twenty-first century version of it. Her protagonist Janey is a social climber, a Victoria's Secret model who wishes to enter high society life in New York, and fulfills her desire by marrying Selden Rose, an up-and-coming manager in a media conglomerate. It goes without saying that she already has a rich sexual past when she marries. In fact, she even has somewhat of a bad reputation. But one specific affair comes back to haunt her. A year prior to her marriage she had a love affair with the Hollywood producer Comstock Dibble, which she hides from her husband. The trouble, however, is that Comstock also paid her an advance for writing a screenplay she has never completed. A tabloid exposes the payment, presenting it as a disguised payment for sex, with acerbic headlines.

A money transfer from a man to a woman is obscene. In Wharton it is obscene because of the sexual insinuations enveloping it. The sexual undertone, however, is inherent to money. Lily had no intimate contact with Gus, though she did elicit the money transfer, arousing his feelings with a masquerade of female helplessness. It was not presented as a gift either. Gus only proposes to invest Lily's money on Wall Street with tips extracted from Simon Rosedale the Jew. Lily does not understand much about Wall Street: "She understood only that her modest investments were to be mysteriously multiplied without risk to herself" ([1905] 1997, 75).

When checks start to arrive from Gus, she remains conveniently oblivious of the fact that she never gave him her money to invest. At one point Gus tricks her to visit him, but when she finds him alone at his house she hurriedly flees. Nonetheless, rumors start to spread. We do not read much about the content of the rumors. There are only rumors about rumors. Grace Stepney maliciously informs Lily's aunt and guardian, Mrs. Peniston, that people are talking about Lily and Trenor. "People always say unpleasant things—and certainly they're a great deal together. A friend of mine met them the other afternoon in the Park quite late, after the lamps were lit" (109–10). When the aunt demands that she explicate her insinuations, Grace feigns reluctance but eventually confesses: "People say that Gus Trenor pays her bills" (111).

A rumor is society crystalized: it makes no difference whether one tells the rumor itself or only reports that other people are spreading a rumor. And the rumor's effects are not diminished, but rather accentuated, when it remains vague. Lily is aware of this. When her banishment from society nears completion, her friend Gerty Farish wants to know the truth: "But what is your story, Lily? I don't believe any one knows it yet" (197). Lily avoids a clear answer and eventually says impatiently, "You asked me just now for the truth—well, the truth about any girl is that once she's talked about she's done for; and the more she explains her case the worse it looks" (197). Being talked about, Lily eventually pays dearly for the money she received.

The opaqueness of money resonates in the opaqueness of the rumors. The plot probably wouldn't have worked so well had Trenor given Lily a thing as a gift. The sexual insinuation is inherent to money. If money changed hands, something must have been given in return. It does not matter if people know this something was sexual. Its sexual meaning is amplified by people *not knowing* what it is: "People say that Gus Trenor pays her bills." Zupančič's insistence on the ontological negativity of sex is most relevant here. We do not know what sex is. The shame and embarrassment that surround it do not cover up what it is, but the fact that we cannot know what it is. "We could perhaps go so far as to say: when—in the human realm—we come across something and have absolutely no clue what it is, we can be pretty certain that it 'has to do with sex'" (Zupančič 2017, 23).

In Bushnell, the money and sex nexus remains scandalous through an inversion of roles. It is not that a sexual insinuation renders the money transfer scandalous, but the other way around: the monetary transfer renders sex scandalous. It is no big scandal that Janey had sex with Comstock, but only that it can be associated with money. As with Lily, the status of the transfer is equivocal. Janey did intend to write a screenplay as part of her ambitions to climb the social ladder but abandoned it after writing some pages. It is a *monetary insinuation* that renders sex scandalous. The twentieth-century sexual revolution separates the two texts. It had dissolved the age-old sex prejudice, but the money and sex nexus emerged from it in a new form, where the focus of obscenity has shifted from sex to money. In a sense, as sex became ethically normalized, the obscenity of the nexus has folded into money.

Two more inversions between the plots suggest a more complex view of the historical change that separates them: paralleling the story of sexual liberation and a movement away from puritan sexuality is a movement into a more explicit manifestation of the sexual economy. First, while Lily's is a story of descent, Janey's is a story of social climbing. Second, Janey escapes Lily's tragic end. By the end of the novel, she completes the screenplay, and production companies vie over its purchase. Ironically, the script, as we learn after a long flashback, is based on her own experience in a sort of sex work: as a poor and lonely American model in Paris, she fell into high-class escorting on a yacht of an Arab arms smuggler. The scandal that envelops her is not altogether unwarranted. Even after coming back from Europe, she has been accustomed to using her sexuality to gain her social ambitions, as a girl from a middle-class family trying to pave her own way in a world dominated by powerful men. Even her marriage to Selden was a partly calculated step in her scheme. The shadow of prostitution has always accompanied her. Noting the difference between herself and her friend and rival, the socialite Mimi Kilroy, Janey is aware that "a rich girl could sleep with a hundred men and people would call her bohemian, while a poor girl who did the same thing was labeled a gold digger or a whore" (Bushnell 2003, 23). Owning the prostitution stigma is eventually what saves her.

There is an economic explanation for the difference between Lily's and Janey's fates. A first clue is the contrast between the different ways in which feminine beauty is expressed in the novels in monetary terms. In the beginning of Wharton's novel, when Lawrence Selden (not to be confused with Bushnell's Selden Rose) accidentally meets Lily in a train station, he has "a confused sense that she must have cost a great deal to make, that a great many dull and ugly people must, in some mysterious way, have been sacrificed to produce her" (Wharton [1905] 1997, 5). Accompanying her out of the station he is "conscious of taking a luxurious pleasure in her nearness" (5). As for Janey, there is neither mystery nor any confused sense of the monetary aspect of her beauty. She directly monetizes it as a model. Her looks are monetary. When Selden Rose brings her to a dinner party, expecting to arouse the jealousy of his peers, all married to successful middle-aged women, he disgustedly admits to himself that she dresses like a whore. He gradually understands that she picks her clothes by their expensiveness.

The two monetary forms of beauty belong to different economies. Lily's is the economy of old money, where wealth is present but not talked about directly. Lawrence Selden, as an external observer of Lily's social circle, explains this clearly: "So it is with your rich people—they may not be thinking about money, but they're breathing it all the while" (Wharton [1905] 1997, 61). That is why the monetary aspect of her beauty is "mysterious." That is also the economic cause of her tragic end. Lily is a prototypical literary portrayal of old money, precisely because she has no money. She was born to a wealthy family and acquired the exquisite tastes and lifestyle that wealth affords, yet before the plot begins her family is financially ruined. She knows "very little about the value of money" yet her tastes demand expensive things—not because they are expensive but because they appeal to her sense of beauty. As the next chapter will elaborate, the economic concept that best captures the phenomenon of old money is Thorstein Veblen's concept of conspicuous leisure. Lily is a literary replica of a social type which Veblen returns to from time to time in his *Theory of the Leisure Class*, representing "spurious" leisure class: "Abjectly poor and living a precarious life of want and discomfort, but morally unable to stoop to gainful pursuits" (Veblen [1899] 2007, 32). Lily's tragic death—half accident half suicide—happens after her social descent forces her to work for a living, a humiliating task she cannot perform. There is, however, another economic cause for her death. At the beginning of the plot, she still spends most of her days at the social events of her circle—a costly activity in itself—but must find a proper match quickly, before her monetary resources as well as her beauty dwindle. It is a puzzle why she had not succeeded in this already, being the most elegant and beautiful young woman in her social circle. In the novel's plot she gets one more chance, a prospective match with a rich and boring heir of great fortune. She most easily charms him, but then half-consciously sabotages the match, accelerating her way down. Putting aside psychological explanations, her deterioration and eventual demise is a result of her adhering too seriously to the values of old money, with its recoil from explicit mention of money. Her refinement cannot withstand the vulgar notion of monetizing her beauty and character through marriage.

The economy of old money is reflected in the "mysterious" connection of Lily's beauty to money. This can be read in reverse. Lily's beauty is an embodiment of the mysterious nature of money in the culture of conspicuous leisure: money which is present everywhere but not to be talked about. Janey, by contrast, personifies the economy of new money and is thus an embodiment of the obscenity, rather than the mystery, of money. The proper economic conceptualization of new money is also found in Veblen. It is captured in the concept of conspicuous consumption. While conspicuous leisure attests to wealth through the cultivation of refined tastes, manners, and lifestyle, conspicuous consumption bears a direct relation to money: it attests to wealth by expensive possessions. Writing at the beginning of the twentieth century, Veblen is already aware of a process that renders conspicuous consumption the dominant mode of display of wealth at the expense of conspicuous leisure. Janey is the culmination of this process. It is not only that her beauty is directly monetized as a model. Like everyone in her social environment, she does not recoil from money. She has her own money, and she thriftily guards it, using only Selden's for shopping. As a personification of new money, she has an escape route from Lily's tragic end. In her environment, there are no taboos sustaining the mystery of money, so she can salvage herself by admitting that she is, in a sense, a prostitute—something that can at most be insinuated about Lily ("people say that Gus Trenor pays her bills").

Finance

The Use Value of Money

Economists tell us that the market establishes correct prices for everything. Prostitution is an inherent exception to this formula, because the specific "thing" purchased in it stands for "everything." Sex consummates the idea that everything can be bought.

It thus reflects how Marx defines the use value of money as embodied in the way "it confronts all the other commodities as the totality of real embodiments of its utility" (1976, 199). While for Marx, this use value "appears only ideally," prostitution is a real embodiment of it. The complementary ideas of market equilibrium and of money as a neutral medium and a universal equalizer rest on a view of the economy as consisting of countless discrete things. This view is disrupted by the inclusion in it of one specific thing that stands for all of them together. Both its elements are disrupted. On the one hand, for male clients prostitution can be a monetary experience no less than a sexual one: an experience of the universal purchasing power of money. Money is present in the two sides of the exchange and thus no longer can serve as a measure and equalizer. On the other hand, prostitution is related to the way money disrupts equilibrium by accumulating, producing surplus in a system where everything is allegedly exchanged for its correct price. This aspect is expressed in the prevalent association between prostitution and finance.

Paul Krugman cited at length in his *New York Times* blog a comment made by an unnamed reader with regard to the question "What do the markets want?"—that is, how to interpret the signals that financial markets elicit. "The markets want money for cocaine and prostitutes. I am deadly serious. Most people don't realize that 'the markets' are in reality 22–27 year old business school graduates, furiously concocting chaotic trading strategies on excel sheets and reporting to bosses perhaps 5 years senior to them" (Krugman 2010). Regardless of the question to what extent prostitution is indeed a part the culture of Wall Street, the association resonates in popular culture in a way which suggests that it encodes a certain kind of economic logic.

The most famous representation of prostitution in Wall Street culture is Martin Scorsese's *The Wolf of Wall Street*, based on the memoir of the stockbroker Jordan Belfort. The movie wallows in the excessive life and work habits of the traders in Belfort's firm, which include a constant abuse of prostitution. The compulsive nature of this abuse, as well as its often public and shared form, suggest that more than pleasure is at stake with it. It articulates the obscene nature of the traders' economic activity, their commitment to making money at all moral and social costs.

The movie is accompanied by a voiceover of Leonardo DiCaprio in the character of Belfort, narrating and interpreting the plot. But it begins with a peculiar infringement of the divide between the diegetic and the extradiegetic. The opening scene depicts Belfort on his way from his mansion to his office, and during the trip DiCaprio unites the two roles of a character and narrator. As he walks to his car he directly addresses the viewers and details his daily use of drugs. At his office he arrives at his "absolute favorite drug." Cutting cocaine with a credit card and sniffing it with a $100 bill, he explains that "enough of this shit will make you invincible, able to conquer the world." Raising his head, he straightens the bill and holds it to the camera to clarify that he was referring to money, rather than cocaine.

This violation of realist conventions suggests an interpretative key: the movie's aim is to show us the money. What DiCaprio explains is that he enjoys the medium: not the drug but the credit card and the bill with which he consumed it. As McLuhan taught us, the most significant effects of media are those entangled with their transparency. We focus on their content and thus miss their message, their effects on us as human and as social beings. The violation of realist conventions in the opening of the movie extracts the medium of money from its transparency. It suggests that whatever we see should be perceived as effects of money, attempts to make money visible. That is true not only for the way the movie addresses its viewers, but also for the use of obscenity within the firm. In the most disturbing scenes, obscenity is used for demonstrative purposes, a sort of perverse pedagogy. In one scene, Belfort demonstrates to his employees their weekly success by offering the firm's secretary ten thousand dollars to shave her head. She agrees, sobbing in tears while being shaved in front of the staff at the office party. In another scene, a trader gets a blow job from a secretary in the building's glass elevator as it goes up.

Prostitution is central to the excessive life and work culture of the traders. It also has a demonstrative aspect and concerns more than sex as a sensual experience. It serves as an intentional, systematic breaking of taboos, a sort of Protestant ethic in reverse, where prostitution consumption is directed at an impersonal aim. It is a part of the firm's common work culture, maintaining a form of sinful camaraderie among the workers. The traders often do it together, sometimes on the office tables. A scene that summarizes the place of prostitution in the work culture of the firm shows a montage of prostitutes going into the office, categorized according to prices and named after stock categories. Belfort's voiceover explains

> In Stratton there were three kinds of hookers: The Blue-chips, top of the line, model material. They cost between 300 and $500, and you had to wear a condom unless you gave them a hefty tip, which of course I did. Then came the Nasdaqs who were pretty not-great. They cost between $200 and $300. Finally, there were the Pink-sheets, skanks. They cost about a $100 or less, and if you didn't wear a condom you'd have to get a penicillin shot the day after and pray that your dick didn't fall off. Not that we didn't fuck them too. Believe me we did.

Intercourse is presented only at the end of the scene, as the narrator arrives at the cheapest category, pink-sheets (stocks of small and suspect companies that do not meet the requirements for trade on the stock exchange). Before it we only see more or less elegant women stepping into the offices surrounded by flocks of employees. It is a process of de-masking the glamorous appearance of prostitution consumption. At its ugliest core, the "skanks," we see a trader fuck a prostitute on an office table, surrounded by his peers, gazing and awaiting their turn, looking mostly bored. At this point it is clear that the abuse of prostitution is no longer about sexual pleasure, or even about pleasure at all. It appears as a compulsive activity, a duty. The workers are committed to experience the whole range of the spectrum, even at risk of their dicks falling off, leaving no possibility unexplored. The traders' abuse of prostitution is about breaking all taboos and all walls of shame together. In this way it becomes a gesture of extreme loyalty to the firm. That is why it is important that they do it together, in public. It is a ritualistic act of doing something utterly wrong, something repulsive and dangerous together—a ritual that unfortunately can bind people more strongly than commitment to shared norms and values. Their lecherous work culture supplements the business credo of the firm, of making money at all costs: "Don't hang up until the client either buys or dies." Through prostitution the traders enunciate their shared inner commitment to do wrong that they practice in their business conduct.

As a celebration of obscenity, one might argue that what the traders do in the film differs from "ordinary" prostitution, whatever that may be. What is brought to an extreme in it, however, what is celebrated, is the monetary aspect of prostitution. That is the reason prostitutes are named according to categories of stocks. It is not that the traders want sex and therefore buy it. What they are after is the *purchase* of sex. MacKinnon, as quoted in the first chapter, writes that in prostitution men "pay for paid sex." She uses the strange phrase to denote prostituted sex as an expression of control and power relations ("you do what I say" sex). The traders in the film bring to the fore the economic meaning ingrained in the phrase "pay for paid sex," where prostituted sex is also an expression of an enjoyment of money. This does not exclude, of course, the motives of control and power over women in their conduct. Yet it frames this motive in monetary terms, as control and power afforded by money. This monetary accent is reflected in the compulsive nature of the traders' conduct. They exert control with money, but also, in a sense, they are controlled by money, driven by it to explore the whole spectrum of possibilities, from the most seductive ("model material") to the disgusting ("skanks"). Like Marx's capitalist, they surrender their personas, their desires, to a nonhuman drive that appears to emanate from money itself.

As noted in chapter 1, prostitution, in either a real or metaphorical sense, designates an exchange where money is present on both sides: paid for something but also reflected in the shape of what it buys. Apart from MacKinnon, this formula appears in different forms in Adam Smith and in Walter Benjamin. It provides an initial explanation for the association between finance and prostitution. In a sense, finance consists of exchanges of forms of money for the purpose of generating more money. The financial instruments that traders buy and sell are not money in the ordinary sense, but they have an affinity to money, as abstract and liquid embodiments of value, detached from use value. Finance involves transformations between various forms of moneyness. For the traders prostitution is an erotic counterpart of finance: an exchange of money for a monetary experience. It is not aimed at generating more money, but it translates the excessive profits to *more than* money, to what money should not buy.

A real-world counterpart of *The Wolf of Wall Street* is found in one of the most bizarre online sexual scenes, the phenomenon of "findom," or financial domination. In findom, the financial form of BDSM relations, men send money and gifts to women, who on their part are required to do "next to nothing in return" (Hosie 2021). All they are expected to do is demand the gift. Money is not paid in exchange for an experience of erotic submission: the payment itself is submission. As the *Independent* reports, in most cases the dominatrix (domme) and the submissive never meet—it's all done online. Some findom relationships consist of one-off payments, but findom afficionados "hand over passwords and total control of their bank accounts to a domme, asking her to devise a minimal budget too" (Hosie 2021). Findom encapsulates the purely monetary dimension of sex work, allowing customers to engage in commercial sex without the mess of bodies and human relationships. An unidentified observer explained to the newspaper that a submissive uses his financial domme "as a tool to access some emotions that provide him with a chemical high that only comes from feeding his addiction to self-destructive behaviour" (Hosie 2021). What's interesting here is that even in findom the clients "use" women. In other words, it is impossible to decide whether in findom money mediates relationships with women or women mediate a relationship to money. The home page of findom.com illustrates the inseparability of the two options, displaying a naked woman lying on a bed seductively looking at the camera, while banknotes are spread over her body and her bed. It is a photo of both eroticized money and a monetized woman.

To understand why prostitution is associated specifically with finance, it is better to turn to Gary Marshall's *Pretty Woman*. As a romantic comedy, it carefully avoids any reference to the reality of prostitution. Julia Roberts plays the role of Vivian Ward, a small-town girl who has fallen to street prostitution in Los Angeles, but has preserved her innocent, childlike demeanor. The movie's fantasmatic nature frames the narrative around a twofold analogy which calls for an economic interpretation: prostitution is analogous to finance, whereas productive capital is analogous to romance. The movie is overly explicit with this point. Edward Lewis (Richard Gere), a corporate raider whose frustrated girlfriend has just broken up with him, hires Vivian after accidentally meeting her, at first to spend the night with him, and afterward to escort him for some business meetings and social events. It makes some sense for him to do this: his ex-girlfriend in any case felt like she was at his beck and call, so a prostitute could fill the role without the annoying emotional weight. After a lunch they have with James Morse, a chivalric owner of a shipyard which Edward plans to liquidate, Edward spells out to Vivian the similarity between prostitution and finance: "We both fuck people for money." Vivian remarks that he seemed to actually like Morse, and he explains that to take over companies he detaches himself from emotions. Vivian naively answers that she does this too with her clients: that is why she does not allow them to kiss her on the mouth. But Edward's attitude starts to change as he spends time with Vivian. First, he refuses his lawyer's request to use his influence to deny Morse a bank loan that could save him. Later on, when Morse eventually surrenders and agrees to sell the shipyard (on the condition that the workers will be compensated), Edward goes through a conversion: he decides, for the first time in his life, to help Morse to recover his company. When he goes back to the hotel he proposes to Vivian that they keep seeing each other. He could put her in an apartment and supply her with enough money to live comfortably. But she is changed too. She has become a respectable woman, a conversion marked, among other things, by her learning to dress and shop (earlier in the movie she is humiliatingly kicked out of a posh store, although she had the money to buy clothes). Although she spent the week with Edward for $3,000, now she wants more than money and declines his offer. His businesslike manner makes her feel like a prostitute. In the final scene Edward completes his conversion and performs under her apartment window an awkward imitation of her childhood dream to be rescued by a knight on a white horse, sword in hand.

The awkward romantic gesture is a solution to an economic problem. The movie could not have ended with a marriage proposal. Such an ending would have only made prostitution and matrimony practically identical (Edward would give her an apartment, provide her money to shop, and continue to use her as an escort to social events). A marriage proposal would simply mean that Vivian managed to get a better deal. Love is necessary to distinguish between marriage and prostitution. The romantic gesture disavows the connection between marriage and prostitution, but it does so in a strange way. It does not present love as a reciprocal relation but encodes the patriarchal notions of possession of women in the imagery of rescue and conquering.

In the conceptual matrix of *Pretty Woman*, therefore, prostitution is to finance as romantic love is to productive capital. Put another way: prostitution is to romantic love-marriage as finance is to productive capital. The economic meaning of these analogies lies in a common pattern of an obscene, disavowed kernel which structures reality in both the economic and the sexual sides of the matrix. In finance money breeds money. Money multiplies through exchanges between financial instruments. From the perspective of real economy, financial accumulation is an illusion. If money begets more money, it is because *somewhere else* profit has been generated through real economic activity, or in Marxist terminology, because surplus value was extracted from labor, and this surplus was shared between the owners of productive and financial capital. Yet from a Marxist perspective, it is a special kind of illusion. It is an illusion that discloses the way real production is organized from the outset for the accumulation of value. Finance is both an illusion and an organizing principle behind the manifest realities of capitalist economy. Recall that Marx first introduces the concept of capital through the M-C-M' form of circulation. This circulation already explains the necessity that capital accumulate: beginning and ending with money, it has no point but in a limitless drive of accumulation. At this stage capital appears as if it results from the fact that money is a purely quantitative measure, lacking qualities or use value. Only after this presentation does Marx explain how accumulation *really* takes effect through the usurpation of surplus value. A financial form of accumulation, from M to M', is an abstract, unreal principle: it is grounded on what money lacks: qualities, use value, or thingness. Yet in capitalist production, this unreal principle governs the way real things are produced and circulated.

A similar configuration informs the relation between prostitution and romantic love. Marriage is not prostitution. Yet insofar as marriage, as part of the real tissue of social life, is also a heritage of patriarchy, prostitution emerges as a shadow that haunts it. Prostitution is the disavowed economic patriarchal meaning of marriage as ownership of a wife. Love is the way the institution of monogamy persisted beyond its original economic meaning. The romantic patterns of conquering and rescue are the way the obscene disavowed kernel persists, inscribed on practices and imageries of love. In productive capital, real things both mediate and conceal an unreal principle revealed in finance. In marriage, romantic love both mediates and conceals the patriarchal heritage, obscenely presented in prostitution.

Although its economic scope is wider, something essential is missing in *Pretty Woman*. Careful of any contact with the reality of prostitution, it presents a mainly theoretical matrix, a homology between love, marriage, and prostitution, on the one side, and productive and financial capital on the other. *The Wolf of Wall Street*, by focusing on the abhorrent core of prostitution, suggests that more than homology is at stake here. Its depiction of the permeation of prostitution abuse into the work culture of finance opens the way to two parallel inquiries: how money is eroticized and how eroticism is financialized.

Erotic Money and Financial Eroticism

Within the general perspective of sexual economy, women pertain to the question of the ends of economic activity. It is a question that economics, the more it wears a scientific form, finds impossible to pose. As Friedrich Hayek writes: "The ultimate ends of the activities of reasonable beings are never economic. Strictly speaking there is no 'economic motive' but only economic factors conditioning our striving for other ends" (2001, 92). More than a century before Scorsese, Henry James explicitly formulated the place of women as embodying the paradoxical end of economic activity in connection with another financier, Christopher Newman, the protagonist of *The American*. Before arriving in Paris from America, Newman's "sole aim in life had been to make money; what he had been placed in the world for was, to his own perception, simply to wrest a fortune, the bigger the better, from defiant opportunity" (James [1877] 2005, 24). His trip to Europe, with which the plot begins, confronts him with a novel question:

> Upon the uses of money, upon what one might do with a life into which one had succeeded in injecting the golden stream, he had up to his thirty-fifth year very scantily reflected.... He had won at last and carried off his winnings; and now what was he to do with them? ... A vague sense that more answers were possible than his philosophy had hitherto dreamt of had already taken possession of him. (24)

Despite his self-controlled character, he falls in love with Claire de Cintré, a young widow of an aristocratic family that has lost its fortune. Due to his wealth, her family reluctantly permits him to court her. When he wins her heart, he understands that she was what he wanted all along, and he phrases it in the language of possession and value: "If you only knew," he said, "how exactly you are what I coveted! And I am beginning to understand why I coveted it; the having it makes all the difference that I expected. Never was a man so pleased with his good fortune.... you come up to the mark, and, I can tell you, my mark was high" (James [1877] 2005 228–29). The family, however, eventually disavows its promise and pressures Claire to break the engagement. She abides, but in protest becomes a nun.

Ostensibly, the delicate Claire cannot be more far removed from the world of Jordan Belfort. But what separates them is only the vulgarity of the latter. Claire belongs to the old world, across an unbridgeable distance from Newman's new world. She embodies what money cannot buy because she belongs to the economy of old money. As her young brother Valentine explains to Newman, the family did try to go through with the match, but it was precisely Newman's monetary skills that made it impossible for them: "They said they couldn't stand a commercial person" (James [1877] 2005, 293). In this, Claire embodies not simply the end of economic gains, but the endlessness of capital accumulation. A woman that cannot be bought stands for the lack of end that defines capital accumulation. The prostitutes at Stratton in *The Wolf of Wall Street* have prices. They nonetheless also stand for the endless drive of capital, but this time through numbers: through repetition, multiplication, and the compulsion to experience everything.

Finance encapsulates the end of capital, or more precisely its lack of end: an end which is a limitless accumulation. All sorts of capital feature this limitless drive, but in the case of productive capital it is masked by the immediate aim of producing *things*. The specific connection between finance and prostitution lies in a movement of demasking. Finance removes the mask of thingness from the movement of capital. It presents it as a process aimed at money, where things are place holders in monetary movements. The association with prostitution expresses the erotic nature of this process. Freud's view of sexuality as repetition beyond purpose is again relevant here. Like thumb-sucking which is erotic as a rhythmic repetition of sucking without actual nourishment, finance is erotic as capital without things.

Sexual economy may explain the conceptual connection between money and capital, or how the logic of capital is already inherent in money. Capital, in a sense, is an erotic relation to money, which pertains specifically to its capitalist form. In a feudal economy, as Marx notes in *The German Ideology*, the extent of things that money can buy is limited. The feudal form of capital is still inseparable from a traditional way of life: It consists of "a house, the tools of the craft and the natural, hereditary customers" (1975, 66). Because of the limited scope of commerce and circulation, capital cannot be easily monetized and descends from father to son, "unlike modern capital, which can be assessed in money and which may be indifferently invested in this thing or that" (66). Money can buy everything in both feudal and capitalist economies, but the meaning of this "everything" is radically different. In feudalism it can buy everything in the abstract, but in practice its purchasing power is limited, bounded by traditional ways of life and embedded in the fabric of social life. In capitalism, the abstract possibility defines the reality of money. It makes money a concrete embodiment of indefinite potential. In contrast with feudal money, capitalist money is not only detached from the fabric of social life but emerges as a negative force within it. As capital, it turns the customary ways of life of workers, represented in the value of labor power, into a source of surplus value. When the abhorrence of prostitution shifts its focus to its monetary aspect, money assumes a parallel place in relation to social life.

Marx formulated this connection explicitly in his early work. In *The Economic and Philosophical Manuscripts* a chapter about "the power of money" brings together an erotic metaphor of money and a preliminary formulation of its relation to capital. Drawing on Shakespeare's *Timon of Athens*, Marx writes "[money] is the common whore, the common procurer of people and nations" ([1959] 1977, 130). Following it is a more conceptual claim: "By possessing the *property* of buying everything, by possessing the property of appropriating all objects, *money* is thus the *object* of eminent possession" (128). This formulation seems vaguer than the language Marx eventually adopts in *Capital*, but it does consist of a conceptual kernel: money is superior to everything it can buy precisely because it can buy everything. Money annuls the thingness of things: anything it buys destroys the infinite potential that defines it. Erotic money ("the common whore") is already capital, as money greater than itself (superior to all its equivalents).

On its economic aspect, the association between finance and prostitution encodes an erotic relation to money. In its sexual aspect, however, it points at financialization of eroticism, at a form of male desire structured by the logic of capital. Today this desire wears an explicit and vulgar form in the adjective *hot* as applied to women. That a woman can be described as "the hottest" already proves the point. In contrast to *beautiful, pretty, attractive*, or even *sexy*, *hot* alludes to a purely quantified measure, a temperature. Capital is grounded on the effacement of qualitative distinctions between things (their use values), articulated in limitless movement of quantitative increase. Similarly, *hot* effaces the individuality of women, which is then articulated in the possibility of desire for "the hottest." Ariel Levy's wonderful *Female Chauvinist Pigs* presents a disturbing and complex portrait of this contemporary erotic map. On the one hand, she points at a semi-transparent eroticization of the economy, evident in the use of the adjective *sexy* as "a synecdoche for all appeal": a new restaurant can be described as sexy, as well as a new job. Women are both an exception and the ulterior principle of this eroticization, because for them *sexy* has a concrete meaning and a highly visible form. When a US Army general describes an air raid on the Taliban as "sexy stuff," he does not really think of sex (or better yet: he does not think that he thinks of sex). For women, being sexy today is more and more expressed in being hot, which as Levy claims, "when it pertains to women, hot means two things in particular: fuckable and salable" (31). The economic terminology she uses is not coincidental. Her book documents a profusion of routes through which forms of feminine appearance originating in commercial sex infiltrate from the margins of society into its decent center: strip-pole dancing as a legitimate form of physical exercise; books by porn stars on best-selling lists; female Olympic athletes who appear naked in Playboy; a Victoria's Secret fashion show aired on national television; successful and accomplished women intentionally attracting attention to their physicality. As a former adult film star has put it: "When I was in porn, it was like a back-alley thing. Now it's everywhere" (Levy 2010, 5).

As Levy explains, there is no real tension between the rise of conservative mood and the eruption of raunch culture into the mainstream. Raunch culture, grounded on a narrow commercial version of sexiness, has nothing to do with sexual liberation, or for that matter, with sex. As she writes: "There is a disconnect between sexiness or hotness and sex itself." Hotness has to do mainly with the appearance of sexiness. This disconnect between sex and its commercial reservoir of imageries is the mark of the infiltration of financial logic to sex. It is expressed in the emergence of eroticism that has severed its last ties with sex, eroticism of an indefinite deferral of the possibility of consummation in sex, which is expressed in a process of pure intensification of the simulations of sex.

Raunch culture is a new phenomenon. The financial grammar of desire, however, secretly informs older and more refined versions of eroticism. A good example is Freud's conception of love as "sexual overvaluation," which resonates with Marx's definition of interest-bearing capital as "money which is worth more money, value which is greater than itself" (1976, 257). Overvaluation, which according to Freud is typical of men more than of women, is the erotic counterpart of ownership. It shapes sexual behavior in different ways, grouped together by Freud as aiming at complete possession of the love object.[1] It is the key to what Freud calls the deviation of the sexual drive: its expansion to various body parts, objects, and even ideas associated with the loved person. In all these "the sexual instinct . . . proclaims its intention . . . of getting possession of the sexual object in every possible direction" ([1905] 1981, 152). However, a rare historical footnote added to the *Three Essays on the Theory of Sexuality* suggests that sexual overvaluation is a modern phenomenon, though it is not clear precisely how modern. "The most striking distinction between the erotic life of antiquity and our own no doubt lies in the fact that the ancients laid the stress upon the instinct itself, whereas we emphasize its object. The ancients glorified the instinct and were prepared on its account to honour even an inferior object; while we despise the instinctual activity in itself, and find excuses for it only in the merits of the object" (149). The grammar of possession informing sexual overvaluation suggests how modern this phenomenon is: it may emerge together with the gradual dissolution of the notion of marriage as ownership. Notice that in the distinction between contemporary and ancient erotic life Freud describes a fetishistic reversal, in the Marxian rather than the Freudian sense of the term. For the ancients a love object is beautiful because I want her, while for us it appears the other way around: I want her because she is beautiful. A relation to an object appears to emanate from the object itself. It is worthwhile to recall again Shulamith Firestone's provocative claim, which today cannot but appear prophetic, foretelling Levy's "female chauvinist pigs": "Women are the only 'love' objects in our society, so much so that women regard *themselves* as erotic" (1971, 148).

The Gift of the Whore

Hanoch Levin is one of the few writers who succeeded in carrying the ingenuity of the literary perspective on money from the nineteenth into the twentieth century. Nineteenth-century realist novelists probably had an easier task. They could clearly formulate a theory of sexual economy in a literary form because they were steeped in a cultural-economic tension between old and new money. This tension made money mysterious and human. With the disappearance of old money as a significant economic category, money seems to have lost much of its aura of mystery. In one of his plays that pertains most directly to economics, Levin brings back the mystery through the theme of prostitution. *The Whore from Ohio* revolves around the weirdest desire, in both sexual and economic terms. Its protagonist, Hoibitter, wants to fuck a whore for free. He is so obsessed with this fantasy, that he is willing to give away all of his savings to realize it. He does eventually give it away, but without fulfilling his fantasy. This strange fantasy is orchestrated like this: Hoibitter is a beggar. At the beginning of the play, he haggles with Brontsatski the whore: it is his seventieth birthday, and he asks her for a gift fuck. She refuses. She won't even give him a discount. He pays the full price but cannot get an erection (his son, Hoimar, also a beggar, is appalled by the waste of money and asks to redeem the unused purchase, but Brontsatski insists that the purchase is personal and nontransferable). Further on in the play, Brontsatski sneaks at night into Hoibitter's bed and confesses that she loves him. Then he gets an erection, somewhat against his will. One suspects that he knows she is fooling him, but the word "love" she pronounces has its quasi-automatic effect. Brontsatski, however, asks Hoibitter to wait: her pimp demands her profits, but she hasn't had clients all day. Hoibitter gives her all his savings, a considerable sum he has stashed in his room. She takes the money and disappears.

So that is the plot: a man pays all he has to fuck a whore for free and does not get what he paid for. The fantasy at the heart of the plot makes no sense, either economically or sexually. If sex motivates Hoibitter, what difference does it make whether it is sex with a woman who is not a whore or sex with a whore for free? If money motivates him, why pay so much to get something for free? The plot makes sense only as a sexual-economic fantasy, disclosing how economy derails sexuality and vice versa. Sex renders money greater than itself, and money renders sex greater than itself. Love is a key ingredient in both transformations, but it is love subsumed within economy. Consider first the sexual side of the knot. The economic context distinguishes free sex with a whore from sex with a woman who is not a whore. Why? Because it renders sex a gift given by a woman to a man. Paying everything for it marks it as the ultimate gift: love encodes sex as an expression of full, exclusive possession of a woman. Prostitution in general pertains to economics for this reason: it is not just a sexual service sold by a woman to man, but an expression of something bigger, a fantasy of possession and ownership. The play thus suggests a provocative economic interpretation of love: love as a gift from a whore. Vulgar as it is, it may pertain to love to the extent it is considered a historical-economic institution, both disavowing and maintaining in a new form the patriarchal tradition of marriage as ownership of a wife. On the economic side of the fantasy, the gift of the whore is eroticized money. As such it is already capital, distinguished by extreme indeterminacy of value. In the sexual-economic knot, this money is clearly different from the economists' money. Rather than an equivalent, it is a medium that circumvents the possibility of equivalence. Its movements are guided by a principle of infinite increase.

Does this concept of money reflect our ordinary money? There are various forms in which money is more than itself. The culture of old money, which surfaced in this chapter, provided one example. Old money is mysteriously associated with the noblest human values. It can be embodied in a figure like Lily Bart, who "must have cost a great deal to make." The next chapter will explore how what money cannot buy is articulated in different ways in consumer culture. There is one example, however, that provides a surprising corollary to the economy presented by Levin. In the online economy we regularly pay everything to get something for free. Consider a thought experiment about Facebook. The company could have made very nice profits if instead of a free service it charged minimal subscription fees of a few dollars a month. Revenues would have been diminished, of course, but the subscription model would also have spared Facebook the need to invest so much in algorithms aimed at hooking us into its services. It would also have been spared its bad, almost evil, reputation and allowed the company to stand up to its original promise of simply connecting people. It would have spared users the emotional turmoil nurtured by algorithms. The impossibility of this commonsensical model is symptomatic of the online economy, where the strongest companies sacrifice short-term profits to achieve complete domination of markets—a business strategy described by Peter Thiel as "zero to one." In this economy we eventually pay everything to get something for free: we get a free service in exchange for a comprehensive surveillance of our activities; we get a free service and pay for it with complete devotion and hunger for "likes."

FIVE

The Eroticization of Consumption

THE EXCLUSION OF MARRIAGE FROM THE SPHERE OF EXCHANGE was one of the factors that reshaped this sphere to its modern form of the market. This exclusion is a focal point in the strange transformation of the ethical status of exchange, from an honorable, uniquely human act to the morally suspicious form it wears today, as expressing selfish and sometimes cynical motivations. One need not decide on a causal direction of this process: whether a transformation in money and exchange rendered them despicable, in need of distancing from anything noble in humanity, or whether it is the other way around, and the exclusion of higher human domains from the market rendered money and exchange despicable. It should be more correctly viewed as a process of overdetermination, in which the meaning of money and exchange is sustained among other things by their relation to love and marriage, and the meaning of love and marriage is sustained by their relation to money and exchange. This reciprocal determination makes clear that the exclusion of marriage from the sphere of exchange is not a thing of the past. It is embedded in our conceptual map determining what properly belongs to the market and what does not. It is ever present in both the despicable nature of money and the noble nature of love.

Moreover, this process is never consummated. The ideas of love and marriage kept evolving throughout the twentieth century, and in parallel so did consumer culture. In relation to love, sociologists speak of passionate marriage as a development of the last decades of the twentieth century. In consumption, brands replaced products. These developments echo each other: the market changes together with what is external to it. This chapter focuses on consumption and traces its overall eroticization.

The Market and Its Outside

Sociologists claim that during the last decades of the twentieth century there occurred a shift from companionate to passionate marriage. Both forms are far removed from precapitalist notions of marriage as exchange, and both are centered on love, but the meaning of love changes between them. The comedian Aziz Ansari and the sociologist Eric Klinenberg demonstrate the change in their book *Modern Romance* through conversations with focus groups of senior citizens and their children. When the seniors were asked to explain how they decided to date and eventually marry their spouses, they said things such as "She was a nice girl" and "He had a good job." Their children had much more dramatic explanations such as "She is my other half"; "I can't imagine experiencing the joys of life without him by my side"; and "He's a one-of-a-kind human being. There is no one in this world like him. He is stunning, and I am amazed by him every single day." There are some obvious socioeconomic explanations for this stark difference. Women's entrance to the work force strengthened their independence and subsequently their range of choice in men. Expansion of higher education prolonged bachelorhood and the span of time dedicated to seeking spouses. Increased geographical mobility and communication also expanded the range of spousal choice. These changes ostensibly explain why young people do not settle for less than a soulmate for marriage.

In a first approach, that is ostensibly how an economy permeates marriage: spouse choice that resembles more and more consumer choice. This framing, however, is misleading. It is the mismatch between the two sides of the analogy that shows the infiltration of economy to marriage. Young people today indeed have a much wider range of possible spouses to choose from—just like wider consumer choice. Yet spouse choice is also the opposite of consumer choice. In the formulations of the younger generation, it does not appear exactly as a choice, but as fate, a suspension of choice: "my other half." There is an economy to love insofar as it appears as an exception to market economy. The intense emotional terminology of the young represents a sort of hysterization of monogamy. Their parents' generation obviously saw marriage as what it is, namely an institution, part of the natural order of things. That does not mean they had loveless marriages, but that love was subordinated to the institutional framework. Marriage is simply what everybody does, and love has to do with finding the right person to fill a preexisting institutional role. In the dramatic descriptions of the younger generation, the intense emotional language entails a partial disavowal of the institutional aspect of matrimony. While the parents found someone they love in order to marry, the children talk as if they decided to marry because they fell in love. It is as if an exceptional individual miraculously explains one more iteration of this age-old social arrangement.

Interviewees from the younger generation present one of the most resilient social institutions in human history as if it were maintained by emotions. Love masks the institutional framework, as if one marries because of the unique qualities of a partner. From a historical perspective this appears as a misperception, yet it is not simply a mistake, but the form of persistence of the institution of marriage today. In a situation of prolonged bachelorhood and an indefinite range of choice, an intense emotional language is a necessary supplement to marriage as an institution. Vis-à-vis this unbearable range of choice, the institutional persistence of matrimony *requires* intense emotions. The explanations of spouse choice by the younger generation express the double role of love, as both a disavowal of the institutional aspect of marriage and a necessary part of it.

The changing emotional landscape from companionate to passionate marriage resonates in a complex manner with the deep transformation in the economic regime of global capitalism that began to unfold in the 1970s, designated by a host of names: neoliberalism, late capitalism, post-Fordism, postindustrial capitalism, globalization, affective capitalism, network society, data capitalism, and more. In many of these terms, choice and its expansion play a crucial role. Neoliberalism, viewed as a political agenda aiming to refashion society in the shape of the market, has turned the economic concept of choice into a worldview, invested with moral and political fervor. The conceptual tools that served neoclassical economics to explain how one chooses between tea and butter have become in the works of Hayek and Gary Becker a comprehensive answer to the question "What is a human being?"—it is a mechanism that chooses between alternatives according to preferences, in the grocery store as well as in family life. The concept of post-Fordism points at the changing role of choice in relation to profit making and consumption. When the Fordist economy, based on mass production of a limited variety of goods, sank into a crisis in the early 1970s, manufacturers turned to what David Harvey termed "flexible accumulation," using, among other methods, diversification of production and increased obsolescence.

Spouse choice, as noted, represents an exception to the language of economics. Facing increased choice, young people describe their decision to marry in terms of fate and destiny, rather than as resulting from a comparison of respective advantages of candidates. This exception, however, pertains specifically to the official *language* of economics. When it comes to economic reality, the language of destiny sometimes infiltrates consumer choice too. Some of the goods we buy are not just preferable to other goods, and we relate to them as specifically meant for us. That shirt "is so you." This mirroring of the language of love in consumer choice suggests that the borderline separating the market and its outside is porous. When this occurs, one can suspect that consumption is eroticized. The shift from Fordism to post-Fordism provides a glimpse into the resonance between consumption and love. Henry Ford's famous quip, "Any customer can have a car painted any color that he wants so long as it's black," reveals a world where consumer desire could wear an explicitly collective form: desiring what everyone desires. Its erotic counterpart is marrying "a nice girl": marrying because that is the way of the world. Deep into the post-Fordist economy, Joseph Pine and James Gilmore (2000) coined the idea of "markets of one," according to which successful companies are those that achieve maximal personalization of their merchandise. Its erotic counterpart is marrying one's "other half."

Throughout the change from companionate to passionate patterns, marriage remains an economic institution external to the market. The upshot of its vicissitudes is that changes in the domain of what money buys resonate in changes in what it cannot buy and vice versa. This chapter follows the mutations of what money cannot buy throughout the twentieth century. It sets aside the direct connection of this category to gender relations to explore how it permeates consumption. Yet it suggests that the articulations of what money cannot buy in the field of consumption result in the overall eroticization of this field.

Previous chapters have shown how the category of what money cannot buy reorients economic thought. Its implicit or explicit appearance in Weber, Sombart, Marx, and at one exceptional point in Smith results in an unconventional conception of economy. Yet the allusions of these thinkers to this category are too general to serve as a basis for a detailed analysis. A potential for a systematic theorization of what money cannot buy is found in the work of Veblen.

Money, Old and New

Veblen's *Theory of the Leisure Class* diverges from orthodox economics in its philosophical foundations. The most radical difference lies in Veblen's conceptualization of private property as thoroughly social. The origins of ownership, according to Veblen, have nothing to do with the satisfaction of needs. In archaic communities, needs were met by collective activity. Ownership entered communities as a social institution alien to needs. Its ulterior principle is the display and signaling of social hierarchies. Its speculative origin, according to Veblen, is ownership of women taken as captives, who served as trophies, attesting to their captors' prowess. Ownership of women later extended itself to include products of their industry, "and so there arises the ownership of things as well as of persons" (Veblen [1899] 2007, 21). There is nothing "private" in private property because the objects of property are addressed to the gaze of others, and their function is the display of superiority. This view of ownership seems to run in contrast to our experience of economic life. Today we satisfy our needs within the realm of property. We buy food and clothes. According to Veblen, however, this situation is only a derivative form, a result of the fact that *everything* has become subsumed within the circle of property. Veblen's ingenuity lies in his masterful demonstrations of the way display remains the secret principle of ownership. The incentive for ownership "was from the outset the invidious distinction attaching to wealth, and, save temporarily and by exception, no other motive has usurped the primacy at any later stage of the development" (23). To see the radical nature of this idea, notice that it implies an alternative formulation for the basic problem of economy in affluent societies. Traditional formulations revolve around scarcity: economy pertains to how people satisfy needs with limited resources. Following Veblen, the economic problem of today is that we satisfy needs with things that serve the role of display; we satisfy needs with luxuries (which does not exclude but complicates the traditional problem: there are still many who cannot satisfy their needs, but this may be the case because they have to satisfy them with luxuries).

The notion of display serves Veblen as a basis for an all-encompassing economic theory, whose scope runs from archaic communities to industrial economies. It is not an ahistorical theory, however. Far from it, the persuasive power of Veblen's arguments lies in the way he traces radical transmutations in the forms of display throughout history. These follow the broad pattern of refinement or sublimation. The barbaric origin of ownership in captive women, to give one example, is transformed to the delicate lady in aristocratic societies. Her conspicuous inability to perform any productive labor serves a similar role as that of the captive woman: she attests to the wealth of her husband, his freedom from the necessity to work. She consumes "vicarious leisure" for him.

Veblen does not use the term *capitalism* in this book and generally tends to avoid it. From his theoretical framework of persistence through change, however, one can extract a unique characterization of early capitalism. It is rooted in the difference between the two main forms of display that he analyzes: conspicuous leisure and conspicuous consumption.

Conspicuous leisure displays superiority and signals status by attesting to the fact that a person is free from the necessity of productive labor. Because mere abstinence from labor does not leave material evidence, conspicuous leisure attests to past leisure through evidence more "spiritual" in nature. It encompasses things that require cultivation but are of an impractical nature: mastery of occult knowledge and dead languages, refined manners, dedication to sports and hunting. To correct a popular misreading of Veblen, it is essential to note that such class markers are not cultivated in order to acquire status. Rather, they assume a sort of moral obligation. Veblen stresses time and again that they fill an economic function precisely because they are considered noble in themselves. Refined manners, to give one example, attest to past leisure invested in their cultivation. Yet the gentleman does not consider his manners as evidence of leisure, but as an "integral feature of a worthy human soul" (Veblen [1899] 2007, 36). While conspicuous leisure displays superiority through practices, habits, and personal qualities, conspicuous consumption displays it through things. It also has its deep historical roots in customary limitations of the consumption of rare goods to superior social groups. In its modern version, conspicuous consumption wears a monetary form in the possession of manifestly expensive things.

A characteristic of industrial economies is the gradual rise of conspicuous consumption as a dominant means of display at the expense of conspicuous leisure. Veblen points at a structural cause of this process. Conspicuous leisure is more effective in a traditional community, where the addressees of display are one's acquaintances. In the urban centers of industrial society, where "one's neighbours, mechanically speaking, often are socially not one's neighbours, or even acquaintances" (Veblen [1899] 2007, 60), there arises the need to impress strangers and passersby with one's "ability to pay." Expensive possessions achieve this goal much more efficiently than refined habits and lifestyle or impractical education.

As already noted in the previous chapter, the two means of display can be mapped onto two cultural-economic tropes: conspicuous leisure is the mark of "old money" or aristocracy, while conspicuous consumption can be associated with "new money," the nouveaux riches or the bourgeoisie. Veblen's theory provides a direct economic explanation of two key themes in literature and theater dealing with the drama of old and new money. One theme is centered on the figure of the impoverished aristocrat: a person who retains the worldview and standards of old money without the material resources to support them. The insistence of such figures on retaining at least a semblance of their habituated lifestyle as well as their inability to work for their living reflects the moral weight of conspicuous leisure, or in Veblen's words, "the sense of the shamefulness of manual labour" which may even "set aside the instinct of self-preservation" ([1899] 2007, 32). The second cultural theme is the desire of the parvenu to enter the social circles of old money, and his failure to achieve it. The canonical figuration of this theme is Molière's Mr. Jourdain, in *The Bourgeois Gentleman*, who hopelessly devotes himself to learn fencing, dancing, music, and philosophy, in a way which only emphasizes his complete ignorance and awkwardness. Christopher Newman, the protagonist of James's *The American* presented in the previous chapter, is a derivative form of this theme. Newman does not want to belong to the aristocracy and even despises its arcane norms. He simply falls in love with Madame de Cintré and wants to marry her. Yet to return to his confession about *how* he loves her, he is charmed precisely by the features of "correct form" characteristic of aristocracy: "You have been holding your head for a week past just as I wanted my wife to hold hers. You say just the things I want her to say. You walk about the room just as I want her to walk. You have just the taste in dress that I want her to have" (James [1877] 2005, 228–29). Without him understanding it, he is charmed precisely by the features of conspicuous leisure.

The failure of the parvenu to enter high society seems to do with a cultural gap. His inability to understand the nuances of this social circle signals him as vulgar, always alien to it. The Veblenian perspective, however, does not distinguish sharply between economy and culture. It presents both the desire of the parvenu to enter aristocratic social circles and his failure to achieve this as basic economic phenomena. The desire reflects the inertia of habits of thoughts and canons of taste. During the gradual rise of the bourgeoisie, the aristocracy still maintained cultural dominance, because cultural values lag behind economic development. The failure of the bourgeois to imitate the aristocratic lifestyle, however, is a direct consequence of the concept of conspicuous leisure. Conspicuous leisure is *by definition* inimitable. To attest to *past* investments of unproductive effort, the marks of conspicuous leisure require time and long cultivation. In other words: they cannot be bought. The bourgeois can buy expensive things to signal his wealth but not the refined tastes and manners of aristocracy. In this way, Veblen provides us with an accurate economic definition of what money cannot buy: it is the gap between conspicuous leisure and conspicuous consumption.

Veblen does not refer explicitly to capitalism, but his theory encapsulates a broad historical outlook of its rise. It encompasses both a rise in the cultural significance of money and the emergence of what money cannot buy as a fundamental economic category. The ascent of the bourgeoisie involves a monetization of conspicuous consumption, where money and prices become the sole key to the dignity it confers. Conspicuous consumption predated capitalism, but in its earlier forms it was not encoded through prices but through social prohibitions, such as a customary limitation of consumption of alcoholic drinks to dominant classes. It is in capitalism that conspicuous consumption becomes encoded exclusively by price. This monetization of culture, however, is supplemented by the emergence of what money cannot buy. With the monetization of conspicuous consumption, conspicuous leisure assumes the form of what money cannot buy. The difference between them pertains to the question of the end of economic activity. During the several hundreds of years of the coexistence of old and new money, the bourgeoisie was busy making money, often drained from the aristocracy, but what motivated it was, in part, what money cannot buy.

All this was true for a large portion of the history of capitalism, yet throughout the twentieth century conspicuous leisure became increasingly marginalized as an economic phenomenon. Good evidence for this is that the display of leisure has become subsumed within conspicuous consumption. People still display their leisure, for example, in photos of vacations in exotic locations posted on Instagram. Strictly speaking, however, these belong to conspicuous consumption, not only because vacations are bought with money, but more so because of the temporality of the display. A vacation photo attests to present leisure rather than to past leisure. It is direct evidence of leisure rather than an indirect one. Nonetheless, vacation photos do manifest a certain sense of what money cannot buy, not in the refined and spiritual form of conspicuous leisure but through a mysterious capability of photography to both replicate reality and produce an image of it that somehow surpasses it. A vacation on a white sand beach with clear blue water can be fun, but in no way does it replicate the peculiar astonishment aroused by a stereotypical photograph of a white sand beach with clear blue water. On Instagram we collectively produce what Guy Debord termed the spectacle: images "detached from every aspect of life" that merge into a common stream and confront us "as a separate pseudo-world that can only be looked at" (2004, 7).

This is the challenge of reading Veblen against the backdrop of late capitalism where conspicuous leisure has become obsolete. The question is how what money cannot buy, which coincided neatly with the difference between conspicuous leisure and conspicuous consumption, has become enfolded within consumption.

Cool

There is in fact a distinct social type that displays a surprising resemblance to the codes of conspicuous leisure. That is the "cool" person or attitude. The qualities that make a person cool are hard to define, elusive by definition. One can list among them, however, a certain nonchalance or an impression of effortlessness which makes cool hard to imitate. These may point at cool as a modern version of the markers of conspicuous leisure. Dick Pountain and David Robins explain the strange exclusionary mechanism embedded in cool:

> If Cool is the new virtue, then the worst sin you can commit against it is to be "judgemental," that is, to make disparaging value judgements about someone else's lifestyle. The next worst sin is to do precisely what we are doing here, namely to attempt to define and analyze Cool. There is a glaring contradiction here, because Cool itself is intrinsically judgemental and exclusive: it can ultimately define itself only by excluding what is Uncool. (2000, 24)

This bears an uncanny resemblance to the social dynamics of conspicuous leisure, as manifested in the dramas of old and new money. Like the codes of old money, exclusion is based on unwritten rules, known only to those who follow them. The poor bourgeois cannot get accepted to the circles of high society not because he breaks social rules, but because he is unaware of them. The resemblance is uncanny because in some basic respects cool could not be more remote from the world of aristocrats that fascinated Veblen. Its origins are usually traced back to the margins of society, to counterculture and the early hipsters, rather than to a dominant class. As

Pountain and Robins define it, the cool attitude is oppositional and expresses defiance to authority, it is "a *permanent* state of *private* rebellion" (2000, 19). What makes the comparison between cool and conspicuous leisure worthwhile is that early on, maybe even at the moment of its birth, cool assumed an economic role.

In *The Conquest of Cool* Thomas Frank shows how the adoption of the cool style in the 1960s marked the birth of advertising as we know it today. In what became known as the creative revolution in advertising, lengthy trite texts accompanying uniformly realistic looking drawings or photos were relatively quickly replaced with imaginative graphic design and sophisticated short copy, often addressing readers colloquially. The transformation occurred in parallel with the rise of counterculture, but it was not a simple act of appropriation of counterculture by commercial interests. As Frank shows, the revolution which brought about the new style, was motivated by a sense of unease which was internal to the advertising industry in a way which echoed the more general unrest that characterized the 1960s. It was a reaction to the Fordist spirit that governed the industry, which adhered to an allegedly scientific approach to advertising, and was produced in agencies characterized by stiff organizational structures. The anxiety over "the organization man" motivated the creative revolution in advertising, just as it hovered over the countercultural rebellion.

Adam Arvidsson attributes to the use of coolness in marketing and production a role in the major turning point in consumption in the twentieth century, namely the development of modern branding. From his perspective, cool is more than a stylistic quality. The production of cool goods necessitates not only deep revisions in advertising, but a complete transformation of the relationship between producers and consumers. While Fordist advertising could be conceived in terms of educating consumers or shaping their tastes, producing cool goods required a new sensitivity to consumers' fluctuating tastes and new strategies to decipher them. Something cannot be simply declared "cool" in an advertising slogan—this, in fact, would be the most uncool thing to do. To be cool, something must express an aspect of rebellion against accepted tastes. In the appropriate conditions, something that at one moment is considered ugly can become cool. Deciphering its logic requires attention to the flexible social web in which goods are embedded. For that reason, agencies specialized in predicting trends, or "cool hunting," employ "expert consumers," young people who "impersonate a trend before it materializes." As Arvidsson notes, these informants are typically not social leaders, but "the slightly awkward or overweight or not conventionally pretty" (2006, 72). It may be that because their position within their peer group is uncertain, they are more attentive to its social dynamics.

These dynamics make clear that the resemblance of coolness to conspicuous leisure is not coincidental. It rests on a similar economic function. Cool embodies what money cannot buy as accurately as the difference between conspicuous leisure and conspicuous consumption did. It embodies this category literally. Buying something because it is "cool" is precisely what in practice makes it "uncool." Buying something cool means that one tries to imitate what is in principle inimitable. It means that the standard of coolness has already begun to shift away from it. Strictly speaking, something is truly cool only at its birth, a moment before it is declared cool. Once declared, it is open to imitation. Put another way, the coolness of an object depends only in part on its aesthetics and more so on the differential social position of its owners. For that reason, for most people, their buying something is precisely what makes it uncool. They pay for what cannot be bought.

The dynamics of cool demonstrate the ongoing relevance of Veblen's thought. As conspicuous leisure was waning, coolness took its place in both a similar social phenomenology of the inimitable and an economy of what money cannot buy. The shift also demonstrates the resilience of this economic category in capitalism. It raises, however, further enigmatic questions. Conspicuous leisure embodied what money cannot buy through the opposition between material things and immaterial practices and qualities, or "spiritual" qualities in Veblen's terminology. One could buy things that attest to wealth (conspicuous consumption), but one could not buy practices that require cultivation (conspicuous leisure): the habits, conduct, or lifestyle of the aristocracy. Within this opposition the category of what money cannot buy is easily understandable: money buys things but cannot buy knowledge, demeanor, or refined taste. It can buy material things but not the spiritual qualities associated with conspicuous leisure.

The reconfiguration of conspicuous leisure in coolness poses a challenge: how can things, objects that people actually buy with money, embody what money cannot buy? Surely, a full answer to the question requires an economic ontological inquiry: a consideration of what a thing is in the economy. It requires considering transformations that took effect in economic things and in the meaning of owning them: how economic things came to assume a spiritual dimension that runs in contrast to their very thingness; how the opposition between material things and immaterial practices that characterized conspicuous leisure has been incorporated into things.

A good way to start is with a closer look at Frank's *The Conquest of Cool* and the revolution in advertising. Frank focuses on changes in the aesthetics of advertising and corollary changes in organizational culture in advertising agencies. Print ads before and after the creative revolution look starkly different. Before the revolution, ads typically showed ideal scenes of consumption, portrayed in a realist mode (a family sitting in front of the television set, couples and families using a car for various leisure activities). By contrast, creative use of graphic design in the new style of advertising marked a divergence from realist conventions. Products were often detached from the immediate context of consumption and presented by themselves, sometimes with no people in view. Short and witty slogans replaced repetitive and pompous texts. These are two utterly different ways to depict objects of consumption. The question, however, is whether the objects themselves have also changed together with the manner of their depiction. Both styles were aimed at selling cars and television sets. As technical objects they remained more or less what they were throughout the revolution. Yet considered as economic objects their status changes once submitted to the social logic of coolness.

Before inquiring into the contents of advertising, we can notice the economic-ontological transformation by listening to the admen themselves. The prophets of the revolution were aware that changes in the mode of depicting goods involved also new relations between the advertisement and the thing advertised. George Lois, for example, ridiculed the "technicians" in the industry who "wildly miss" the main point about advertising, namely "that the product of advertising, after all, is *advertising*" (Frank 1998, 80). In the new approach, advertising *produces*. It has a product, and this product is advertising. What does this mean? The rebellion against the "technical" approach of advertising was at the same time a rebellion against the conformist pressures of 1950s mass society and its homogeneous consumer culture. As Frank notes, the prophets of the revolution recognized that the basic problem of advertising was how to make products that are materially very similar to each other seem "unique." Advertising could succeed in this "if it, too, is made somehow to stand out from the blizzard of other ads, each vying for the consumer's attention" (89). Making an advertisement unique was the way to present the commodity as unique. The economic-ontological implication of this new way of thinking is a slippage between the thing and the advertising for it: advertising is no longer a transparent medium that presents finished products and has become a part of the process in which goods are produced. In a sense, the concept of realism pertains to both approaches: realist conventions in old advertising depicted products as the material objects they were; new advertising presented what products *really are* in distinction from their mere material existence.

The revolution in advertising can thus be seen as a part of a transformation in the libidinal structure of consumer economy, a transformation in economic objects as media of desires. The realist conventions of older advertising appear to us as banal and repetitive. That does not mean that admen didn't know their job or lacked talent. Their work appears to us naïve and dull because they belonged to a very different economy from ours. Their work expressed an economy where consumer desire wore a collective form: an economy where things stood for what everyone desired. It is hard for us to imagine such an economy, because in our economy, this collective form which is never really absent, is masked by its inverse form, where goods stand for the desire to be different from everyone. What is hard for us to imagine is a desire for homogeneity.[1]

The rebellion against the old practices of the industry was sometimes expressed in a reflexive form of advertising. A Volkswagen ad was patterned as a list of guidelines for how to create an ad: "4. Call a spade a spade. And a suspension a suspension. Not something like 'orbital cushioning'" (Frank 1998, 63). The ridicule directed at the pompous language of old advertising allegedly highlighted the honest and direct address of the new approach to the art. More importantly, it also reflects a change in the basic role of advertising. Old practices could be ridiculed as aiming to fool consumers because their basic imperative was that of persuasion: persuading customers to buy an existing object. The new approach, by contrast, could explicitly refer to the fact of advertising, because it no longer fell within the category of persuasion but that of production. The ad is one more locus in the process of production of the car. Admen attributed a liberating role to their work: "Marketing should be an emancipator. It should unlock locks and cut bonds by suggesting and implying, by hinting and beckoning, not by defining. It should be the agent that frees, not the agent that imprisons" (Frank 1998, 93).

Hinting rather than defining: that is how the change in the role of advertising is entailed with a change in the ontological status of the economic object. The iconoclastic Volkswagen campaign from 1959 demonstrates this most clearly. In place of the conventional realist depiction of a car alongside owners or potential buyers, the ad displayed a diminutive image of a Volkswagen Beetle set in white abstract space that fills a whole newspaper page. The slogan reads "Think small." It is an ironic design: the white space that occupies most of the page is a gesture of waste, in contrast to the invocation of smallness and modesty. Accordingly, asking what the ad means would miss the crucial point. Its effectiveness lies precisely in the ambivalence of its message, in the wide range of meanings consumers can attribute to the imperative in the slogan. "Think small" may mean "be different," "think different," or "go against the trend" but also "be self-sufficient," "be modest," "be a realist," etc. The change in the ontological status of the object is not simply that a material object carries a social meaning. That was true for most, if not all, economic objects at any time. The change is in the manner of the conjunction of objects and meanings, which for the first time wears the form of a question. What exactly does a commodity mean? It is posed as a personal, existential question. Alongside their practical uses, goods always expressed something about their owners. The revolution in advertising gave way to objects that answer the question "Who am I?" in a nondefinitive way, itself shrouded in question.

The notion of youth rebellion, hovering over the revolution in advertising, demonstrates how what money cannot buy is embodied in things that money buys. During the 1960s advertising increasingly turned to the iconography of youth, especially in connection with the rising counterculture. The standard explanation for this turn invokes demographic and economic factors, such as the growing share of youth in the population and the increase in the purchasing power of young people. As Frank notes, this is at most a partial explanation. Advertisers did not turn to youth as such, but mainly to the association of youth with nonconformism. They ignored the large portion of young people who did not identify with the counterculture. In parallel, the iconography of youth was applied to all types of products, including those marketed to older people. Youth represented an attitude rather than an age group: creativity, nonconformism, rebellion, etc. For that reason, admen adopted the phrase "think young." As one of them quoted by Frank writes: "We see old men of 35 walking into our office, and we see young men of 50 coming in. It all seems to be based on a state of mind—a healthy enthusiastic approach to life in which you never seem to run out of *elan vital*" (1998, 111). One must pose here a naïve question: if youth is an attitude rather than a demographic group, and if this attitude does not characterize all young people, then why call it *youth*? The economic role of the youth iconography resides in this act of naming: it draws on the ephemerality of youth to inscribe an unachievable goal on consumption. Older people can maybe "think young" and behave *as if* they are young, but it is a basic condition of human existence that they will never be young again. Their conduct is thus colored by the gravest sin against coolness, namely imitation: trying to imitate the inimitable. Youth in its consumerist rendition is thus a marker of what money cannot buy. Notice that it embodies this category through a complete reversal of temporality in relation to conspicuous leisure. In the latter, what money cannot buy was entangled with the temporality of tradition and persistence, not only because the practices of conspicuous leisure required time and cultivation, but also because they were consecrated through the passage of time, which turned them from direct evidence of power to meritorious in themselves. Cool articulates what money cannot buy through things that money buys, by inserting them in the context of ephemerality. It sets things against a background alien to their very thingness, whose basic premise is persistence. Persistence is what makes a thing a thing. Injecting ephemerality into consumption, cool replicated the contrast between material things and "spiritual" or immaterial practices within the world of things.

The ephemerality of objects is a distinct economic feature of post-Fordism, where profit-making techniques require that much of what we buy becomes garbage once we have it. A clear phenomenological expression of it is found in Marie Kondo's techniques for tidying up, in her reveling of throwing massive amounts of stuff away. Her methods guide one to reach the understanding that "a particular article of clothing has already completed its role in your life." In that case "you are free to say, 'Thank you for giving me joy when I bought you,' or 'Thank you for teaching me what doesn't suit me,' and let it go" (Kondo 2014, 60). The vanishing object is spiritual.

The notion of rebellion is another way goods embody what money cannot buy. The cool attitude always entails an act of defiance. In its application to marketing it means that cool goods acquire their value by an implicit rejection of accepted taste. They are not simply what they are as objects but also an embodied negation of other objects. The in/out lists that were once popular in the press illustrate this status of goods as well as its economic resonance. Declaring that something is "in" is meaningless unless it renders something else "out" (due to the dynamics of coolness, however, such lists are today themselves "out": declaring that something is "in" is uncool). In a sense this role of objects applies to all goods insofar as they carry a symbolic meaning. Following de Saussure, a sign always receives its meaning from its relations to other signs. What makes the signification process associated with coolness unique is its intentional and active form. To follow the linguistic analogy, cool involves not the use of goods as preexisting signs, but intervening in the semantic web, actively producing a new sign that changes the web of meanings. That is another way in which cool inscribes the Veblenian opposition between things and practices within the domain of things. Under the regime of cool, things *are* practices: they are acts of defiance against prevailing taste.

Eroticization

A simple description of the uniqueness of the domain of sexuality in human beings is that language lacks proper names for all things sexual. Languages usually hold vast vocabularies for sex. They are vast, however, because they consist of epithets rather than names. Words that refer to sexual organs and acts are all colored in various ways: some are clinical, some vulgar, some euphemistic, some infantile. None of them is transparently connected to a thing as the word *table* is to tables. When the relatively disciplined ritual of dating gave way in American colleges to the more promiscuous hook-up scene, a host of new alluding words emerged, starting with *hooking-up* itself, which as Kathleen Bogle (2008) notes means different things in different places, and continuing with further vague terms such as *talking* and *hanging out*. Something similar happened to the word *cool*. The very use of the term in this chapter may confer an awkward, somewhat outdated overtone. A strange fact is that the word *cool* has become itself "uncool." This does not mean that the dynamic of cool has become obsolete, but the opposite, it marks its intensification. As John Brandon wrote in *Inc.* business magazine, cool has become "a dad word." He recommends extracting it from emails and conversations lest "you will end up sounding a bit dated, out of touch, and maybe even not that relevant anymore" (Brandon 2015). It is most telling that he does not instruct his readers with what to replace it. That would have marked him as uncool: instructing people how to imitate the inimitable, how to behave as if they are young in spirit. The disappearance of the word suggests that coolness has subsumed consumer culture as a whole. It may also suggest that this subsumption has to do with a comprehensive eroticization of consumption.

Before dwelling on its specific forms, an overall eroticization of consumption is suggested from a macro perspective in a blurring of the distinction between luxuries and necessities that characterizes contemporary economy. As we have seen, luxuries are more easily understood as eroticized. This insight is developed in parallel to mainstream economic thought from Mandeville, through Sombart, to Benjamin. Luxury can be seen as eroticized because it consists of a vague excess. There is more to the luxury item than mere use, and it is unclear what this "more" alludes to. Throughout the twentieth century, however, the distinction between luxuries and necessities seems to have lost its edge. The blurring of this distinction reflects an expansion of luxury over most of consumer economy. Veblen was aware of this already at the beginning of the twentieth century, writing that "there are to-day no goods supplied in any trade which do not contain the honorific element in greater or less degree." A frugal consumer who would insist on avoiding any extravagance "would be unable to supply his most trivial wants in the modern market" (Veblen [1899] 2007, 104–5). Paradoxical as it may seem, this point is reflected today in the economic definition of brands. In standard economic terms, brand equity is defined as "a value premium that a company generates from a product with a recognizable name when compared to a generic equivalent" (Hayes 2023). The intriguing point is that for many categories of consumer goods the notion of "a generic equivalent" is a pure fiction, because all goods in the category are branded. There is no generic equivalent of Nike sneakers, only brands with lower brand equity. In this case there are markets of everyday consumer goods composed exclusively or chiefly of luxuries. Paradoxically, there are markets where everything is expensive. That would be an absurd statement if expensive is understood as a comparative term. It is meaningful only if expensive is an inherent property of goods. Eroticism is one way to explain this. All goods are expensive to the extent that they are all more than themselves, that they include a certain undefinable excess, erotic precisely because of its vagueness. This eroticism is the expression of a unique economy: goods that stand for what money cannot buy, articulated in money that traverses exchange to become a quality of the thing it buys.

Returning to the moment of birth of contemporary advertising style, the use of cool in marketing shows a phenomenological counterpart to a process of overall eroticization of consumption. When the new style emerged in the 1960s, goods confronted consumers on an existential level, as marked by the many versions of the formula "be yourself" that recurred at the time in advertising. In a sense, goods always provided an answer to the question of who we are. What rendered the cool answer erotic is its nondefinitive form. Due to the inherent ambivalence of its message, cool does not provide an answer to the question, but replies to it with further questions: What is this thing to me? In what way does it represent me? In this, cool replicates the way human beings assume their gender according to the psychoanalytic theory. Freud's often misinterpreted maxim "anatomy is destiny" does not equate gender with biological sex. Destiny is not what we are but what we cannot escape. What the maxim thus means is rather that one can never simply *be* a man or a woman. These sexual identities are to our psyche external fates, something one can neither escape nor fulfill; something we are but cannot fully comprehend exactly how.

Ernest Dichter, one of the prophets of the revolution in marketing, presented most clearly the economic and existential questions involved with new patterns of consumption, which he labeled as an impending "consumer rebellion." The title of his 1965 article, "Discovering the Inner Jones," resonates with Veblenian terminology. It begins with a renunciation of the Veblenian framework, colloquially identified with the idea that consumers are motivated by the wish to "keep up with the Joneses." This competitive motivation, he argued, was becoming obsolete, to be replaced by a search for inner satisfactions. The "inner Jones" in Dichter's title alludes to a rebellion against implicit forces of social coercion but unwittingly it also suggests a form of their internalization and intensification. This ambiguity is not accidental. Dichter presents the search for inner satisfaction as infinitely more demanding than the pressures of social comparison. On the one hand, he concludes his forecast with the claim that the person who will be admired by the new Joneses is he "who more truly becomes himself." On the other hand, "becoming oneself" involves more intense, and actually insatiable, patterns of consumption. While formerly human needs could be visualized in the form of a pie chart, implying the possibility of satisfaction, of a static balance, in the new regime, "the model one has to imagine is that of an ever-expanding rubber balloon; no sooner have we reached a desired goal than we think of another need to be fulfilled" (Dichter 1965, 7). Most interesting is Dichter's description of the new consumer: "We are rapidly reaching a stage, not least as a result of successful advertising, where the consumer asks, in effect, not just how long will the washer last, but what will it do for his 'soul'" (7). The blatant incompatibility between "washer" and "soul" is not a slip of the pen. Washers are not supposed to do anything for the soul, but that is precisely what makes the question open-ended and enticing. To recall again Zupančič's terminology, the impossible consumer's question is also erotic: "We could perhaps go so far as to say: when—in the human realm—we come across something and have absolutely no clue what it is, we can be pretty certain that it 'has to do with sex'" (2017, 23).

The abandonment of realist conventions of representation in the creative revolution in advertising should be taken at face value. It reflects the way that goods are imbued with unrealistic, exaggerated expectations. That is the key to Dichter's question of what a washer will do for our soul: it means demanding from goods the impossible. This new way of using goods in order to become ourselves replicates the outline of the assumption of gender in psychoanalysis. It invests in an external thing, a part of us which we ourselves cannot comprehend. According to psychoanalysis one is never simply a man or a woman. One *becomes* a man or a woman in a process that is never consummated. This becoming involves confronting one's own body as an external reality. That is the gist of the concept of castration as the principle of masculinity. The male boy starts becoming a man in psychic terms when he confronts the possibility of bodies without penises. His gender overlaps his biological sex though it is different from it and not derived from it: it evolves from a mediated relation to one's own body, a perception of it through its difference from other bodies. Being a man or a woman means *knowing* that one is a man or a woman, absent the possibility to back that knowledge with experiential content.

Adam Arvidsson traces the emergence of modern branding to a new conjunction of goods and identities. Branded goods, he argues, do not express preexisting, stable identities but are used by consumers as symbolic tools to fabricate and innovate identities. What people pay for when they buy a brand is "what they can become with it" (Arvidsson 2006, 68). A small correction is required to highlight the existential and erotic weight of this play of identity. A better formulation is that people pay for what they cannot become, which is nonetheless a fundamental aspect of who they are (one could say their fantasy). The iconic ads of Marlboro cigarettes, which Arvidsson presents as initial steps toward modern branding, are the perfect example. In place of ideal representations of real-life situations, Marlboro ads displayed spectacular landscapes of the mythic American western frontier. Through such images Marlboro cigarettes became symbolic tools through which male consumers expressed or imagined masculinity (62). That is obviously true, yet what should be added is that the contrast between such images and consumers' everyday experience presents masculinity as an unattainable goal. That is the mark that the identity expressed by them belongs to the domain of the sexual: it has to do with a failure to be a man, which is at the same time one's way to be a man.

Marie Kondo's books are such a success because her techniques for tidying are techniques of the self ("Tidying is a dialogue with one's self," "The moment you start to reset your life"). The joy of throwing stuff away is the joy of knowing oneself. At the heart of the process objects mysteriously reveal this to us: "Take each item in [your] hand and ask: 'Does this spark joy?' If it does, keep it. If not, dispose of it" (Kondo 2014, 39).

The Failure to Be Oneself

Dichter's characterization of the ideal new consumer as the person "who more truly becomes himself" deserves further thought. How can "becoming oneself" designate an ardent task? Isn't it the simplest thing of all? A perspective from media provides an answer. The history of visual media in the twentieth century in its progress from movies, through television, to new media, is an evolution of the demand to be oneself and of the different forms of failures to fulfill it. To start in the middle, television began to stage this demand most explicitly with the reality genre and the value it places on authenticity. *Big Brother*, being an all-encompassing, ruleless game that deserves the title of the genre's masterpiece, stages the demand to be oneself in the most complex manner. The allusion to Orwell resonates with totalitarian imagery, which the show partly realizes in a thoroughly monitored living space, as well as in the stream of capricious orders and tasks that the big brother presents to the participants. Yet in place of the homogeneous, lifeless conduct we associate with totalitarian regimes, the show displays a celebration of transgression. The strangest contrast to the totalitarian connotation, however, is the way participants typically understand their challenge. Absent any strategies or criteria for winning, they often explain their ulterior mission in the show in terms of being themselves. That is the late capitalist Big Brother in a nutshell: a totalitarian regime that demands authenticity, an "inner Jones."

Dichter's tracing of a similar demand to marketing points at a context that renders this combination plausible. The demand to be oneself can be seen as a regime, rather than simply a liberating call, insofar as it answers the interests of business, and not just the wishes of consumers. It is worthwhile, however, to look into the mechanisms that *Big Brother* utilizes to render this demand meaningful. Such mechanisms are the tasks that involve absurd role playing (cops and thieves, rich and poor, ruler and subjects), where the "authentic self" of a participant emerges through their unique way of failing to play their role, highlighting the performative aspect of their authenticity. More generally, participants are cast as both ordinary people and social types, representing different and sometimes antagonistic social groups. Because they do not share what Erving Goffman described as "the definition of the situation," the implicit knowledge of how people "naturally" perform various social roles, their conduct is bound to appear to each other as artificial, performed. This suspicion of inauthenticity may even seep into one's own self-perception. In the second Israeli season, after ranting to the big brother about the constant masquerades of his peers, a participant suddenly burst into tears as he began talking about himself: "And after two weeks here, I even feel that I am fake myself. I do the things I always do. I live the way I live for years, and suddenly all I do seems to me fake."

This use of difference reveals the logic of the regime of authenticity and its deep connection to post-Fordist capitalism. Authenticity can be the subject of a demand insofar as being oneself is naturally taken to mean being *unique*, different from others. The conjunction of authenticity and difference is far from being a logical identity. Authenticity can have a socially liberating meaning when it designates the permission to be oneself *irrespective* of others, which entails the possibility that one is oneself even when coincidentally one is like others. The rendition of authenticity in terms of difference designates rather the intimate presence of others in one's sense of self. Formally speaking it designates a more intrusive social regime than the pressures of conformism and homogeneity. The latter leave intact the possibility of a true self hidden behind the social conformist mask. The regime of difference, by contrast, involves the imperative to display an inner self in its difference from others. It thus implies a more intimate presence of others in one's perception of self. A Twitter catchphrase captures the intrusive nature of this regime: "You are X. I am Y. We are not the same." The formula typically involves exposing a difference behind ostensible similarity. The virality of the formula is evidence of an identity regime where ostensible similarity to others is perceived as threatening to the integrity of the self. The regime of authenticity as difference is a direct corollary to the brand market. Brands are tools of differentiation. There can be so many types of beers or soft drinks in an average supermarket because of the logos they carry. Differences in flavor could not alone account for such a variety, while the visual field opens an infinite space of differentiation. If, as Naomi Klein (2009) has argued, in modern branding the brand has taken the place of the product, then what we buy *are* differences: objects that stand for differences and thus can express our unique self.

The launching of a new iPhone model is accompanied by lines of people camping overnight outside Apple stores, waiting to buy the gadget. Ostensibly, this makes no economic sense: why wait a whole night if after a couple of days one can simply enter a store and buy the thing? In truth this idiotic behavior expresses the real economic meaning of the thing: an iPhone holds the promise to make us unique, which it obviously cannot fulfill once everybody has it. The only way to really possess an iPhone, even if for the shortest time span, is to wait through the night to be the first to have it.

It is no accident that *Big Brother* displays so explicitly the regime of difference and authenticity. The evolution of this regime can be glimpsed at the margins of the history of visual media in the twentieth century, from cinema through television to new media. This history can be told from the perspective of the evolution of the typical personas that populate them: from movie stars through television celebrities to social media influencers. This perspective highlights how the different screens (movie, television, smartphone) are involved in different ways in our ways of being ourselves. Media personas are in truth ways of being of the crowd. Stars, celebrities, and influencers are three answers for an existential question of someone else. The fact that a person is a movie star, a celebrity, or an influencer is strictly speaking a fact about *other people*, for whom this person is a star, a celebrity, or an influencer. And it is a fact that belongs to an intimate level of being: of who we are, who we want to be, and who we fail to be. Media personas are embodiments of ethical demands. It is not simply that they present models of the good life or that everyone wants to be like them. More importantly, their very existence as stars, celebrities, or influencers materially implies a perceived deficiency or failure on the part of the viewers who accept them as stars, celebrities, or influencers. Their existence materially implies what viewers perceive themselves as lacking. Yet this lack wears different forms vis-à-vis different media personas.

Movie stars are marked by distance. Their lives are glamorous. Their persona, insofar as one confronts it in movies, exists in separate sphere from that of the crowd. In the movies the characters they play never address the audience (Marshall 2014, 119–21). Glamour is of course an illusory concept, but this does not exclude its unique mode of reality. The question it raises is how its illusion is sustained. Glamour simply means that viewers perceive themselves as ordinary, leading unglamorous lives. This matrix is simple enough, but it becomes complicated with the emergence of television celebrities, who are marked precisely by their nearness and ordinariness. This paradoxical feature of celebrity was already noted by Daniel Boorstin in the 1960s. In his seminal book *The Image* he defined celebrities as "known for their well-knownness." Their claim to fame contains nothing but fame itself. Contrasting the celebrity to the hero, the traditional focal point of mass identification, Boorstin highlights the former's paradoxical nature. We admire celebrities as ordinary people, neither better nor greater than ourselves: "In imitating him, in trying to dress like him, talk like him, look like him, think like him, we are simply imitating ourselves . . . reaching to become more emphatically what we already are" (1962, 83). To read this literally, the celebrity is our failure, not to lead glamorous lives, but to be ourselves. The skills that are required from the celebrity, Boorstin writes, are those of differentiation, the ability to display a unique personality. Celebrities "succeed in skillfully distinguishing themselves from others essentially like them. They do this by minutiae of grimace, gesture, and voice" (74). This paradoxical form ingrained in the phenomenon of celebrity became explicit with the reality genre, when television began to "mass produce" what Graeme Turner called "ordinary celebrities." Traditional celebrities typically had a certain talent or achievement allegedly explaining their status. Reality TV celebrities, who need only to "perform their ordinariness with some degree of specificity or individuality" (Turner 2010, 22), prove that such talents or achievements are no more than pretexts, external to the form of existence of the celebrity. The existence of celebrities implies viewers who perceive their own ordinariness as lacking specificity or individuality. The celebrity is thus a channel of the ethical demand to be ourselves, expressing our failure to be ourselves as distinguished from others.

The difference between stars and celebrities is a corollary of the difference between the libidinal economies of Fordist and post-Fordist consumption. Stars embody a collective form of desire: a desire shared by everyone to be like someone who raises above the crowd. Celebrities embody the desire to differentiate oneself from others. In the early days of television Andre Bazin formulated a similar distinction in erotic terms. He distinguishes between the movie screen and the television screen through the different eroticism of their typical female personas: the movie starlet and the television hostess. The former can be explicitly erotic while the latter cannot. The distinction has to do with social and technical differences between the screens. On the movie screen we see only an image of the starlet, while television, that is, *live* television, maintains a sense of spectral presence of its personas in the living room. It is as if we see the people on it through a set of mirrors, which would make an explicit eroticism too obscene to bear. The "unreality" of the starlet image opens the possibility for a collective erotic fantasy: "In the darkened cinema, I have the feeling that the starlet incarnates my dreams because she incarnates the identical dreams of the several hundred people who surround me" ([1954] 2014, 112). The television hostess, due to her place in the family home as well as to the sense of her presence, cannot be too explicitly erotic. If the male viewer has an erotic relation to her, it can only be personal, implicit and somewhat shameful: "I am conscious that it is I who am looking at her.... This extraordinary power, which brings me control over her, entails something indecent by its very nature" (112).

New media influencers present a further stage in the development of media personas and the corollary ethics they imply. Influencers are typically marked by an idiosyncratic quirkiness. Josh Ostrovsky, nicknamed "the fat Jew," an influencer with more than ten million followers, explains in the documentary *The American Meme* (dir. Ben Marcus 2018): "Everywhere I go, I want people to think, 'what the fuck!' If it makes sense, I don't want to be there. No one on the internet can be normal. Everyone on social media is so extreme, right?" At first sight, influencers represent a democratization of fame, the possibilities that social networks afford to individuals to produce fame by themselves. The need of influencers to revert to extremes, however, reveals the limits of this self-made fame. It shows the difference of their persona from that of the celebrity, who can appear as both an ordinary human being and as distinguished from ordinary people.

Netflix's mockumentary *Haters Back Off* draws its pleasures from this difference, marked by the new possibility of becoming famous for being ridiculous. Its main character, Miranda, is afflicted with the idiotic desire for fame, which she tries to realize by shooting video clips of herself for YouTube (to be honest, everyone is afflicted with this desire: otherwise, there would be no celebrities). Her performance is utterly off-putting: her voice is squeaky, her singing off-key, her gestures are grotesque emotional expressions, and her makeup makes her ugly. What makes her particularly cringey is her total lack of self-awareness: she behaves as if she is a "natural" star. Through a twist of fate and algorithms, her sheer idiocy earns her a measure of fame. She fails however to achieve the status of "real" celebrity when a talent agency that wanted to sign her up discovers that her media persona is not a sophisticated farce but her real personality. Of course, the difference between celebrities and influencers does not really reside in their personalities, but in the social ontology of their respective screens. Broadcast television's screen is shared by definition. We watch it together with an anonymous crowd even when we are alone, and for that reason any person that appears on it is potentially known for her well-knownness. If she is a celebrity, she simply embodies this feature of the screen. Influencers have a following, measured sometimes in millions. The fact that this following must be explicitly noted proves that it is not implied by the screen and enfolded into their persona. Celebrities and influencers thus portray the failure to be oneself from both sides. The celebrity, who exists in the sphere of centralized media accompanying and confronting our everyday reality, embodies the demand to be oneself as unique. The influencer, who shares with us the same social space saturated by screens directly entangled with everyday reality, represents the failure to meet this demand. To distinguish themselves from others they cannot be ordinary. They succeed by a certain eccentricity—by appearing fake, bizarre, or some other feature which does not typically mark them as bigger than the ordinary, but in a sense lesser than ordinary.

The difference between celebrities and influencers suggests that the medium of television still maintains what Walter Benjamin termed *aura*. This might sound strange, because television can be easily identified with the causes of the decay of aura: the desire of the masses "to bring things 'closer' spatially and humanly" and their "bent toward overcoming the uniqueness of every reality by accepting its reproduction" (Benjamin [1968] 2007, 223). Yet, broadcast television creates in new ways the conditions of aura which characterized art before mechanical reproduction. Aura is what gets lost in a perfect reproduction of a work of art: "Its presence in time and space, its unique existence at the place where it happens to be" (220) (it is because aura is what disappears even in a perfect reproduction that it should be understood as a condition of seeing rather than as visual content). Television indeed has no unique place—it is everywhere—but retains the sense of a unique presence in time. In broadcast television every moment is unique, irreproducible. One can record it, or find it on YouTube, but then it is no longer live. The liveness of television is the secret of its sense of presence. It lies in the awareness that the news anchor ostensibly talking to me is indeed talking somewhere right now. It is no coincidence that the rise of the reality genre parallels the rise of new media. The genre is the way of broadcast television to differentiate itself from competing screens, and it plays on different senses of presence that characterize television. Its mesmerizing effect lies in the conjunction of the real and the unbelievable: in the acknowledgment that the participants are real, ordinary people who really performed their bizarre, surreal acts in front of the camera (or better yet: because of its presence). Celebrities, however, are the best evidence of the persistence of aura because they give concrete meaning to Benjamin's enigmatic description of its impression: "the unique phenomenon of a distance, however close it may be" ([1968] 2007, 222). One would probably try in vain to recapture this feeling standing in front of the *Mona Lisa*. Celebrities, by contrast, confer on it immediate meaning: however close they are to us (on the screen in our living room, speaking about ordinary things) they remain distant.

The aura that distinguishes television from internet-based media is reflected in the goods marketed through them. Ads on social media cannot be more different from television commercials. On television ordinary things can appear magical (consider the countless supernatural phenomena associated over the years with a mundane object like a Coke bottle). On social media, by contrast, things typically appear as what they are. Yet internet advertising has not forsaken completely its affinity for the supernatural. It is now enfolded into the goods themselves, as evidenced by the plurality of ads for miraculous, wonderful gadgets: a double-sided duct tape with enormous adhesive power; a tiny microscope connectable to smartphones, inviting us to explore wonders in our immediate surroundings; an orthopedic device promising to recover in ten-minute exercises a healthy upright posture, harmed by hours of working on laptops. Like influencers, such goods cannot but take literally the demand of extraordinariness, at the price of being bizarre.

SIX

Women and Capital

IN THE *COMMUNIST MANIFESTO* MARX AND ENGELS describe the entanglement of marriage and property in the erotic economy of nineteenth-century bourgeois society:

> But you Communists would introduce community of women, screams the bourgeoisie in chorus.
>
> The bourgeois sees his wife as a mere instrument of production. He hears that the instruments of production are to be exploited in common, and, naturally, can come to no other conclusion than that the lot of being common to all will likewise fall to the women. (Marx and Engels 1965, 54)

The bourgeois's conception of marriage is colored by the logic of property (and vice versa: his conception of property is secretly erotic). Within this framework, however, lies the Victorian double standard, in an implicit *suspension* of the official code that sanctifies both family and property. The "community of women," has in fact existed "almost from time immemorial": "Our bourgeois, not content with having wives and daughters of their proletarians at their disposal, not to speak of common prostitutes, take the greatest pleasure in seducing each other's wives." (54)

Western sexual mores have changed since the nineteenth century, yet the sex and property knot that Marx and Engels describe persists in new forms. In some senses, liberal sexual morality has only made it more explicit. The covert perception of the bourgeois wife as a "mere instrument of production" has morphed into the concepts of sexual capital and erotic capital which have gained currency in academic discourse in the last decade or so. Originally coined by Catherine Hakim (2010), the concept of erotic capital literalizes the sexual-economic matrix that Marx presented in the manifesto. While for Marx and Engels the logic of capital secretly informs the relation of the bourgeois to his wife, for Hakim erotic capital is a real asset that people have in their own personas. Attractiveness, alongside money, education, and connections, can help people "succeed in life." The gender asymmetry that characterized the Victorian sex and property knot, however, still informs Hakim's theory. It is primarily women who have erotic capital. Due to male "sex deficit," women, much more than men, can cultivate their erotic capital to their advantage in job markets and other contexts, or as the sordid pun in the subtitle of Hakim's book phrases it "the power of attraction in the boardroom and the bedroom." In Marx and Engels, a certain sense of erotic capital was a dirty secret ingrained in the bourgeois's relation to his wife (and to his capital). In a sense, what Hakim recommends to women is to explicitly utilize the logic of capital embedded in male desire ("men always want more") to turn themselves into capital. Hakim probably does not recommend to women to have sex with men to advance their careers and material wealth. This only shows how capital increasingly informs sexuality through a widening gap between sex and eroticism. A deferral of consummation both sustains the independent domain of eroticism and confers on it the logic of capital.

Because the academic discourse on erotic capital seems both ideologically motivated and euphemistic, let us start from a vulgar representation of it in Sarah Dunn's novel, *The Big Love*.[1] It formulates bluntly the gender asymmetry of erotic capital. Looking back at the frustrations of her search for a relationship, Alison, the first-person narrator of the novel, dedicates her newspaper column to her theory of "Romantic Market Value": a value system which implicitly regulates romance, matching men and women with more of less equal values. As she admits, her theory is somewhat of a cliché. She cannot recall what part of it she heard from someone else and what she developed herself. Yet it is a good starting point because this theory spells out a fundamental economic asymmetry in the erotic field: "Men and women's Romantic Market Value is based on different things; women are valued for youth and beauty, men for wealth and power" (Dunn 2004, 106). Notice that these are not simply differences in types of "assets" men and women possess in erotic contexts. The more significant gender difference lies in the relation between being and having. Insofar as there is an economy to eroticism, the value of men refers to what they *have*, while the value of women to what they *are*. This crude theory is thus a contemporary version of the patriarchal notion of women as assets.

Chapter 1 dwelled on some erotic metaphors that Marx applies to the relations between money and commodities, where "the use value of commodities attracts the gold," and "commodities are in love with money" (1976, 202, 203). These metaphors are important because they point at the metaphorical nature of money itself, grounded in a double relation between money and commodities: exchange alongside expression. As discrete objects, commodities are exchanged for money. Yet beneath exchange lies a relation of expression where commodities and money permeate each other, undermining their discreteness. On this level, what each object *is* relies on its relation to other objects. A thing is a commodity insofar as its value is expressed in money. Another thing is money because all commodities express their value in it. Dunn's crude theory of romantic market values literalizes Marx's erotic metaphors in the context of relations between men and women (or what amounts to the same thing: in adding one more layer to the metaphorical nature of money). What a woman is (youthful and beautiful) expresses what a man has (wealth and power). From the perspective of this theory, a woman is the use value of money, standing for the "the totality of real embodiment of its utility" (Marx 1976, 199). Commodification of women is obviously at play here. Yet in contrast to our established critical instincts, this version of commodification is not opposed to love but expressed through it. Dunn's romantic value theory is a commodification mediated through love. There is no exchange involved in this theory: the youth and beauty of women is not exchanged for the wealth and power of men. Marx already foretold this, when he used the metaphor of love to designate relations between commodities and money *other than exchange*. Similarly, Dunn's romantic value theory brackets exchange and points at the level of expression. In this theory women mediate men's relation to their wealth: their way not simply to *have* it but to *love* it.

Prurient Puritanism

The double standard implicitly granted men a measure of sexual freedom that was severely forbidden of women. Keeping in mind that normative sexual relations in Victorian times involved one man and one woman, what the double standard practically achieved was to transport the moral burden of sex, the feelings of shame and disgust that enveloped it, from men to women. It stigmatized women precisely for conforming to male desire. It made women "sexual," identified with sex differently than men. In a way, sex became what women *are* and men *do*. As Kate Millet writes, "Patriarchal religion and ethics tend to lump the female and sex together, as if the whole burden of the onus and stigma it attaches to sex were the fault of the female alone" (1970, 51). The sexual revolution of the twentieth century has discarded much of the puritan sexual ethics that supported the double standard. The intriguing point is that it did not result in a dismissal of the double sexual standard, but rather in its reappearance in a lewd version. In this sense we live in an era of prurient puritanism.

One of the female college students interviewed by Peggy Orenstein for her book *Girls and Sex* gave a succinct characterization of the workings of this new version of the double standard in the context of promiscuous college party culture: "I think that every girl's goal is to be just slutty enough where you're not a prude but you're not a whore" (2017, 125). Just slutty enough: that is a fine line to tread! That is how the double standard persists through the transformation from a puritan to a hypersexualized culture. "Slut" is both a principle of female erotic appearance conforming to male desire and a humiliating pejorative for conforming too closely to male desire. In contrast to the Victorian double standard, which enveloped sex in secrecy, its hypersexualized version wears a public form. Female students interviewed by Orenstein repeatedly explained that their "hot" party clothes—tank tops, short skirts, stilettos—made them feel empowered, liberated, proud of their bodies. Yet if they spent a night with a male student, the clothes became a source of embarrassment:

going to classes with them was referred to as "the walk of shame." The clothes attested in plain sight that a girl had sex last night (boys are exempt from this problem because they wear the same kind of clothes to parties and classes).

The hook-up scene, as described by Kathleen Bogle (2008), demonstrates a similar double movement in relation to economy. On the one hand, hooking up severs the last concrete connections between intimacy and economy. On the other hand, it reveals an obscene kernel of economy informing sex itself. Dating, which before the emergence of hooking up was the main social script for intimacy in college life, entangled sex and economy in a direct but somewhat mysterious manner. For some reason, not fully transparent, a negotiation of intimacy in dating had to involve the purchase of *something* (a movie ticket, dinner, etc.). Dating was a triangle: a man, a woman, and a commodity. Some basic sexual-economic questions ensued: "Who pays for what?" and its obscene supplement, "To what does payment entitle one?" These questions lost their meaning in the hook-up scene, which typically occurs as part of a collective activity and does not necessarily involve an economic transaction. It often takes place at parties and bars, which students attend in peer groups and where some couples are formed for a short-term sexual encounter. Yet alongside the separation of intimacy from consumption, in hooking-up an economic aspect informs sex itself: it is still what men get and women give. Moreover, men are expected to get as much of it as they can—those who excel at it are recurrently referred to as "deal closers"—while women are expected to be careful in allocating it, for fear of their reputation. A shadow of the sex and ownership knot still looms over this lewd version of the Victorian double standard. It is most apparent in the significance imputed to male exclusivity in sexual access to women. One of the gravest mistakes for a young female student is to hook-up with a friend of someone she had formerly hooked-up with, and it is worse still to hook-up with two men from the same fraternity. In one of the fraternities Bogle studied, such women were nicknamed with the breathtakingly vulgar pejorative "house rats." One of the students interviewed explained: "How do you expect these people not to talk [when] they're friends? . . . She would have to realize that these guys are close buddies and of course they are going to know. I'd almost say that would be her fault" (Bogle 2008, 108). Her sin is not exactly sexual but rather economic: she has not behaved as property should.

Marx and Engels describe the bourgeois erotic-economic imagination as haunted by the nightmare of "a community of women," expressing the fear of communism and disclosing a secret code of bourgeois society itself. Both these aspects inform the male imagination in the hook-up scene. The fear of sharing women rests on imagining them as trophies for men. The hook-up scene, however, materializes the nightmare in its public nature, where everybody knows who hooked-up with whom. The nineteenth century's double standard was prudish because it was entangled with the privacy of the household. John Stuart Mill attributed the resilience of women's subjugation to this unique locus where the female subject of male power "lives under the very eye . . . of one of the masters—in closer intimacy with him than with any of her fellow-subjects; with no means of combining against him" ([1869] 2009, 21). In the hook-up scene, intimate encounters are publicly acknowledged, and the eye that surveils them is straightforwardly collective.

The sex and property nexus takes effect in both the prudish and the lewd versions of the double standard. What changed is the relation of expression between the two sides of the knot. In its original form, the sexual double standard monitored the modesty of women. What they were punished for was a suspicion of a breach of sexual mores. This made eroticism the secret code of ownership. The lewd double standard is grounded on a liberal approach to sex, which is nonetheless limited only by the shadow of property. Women should beware of hooking-up too much, thus embodying the nightmare of communal property. They are punished for violating the secret code of ownership informing sex. The poles of the nexus have switched places: ownership has become the open secret of sex.

Marriage, a Shadow That Haunts Sex

For generations, marriage articulated sex and ownership. Maybe it still does. What is new, however, is that nowadays a renunciation of marriage also serves the purpose of skewing the erotic domain around male orientation.

After sleeping with her new boss, Henry, a couple of times, Dunn's Alison enters his office to talk about the nature of their relationship. "Relationship?" he replies, "What relationship?" Pressed further he says, "I don't know. I hadn't thought about it. I didn't know it needed a name," and he eventually settles for "It's a bit of fun" which is "somewhere between 'just a fuck' and 'a relationship.'" Humiliated and embarrassed, Alison turns to go saying she is not interested in "a bit of fun," so Henry draws the trump card:

> "Are you asking me to marry you?" said Henry.
>
> "*No.*"
>
> "Are you asking me to ask you to marry me?"
>
> "*No.*"
>
> "Would you like to move in together?"
>
> "*No.*"
>
> "So I don't see the problem," said Henry. (Dunn 2004, 93)

Bringing up the topic of marriage presents the attempt to "talk about the relationship" as a symptom of female uptightness. The derision of marriage, rather than marriage itself, has become a disciplinary tool exerting pressures on women to conform to male desires for casual sex, free of emotional involvement. Alana Massey (2015) describes it as the "chill" attitude. Chill is relaxed and easygoing, posing no demands on others, and it is precisely these qualities that make it the contemporary version in a lineage of disciplinary mechanisms addressed at women. In Massey's words: "Chill is a sinister refashioning of 'Calm down!' from an enraging and highly gendered command into an admirable attitude." It envelops romantic relations with vague language—"talking," "hanging out," "we are not a thing"—consummated in the typical evasion from any inquiry after the meaning of a relationship: "I don't really like to put labels on things."

Ostensibly, the chill attitude is the farthest away from the patriarchal tradition. It expresses men's desire to *not* own women. From a certain perspective, however, it realizes more explicitly the bourgeois's view of his wife "as a mere instrument of production." It marks a progression in the imaginary status of women from mere property to a unique form of capital, whose owner must repeatedly let go of in order to amass more. As Marx put it: "The ceaseless augmentation of value, which the miser seeks to attain by saving his money from circulation, is achieved by the more acute capitalist by means of throwing his money again and again into circulation" (1976, 245–46).

Simone de Beauvoir (1956) described prostitution as "a dark shadow" over marriage. Today it may be that the reverse also holds true: marriage is a dark shadow that orients the liberal sexual domain around male desire (or more bluntly: a dark shadow over sluttiness). Bogle notes a difference between male and female attitudes toward marriage. Throughout the twentieth century marriage was continuously postponed to older ages for both men and women. Yet Bogle points out two different understandings of this postponement: while male students typically indicated they would like to marry "*no sooner* than [age X]," female students tended to say they would like to marry "*no later* than [age Y]" (Bogle 2008, 53). That is how postponed marriage casts its shadow over liberated sex. The difference between "no sooner" and "no later" is a difference between amassing and allocating.

The clearest expression of the way capital informs male sexual imagination is pornography.

Pornography

Pornography objectifies women. Yet one needs to ask into what kind of object? It is an object of a particular kind: an object that wants. Kate Millett's ([1970] 2016) reading of the seduction scene in Henry Miller's *Sexus* is a perfect example. Val seduces Ida, the wife of his friend Bill Woodruff, at their home in the morning after sleeping over there and after Woodruff had left for work. The seduction as well the sex itself involve force and humiliation, affirming Val's mastery and virility. Yet in the pornographic imagination force is not opposed to seduction. It is a proof that Val knows what Ida really wants and what she really is, namely a whore. Throughout the sexual act, Val remains poised while Ida, overwhelmed by her own pleasure and desire, loses all self-control. Enjoyment plays a paradoxical role in the scene. Ida is enthralled in sexual pleasure while Val is occupied mainly by thoughts of his own prowess. That may be the archetypical pornographic fantasy of modern times: a man can find a way to "activate" women, to arouse their desire to the point where it overrides their conscious will.

Women in pornography turn into mechanisms that know no limit to desire. That is the answer to the question into what kind of object they are objectified. They are objectified into capital. The allocation of desire and enjoyment between the man and the woman in the pornographic imagination recapitulates in a precise manner the relation between the capitalist and his capital as described by Marx. A capitalist is not simply a greedy person, someone who wants more money. Rather, he is a subject that behaves as if capital itself possesses a drive for limitless accumulation. The capitalist is "a rational miser." His rationality, however, consists in the fact that like Val he transfers his desire to the object, behaving as if it is the objects that wants. It consists in suspending his own human desires, surrendering them to the abstract drive of capital, aimed neither at things nor at money. That is why Marx can describe capital with a metaphor of perverted eroticism, foretelling Miller's pornographic fantasy. Quoting Goethe's *Faust*, he describes capital as "an animated monster which begins to 'work,' 'as if its body were by love possessed'" (Marx 1976, 302).

The extremely misogynistic culture of pick-up artists, which aims at realizing the pornographic fantasy in practice, demonstrates the various ways in which capital structures male sexual desire. Reading Neil Strauss's bestseller, *The Game*, one gets a strange impression that having sex is not the real goal of the members of "the secret society" of pick-up artists. It is rather this society itself to which their libido is attached. They are indeed obsessed with "getting" women, but mainly as a vehicle of male camaraderie and competition. They embark on seduction expeditions at bars together, share "knowledge" (sometimes referred to as "technology"), and seem to derive immense pleasure from the skillful use of a wealth of abbreviations coined to describe techniques and people (LMR—last minute resistance; SHB—super-hot babe; AFC—average frustrated chump). A reader unacquainted with this subculture might be misled by the air of sophistication conveyed by such terminology. In truth, a familiar sense of masculine infantilism envelops the "knowledge" of pick-up artists (PUAs). One of Strauss's favorite "techniques" is the ESP trick: ask a woman in a bar to think of a number, then impress her by guessing "seven." This gap between the sophisticated language of technology and the infantile tricks it refers to underscores the same point: what the PUAs really want is not merely sex. What they want is a method: an impersonal technique of getting as many women as possible to have sex with them. Their obsession with sex is a mirror image of the capitalist spirit, as Max Weber defined it: not simply a desire for riches, but a drive toward a systematic, rational production of profit ([1930] 1992, 22). Indeed, male camaraderie is also the substrate for competition where quantitative success grants members with a higher, and sometimes "legendary," status within the circle. Of one legendary PUA, it is told that his techniques are so powerful that he makes women pay to give him blowjobs (Strauss 2005, 12). What a legend! It is futile to ask whether it is the money or the blowjob that he wants, for it is the combination that moves his desire. It is a tense combination articulating sex as a form of control in a paradoxical way. The price delegates desire to the women: it is they who want it, while he only acquiesces. At the same time, the price also serves as a defense mechanism against the horrifying image of the female monster who knows no limit to her desire: there is only so much she can afford.

With its shift from old media to the internet, the change in the contents of pornography shows how the logic of capital increasingly permeates the imaginings of sex. Rule no. 34, coined by a British teenager sometime in the beginning of the millennium, states that "If it exists, or can be imagined, there is Internet porn of it" (Dewey 2016). The rule refers to the overwhelming diversity of pornographic themes on the internet, which encompass not only aliens, robots, and goats, but also things like trombones and Tetris blocks. Yet beyond this diversity, rule no. 34 speaks of an ethics, similar to the one that renders money capital: any potential must be realized. Weber's definition of the capitalist spirit is again helpful here: an ethic is enfolded in money once its mode of existence is recognized as that of potential (when forgoing a potential profit should be counted as a real loss).

Not only diversification of themes is involved with internet porn, but also what many critics describe as a process of escalation, among which is an escalation in the degradation of women. Orenstein lists some extreme yet popular themes: ass to mouth (anal sex immediately followed by an oral sex), Bukkake (multiple men ejaculating on a woman's face), triple penetration, oral sex aimed at making a woman vomit, penetration by multiple penises in a single orifice. Notice the strange role that numbers play in this process of escalation. It speaks of a certain abstract nature of the desire motivating and driven by pornography. Numbers can grow infinitely, and thus they express the "more" of desire, its insatiable aspect. Following Freud, and especially his Lacanian interpretation, this aspect may be characteristic of desire as such. Numbers express this surplus of desire in its purity, in a way which paradoxically annuls the bodily aspect of sex. The obscenity of images rotates from sex to numbers alluding to infinite increase. In this way, the sexual content of the images stands for its own insufficiency and becomes subservient to the drive for pure increase. This is again a mirror of the desire of capital, aimed neither at money nor at things, but to a movement between them which renders each of them partial.

The process of escalation in porn is characterized by constant transgression. As psychologist Victor B. Cline writes, "pornography, which was originally perceived as shocking, taboo-breaking, illegal, repulsive, or immoral . . . in time came to be seen as acceptable and commonplace" (quoted in Paul 2007, 227). Pamela Paul traces this process in conversations with porn addicts, for some of whom the escalation of their taste in pornography made real sex nearly impossible. As one of them recounts, having sex with his wife became a pale shadow of porn. Fantasizing about porn while having sex with her, he says, meant that "I was really just using her—she was like a masturbatory accessory" (233). This constant transgression of boundaries is another reflection of the logic of capital in the domain of sex, of capital as "the endless and limitless drive to go beyond its limiting barrier" (Marx 1973, 334).

The porn addicts that Paul interviews replicate the interplay between domination and subservience characteristic of the relation of the capitalist to his capital. They admit that they objectify women and at same time are themselves haunted by this objectification. For the addict, Paul writes, pornography is "the means to 'get' someone, to 'have' her and control her" (2006, 221). At the same time, their basic condition is one of helplessness in front of the object. They cannot resist it. They are penetrated by it ("There were times when I thought women could tell what I was thinking," one of them reports, "they knew something was wrong with me" [222]). They are appalled by the inner monster that porn consumption brings out in them (after coming across kiddie porn, another one reports, "It was scary for me because I was turned on and also because it obviously depicted kids who had been abused and tricked" [227]). Capital empties things of their essence. Being not a thing but a constant change of forms between commodities and money, it robs things of their thingness, rendering them placeholders of abstract value. The same goes for the porn addicts ("For me," one of them explains "sex became less and less gratifying" [228]).

Critics are alarmed by the unrealistic contents of pornography, especially in light of the fact that young men sometimes say they watch it for information and knowledge about sex (Srinivasan 2022). Orenstein suggests that realistic videos of enjoyable sex might be a good idea and explains that these are hard to find because of the financial interests of the huge porn industry, which is intent on producing as much traffic as possible at all costs. This explanation deserves careful attention. It is meaningful insofar as it points to finance as the secret form of internet pornography. From a standard economic perspective, Orenstein's explanation makes no sense: if some young men watch porn to learn about sex, the financial interests of the industry should have led to the creation of a substantial trend of "realistic" pornography. It makes sense, however, if the financial forces that drive the porn industry are reflected in its contents: finance is the secret of its unreality, in the same way that finance is opposed to real economy.

Two points can explain why there is no realistic pornography on the internet. First, a more general point: according to the psychoanalytic approach, it is impossible to simply "show sex." As Zupančič writes, "Culture is not simply a mask/veil of the sexual, it is the mask or, rather, a stand-in for something in the sexual which 'is not'" (2017, 23). The masks that cover sexuality do not hide a factual knowledge of sex, but the paradoxical fact that there can be no factual knowledge of it. Conservative societies envelop sex with secrecy and shame, but there is no "real" sex behind these veils, because secrecy and shame are constitutive to sex. And what about our hypersexualized societies? That brings us to the second point. Pornography is our own way of masking sex. This may be true of all pornography, but it is true in a unique way for the internet, where pornography is ubiquitous and no longer hidden behind walls of shame. The escalating content and the fascination with numbers is pornography's contemporary way to mask sex.

Patricia Nilsson (2022), in a fascinating series of investigations for the *Financial Times*, exposed how the internet caused a comprehensive shift in the pornography industry. A small group of internet entrepreneurs took over much of the revenue of porn by creating an enormous web of free sites, consisting mainly of illegally copied videos uploaded by users, with the aim of profiting from increased traffic, either from ads or from a minority of paying users. In an interview with Jon Ronson, old-time porn director Mike Quasar explains how this new financial scheme changed the contents of porn: "Everything needs to be searchable by a particular fetish, so keywords like interracial, anal, whatever . . . they typically go into the title of the movie" (Ronson 2017). As a result of the work of engineers and programmers who have nothing to do with porn, generic movie titles like *Women of Influence*, or *Playing with Fire* disappeared and were replaced with highly focused ones like *Cheerleader Stepdaughter Orgy* or *Bad Babysitters*. Interestingly, female performers in their twenties, even attractive ones, can no longer find work in the field, falling in the space between the keywords *teen* and *milf*. As Quasar explains: "Just attractive is not a keyword." The monstrous plurality and specificity of themes is how internet porn expresses the impossibility of showing "just sex." On the internet one finds all imaginable kinds of sex, except sex itself.

There is in fact an exception to this last exception: in the early days of the internet, amateur porn was a popular theme, which relied on the desire for representations of "real sex" (as defined in contrast to "professional sex"). Today, this niche is occupied by OnlyFans, a social network which has made an extraordinary financial achievement: in an environment flooded by free porn, it succeeded in inducing people to pay for sexual content that is typically milder, and sometimes weirder, than typical internet porn. The immediate explanation for this is that people pay because the sexual content there is somehow real. That in itself is interesting, because it renders reality as one more fetish, or even the ultimate fetish, one worth paying for. But the explanation is also partial. It is not that people pay for real content, but the other way around: paying makes the content real. The visual content itself cannot vouch for its unique reality. It is the fact that one directly pays the performer, who communicates with him and incites him to pay, that makes the visual content real.

Money is the principle of reality and unreality of sex in internet porn (it is one combined principle, not two: if money is the "real" of sex, it is because sex cannot be real). It is reflected in a financial form of porn. The obsession with numbers and the drive to transgress all boundaries make finance the "real" of porn and renders sexual content subservient to it. The principle is further reflected in the consequences of new financial schemes that changed the nature of pornography on the internet. The obsession with keywords is an integral part of the scheme, making the search for content particularly efficient and addictive. Its result is a unique way of masking sex. The correct name of those keywords, as Quasar uses it, is "fetishes." The content does not show sex, but one's specific quirkiness in relation to sex. What one sees is his specific keyword, or fetish, which in psychoanalysis serves precisely as a mask. Viewers get as much free porn as they want, but the financial scheme that brings it to them circumvents the possibility of "normal sex" (from a psychoanalytic perspective, of course, there is no such thing as "normal sex," but internet porn is one specific form of its nonexistence). Finally, money is the principle of reality of amateur porn. Reality, as the ultimate fetish, distinguishes amateur content from the ocean of free porn. Yet one does not exactly pay for a sense of reality but rather pays to confer reality on images. It makes normal the ultimate pervert.

Coda: The Economy of Nonbuying

In the porn industry, "the money shot" is a video capturing an ejaculation. An intriguing question is what does this phrase teach us about money? As its name attests, the money shot is considered a necessary component for a successful porno movie (in action movies a money shot may refer to an expensive sequence of spectacular devastation, which is also essential for success). Its importance lies in the fact that ejaculation cannot be mimicked and therefore serves as a proof of reality. The money shot proves that *someone* enjoyed. Pleasure, reality, and money. The money shot presents a transmutation of this triangle vis-à-vis the standard economic meaning of its terms. In economics, money marks an unreal dimension, as expressed in the contrast between real prices and nominal prices. The nominal price of a thing, its money price, is considered less real than a price expressed in terms relative to other goods and services. Pleasure has to do with this distinction. Money itself is not enjoyable, or at least is not supposed to be, only other goods and services are. The concept of a real price therefore expresses the economic view of the human being as an autonomous pleasure-calculating mechanism, comparing solipsistic pleasures afforded by different goods and services. In the ejaculation shot, by contrast, money is the name of both reality and pleasure. The transmutation of the triangle is not a simple negation of the standard economic opposition between money, reality, and pleasure. It is rather made possible by a *double* negation, whereby pleasure is replaced by knowledge. Money does not denote pleasure but proof of pleasure of *another* (which means that pleasure, like money, is inherently social).

While the term "money shot" is metaphorical, a similar triangle informs in a more literal way the strange economy of sex in the global party circuit of the superrich, as described in the fascinating ethnography by Ashley Mears, *Very Important People*. This economy, colloquially referred to as "models and bottles," works like this: image promoters, many of them nonwhite, are paid a few hundred dollars a night to bring women to parties in clubs. It is best if they invite models, whom they use elaborate ways to meet, and among whom Victoria's Secret models are the most sought-after prize. Second best are women who look as if they could be models, who in the lingo of the trade are referred to as "good civilians" (in contrast to mere "civilians" or "pedestrians" who play the role of "fillers": ordinary people with the proper style who are let in to fill the dance floor of the club). The presence of models is necessary to attract rich people to order one of the tables set at a highly visible area of the club, apart from the dance floor and the bar. While "fillers" crowd the bar to order drinks, at the tables, drinks are served in bottles sold at exaggerated prices, sometimes reaching up to $40,000 a piece. The models are not paid, but their food and drinks are comped by the club. The whole intricate apparatus revolves around this nonpayment. The theoretical challenge that this social scene poses is how to understand nonpayment as an economic fact. Ostensibly, the apparatus would have been made redundant if the clubs could simply pay models for their presence. They cannot. It is crucial that the models are there to party, rather than to work. Their "fun" is a necessary condition for superrich clients, called "whales," to spend enormous sums, sometimes ordering dozens of bottles of champagne. Of one legendary whale it is told that he spent $1.5 million dollars in one night at a club. Interestingly, some of the whales, as well as some celebrities, do not pay for their drinks and food. Their attendance in the club reassures some less rich clients that they are in the right place, in the presence of "the cool people," and encourages them to pay the scandalous prices. Some parties show off with "bottle trains" where bottles of champagne, with lighted sparklers attached, are delivered to the tables in a procession, carried by beautiful, tall, and scantily clad waitresses. The crowd on the dance floor cheers at the sight, and people hold up their phones to take photos and immediately post them on Instagram.

As Mears writes, much effort is invested in the orchestration of the party. It gives the impression of a systematic mechanism, worthy of the name "economy," although foreign to the standard meaning of the term. The derisive vocabulary of the club operators (civilians, pedestrians, fillers) attests that it is an economy in the form of an X-ray photo, discovering the real skeleton masked by appearances. The intricate economic apparatus produces an erotic atmosphere conducive to grand gestures of waste. The crucial point, however, is that sex, in contrast to eroticism, is not a part of the scheme. The rich clients do not typically have sex with the models, and if they do, it is coincidental to the club economy. That is the key to the fundamental difference of this economy from standard economic terminology. The club economy cannot be fully captured in terms of exchange. There are exchanges of course: bottles are bought from the club; promoters are paid to bring women; models get free drinks. But exchange is supported with another relation in which money is involved: a relation of proximity. The exchanges that do take place are motivated by proximity: wasting money in the presence of a model partying, partying in the presence of rich men, buying expensive things in the presence of people richer than oneself. This effect of proximity is what makes the club economy so strange to the standard economic perspective and reveals the contours of the sexual economy of capitalism.

As in the money shot, pleasure in the club scene is partly replaced by knowledge, which marks pleasure as inherently social. Parties may be fun.

But for the economy, there must be evidence of fun. People must see the models having fun and the rich men spending lavishly beside them. It is even better if they take photos (why aren't *these* called money shots?). Fun is less important for the club economy than its public display. One of the strangest facets of the significance of knowledge of fun over simple fun is the obsession with "real models" rather than beautiful women or even "good civilians," women who look like models. As one club owner explained to Mears: "Someone spending $15,000 a night in a nightclub wants the real thing, just the peace of mind that he is now part of that A list, that social elite" (2020, 18). Real models are required because their beauty is *objective*. It is objective in an economic sense: outside the clubs, they monetize their beauty. Money traverses relations exclusive of exchange: it is wasted lavishly in the proximity of monetized beauty, though nothing changes hands. Marx might have called this "a change of form" underlying exchange. The models' beauty is objective in a social sense, namely as intersubjective: one recognizes a model as someone whom everybody knows from billboards and ads and maybe many fantasize about (maybe that is why Victoria's Secret models are most desirable for image promoters: people know that they have tread the catwalk in underwear in the presence of a gazing crowd). Because their beauty is objective, models do not even have to appear beautiful. A New York club owner told Mears that "models weren't even that pretty." To him they are strange. "But it pops in the club because they are seven feet tall." A former club owner said that "only really sophisticated people can tell the difference between models and hot girls" (Mears 2020, 44). Image promoters train their assistants, or "subs," to ignore their personal tastes in female beauty and focus on the model look which boils down to four narrow parameters: height, slenderness, youth, and face. This narrow, objective interpretation of beauty is reflected in the violently misogynistic terminology that promoters and club personnel use to refer to women who diverge from its stiff standards: midgets, muppets, ugly dogs, troll, elf, hideous, disaster, monster—pejoratives which mean nothing more than that their object is an "ordinary" (i.e., not model-like) woman.

The obsession with "real models" brings to the fore a theoretical economic puzzle: what is the "real economy" in the clubs? In economics, the notion of real economy involves going beyond nominal prices to an ideal view of the economy as consisting solely of "real things" (goods and services as they are to individual autonomous agents). In the clubs, the notion of real economy involves the opposite movement: from things to their underlying monetary nature. On the surface, one sees a party: men and women having fun, eating, drinking, and dancing. The real economy lies underneath, in the way money permeates the whole scene, embodied in different ways in different persons and objects. A bottle of champagne is in reality a means of an extravagant waste of money, the man who bought it is rich, and the beautiful women near it are models, professional women, women who make money from embodying a certain ideal of womanhood. Even the fun of the models is monetary. It is no doubt real fun. A member of closely knit group of models of one of the promoters told Mears: "It's the most insane night for our group. . . . everyone in the club, when we start yelling and screaming, they all turn and look at us like, 'what the hell.' We get crazy. We have so much fun." Her friend added that "the managers love us . . . we bring the energy" (2020, 84) (notice that even for them fun is inseparable from attention). Yet from the perspective of the real economy, it is a monetary fun precisely because it is not simulated for payment. It is related to money through the intricate mechanism of nonpayment. It is the pleasure of money. From the narrow perspective of mainstream economics, focused exclusively on exchange, money cannot be pleasurable. It *buys* pleasures and for that reason is not itself pleasurable. The relation of proximity, however, renders the fun of the model a pleasure of money, precisely because it is situated *beyond* exchange. Their fun is a metonymy of money. When we buy things, we do not enjoy money, but what it buys. The pleasure of money involves what it accrues *without* buying (the rich men are recurrently referred to, by promoters and models alike, as "amazing people").

This brings us to a second distinction of the "real economy" of these parties. Rather than the standard economic meaning of the term, it is closer in form to the Lacanian concept of the real, as what cannot be directly represented, yet informs social reality; the real which cannot be directly approached yet is alluded to through inconsistencies and gaps in the symbolic order. We need not dwell too much on Lacanian formulations, because the club economy presents a concrete and simple incarnation of this formal structure. It is an economy structured around absence. Two things that don't happen are the ultimate keys to its reality: models are not paid, and rich clients do not have sex with the models. The whole orchestration of the party revolves around them. The first thing to note regarding this notion of "real economy" is the out-of-the-ordinary atmosphere of the parties. In some sense it can even be described as traumatic: in interviews outside the club scene, participants often distance themselves from the lavishness of the parties; some of them express derision and even disgust with the extravagant spending of whales (this derision, as Mears notes, helps them justify their own lavish yet smaller spending). These reactions are understandable: at the parties, ordinary, decent men are confronted with an explicit staging of the obscene image of the harem, of powerful men possessing flocks of women. The "fun" of the party revolves around this obscene kernel and sometimes approximates it: unable to consume the tremendous quantities of champagne they order, rich clients habitually use them to spray the dancing crowd (a purpose for which some clubs offer cheaper substitute bottles of sparkling wine—this economy of thrift hidden within the spectacle of waste being yet more proof that waste has its own economy). In one case Mears witnessed a whale physically forcing models to drink straight from a bottle he brought to their mouths. The stigma of prostitution also has an ominous presence in this social environment, and models actively distance themselves from it. They distinguish between "party girls" who only seek "fun" and "paid girls" who monetize their beauty. Among the latter are "table girls" who try to solicit men to order a table or bottles and are paid a commission by the club. They too do not exchange sex for money but are nonetheless stigmatized as "hookers." They get too close to the obscene kernel that must be avoided. The same goes for women who try to utilize the opportunity of connecting with rich people for their own interests. Occasionally, after a uniquely successful night, promoters share some of their profit with models. Yet to render this a gift rather than payment, through an unspoken understanding the shared profit is dedicated to shopping sprees of clothes and accessories.

The club economy, however, is not to be identified with these obscene kernels of the harem and prostitution. Economy is nothing but the way these kernels are avoided, circumscribed, or disavowed. Lavish waste on one side and ecstatic female fun on the other: together they disavow the obscene kernel of the party. On the economic side: accentuated waste (not only champagne, but in scandalous prices, and using it partly for spraying rather than drinking) disavows—the more vocally the merrier—the possibility of exchange. It is further disavowed on the sexual side by the fun of the models. The absence of sex (between rich clients and models) is expressed in certain form of eroticism. Sex looms over the parties. The work of promoters is in truth quite demanding. Attending parties a few nights a week is exhausting, and promoters have to invest much effort in maintaining the commitment of their models. They attend to their needs during the day, run errands for them, hang out with them, and dine with them. Many promoters have sex with some of the women in their entourages. From the economic perspective, that is one way to strengthen their commitment and generate the required erotic atmosphere in the club. Sex is excluded, however, from the set of monetary exchanges composing the club economy. This exclusion is the key to the unique erotic atmosphere of the party: an eroticism founded on the deferral of consummation in sex.

The "models and bottles" economy encapsulates the basic features of the sexual economy of capitalism as described in this book. From a broad historical perspective, capitalism coincided with the formal exclusion of sex from the economy. The basic argument of this book is that this transformation could not have taken place without fundamentally changing the *two* fields it involves: sex and money. On the sexual side it involved new forms of love, marriage, eroticism, and gender relations, articulated in some ways with new economic practices. Yet the change involved not only the economic aspects of gender relations. It is reflected in the transformation of economic fundamentals themselves: money, ownership, capital, and exchange were also transformed with the formal exclusion of sex from the economy. A central axis of this change is the emergence of what money cannot buy as an economic category unique to capitalism. The club economy as described by Mears is a microcosm that shows how this transformation keeps playing out. A complex economic apparatus organized around nonpayment to women, it shows how the nonbuying of women can be an active economic phenomenon, having dramatic effects expressed in money and goods. Nonpaying is expressed, on one hand, in the fun of women, and on the other hand, in extravagant waste as eroticized money.

In some senses, eroticized money is already capital. Not simply because it is the money of rich men or because of its quantity. The complex economic apparatus of the club party, rather, inscribes a qualitative difference on the rich man's money. It is closer to capital than to everyday money because it accrues surplus. It is bigger than itself. The partying models are one form of this surplus: related to money not through exchange. That the rich men are "amazing people" is another form of this surplus: a quantity which has become a quality. Unlike capital, the eroticized money at the parties is related to waste rather than to accumulation. Yet it shares with capital a basic feature, where the means of universal equivalence circumvents the possibility of equivalence.

On its theoretical side, Mears's otherwise wonderful book, has some shortcomings. It is important to dwell on them because they are symptomatic to some dominant sociological approaches to contemporary economy. Mears oscillates between two incomplete ways to put together sociology and economics. One way is to append sociological and anthropological insights to an economic analysis, thus "enriching" the economic outlook with "softer" subject matter. The other is to apply to her subject matter concepts from economic anthropology, originally developed in the context of precapitalist societies, in place of standard economic concepts. Both miss the real challenge that sociological and anthropological studies can pose to economics. The stronger option omitted between these two is to put in question the very distinction between sociology and economics. The two disciplines are clearly distinguished in their techniques, concepts, and methods of inquiry, but what should be kept in mind is that the obvious disciplinary difference does not reflect a distinction in subject matter. While sociology and economics are easily distinguishable, there is no theoretically tenable way to distinguish between economy and society. From this perspective, if economics fails in comprehending a social interaction, it is not necessarily because its outlook is partial and needs enrichment, but maybe because it is simply *wrong*.

The strategy of sociologically enriching the economic outlook is most evident in Mears's use of the term *status* as explaining the crazy conduct of rich clients throwing away fortunes. To say that in wasting money they acquire status solves the mystery that this conduct poses for economists, but it does so at the price of subjecting sociological inquiry to the idiotic individualist utilitarian framework of economics. It is to use sociology as a means to do away with the social. Status becomes one more form of utility, and it shares the tautological form that this concept has in economics (people pay for things because they have utility, and we know they have utility because people pay for them). This strategy sterilizes the critical potential that sociological and anthropological studies hold vis-à-vis economics.

A more serious challenge to mainstream economics is found in Mears's use of the concept of potlatch: a hostile gift exchange, where a gift must be reciprocated with a bigger one until one party is humiliated with the depletion of his resources. In some club parties, potlatch seems to come back to life in competitions between rich clients who treat each other's table with bottle trains. The clubs, obviously, profit from this practice, and they actively encourage it: the DJs stop the music to announce a purchase and its price. This simple fact points at the real challenge that anthropology can pose to mainstream economics. It lies not in naming the practice as potlatch, but in its *difference* from potlatch. In tribal potlatch, wealth is destroyed. In its modern simulation, it is not destroyed but consumed. It cannot be destroyed because it is embedded in a monetary economy, where destruction is impossible: any grand gesture of waste is registered somewhere else as a profit. The *simulation* of potlatch thus signifies a *double* difference: a difference of capitalism both from precapitalist economies and from itself (i.e., from its official image in the language of economics). It shows how capitalism carries residues of archaic economies, foreign to the language of economics. At the same time, it shows how these residues are different from their archaic origin precisely because of their reappearance within a capitalist context.

Mears's analysis gestures at this direction. Alongside invoking the image of archaic economy, Mears interestingly describes the club scene as a uniquely new economic phenomenon, made possible by the conditions of hypercapitalism. The profligate parties are symptomatic of the emergence of a new economic elite: a global class of the superrich, untethered from local communities and the ethical forces they exert. Moreover, joining this class is predicated on wealth alone. One only needs the right credit card to enter the club. In other words, this class represents the consummation of the process that Veblen identified in the beginning of the twentieth century, where conspicuous consumption replaces conspicuous leisure; where vulgar, anonymous "new money" becomes culturally dominant at the expense of "old money," entangled with ethics, refinement, tradition, and community. Mears's analysis gestures at an answer to the question "What is new in new money (or in hypercapitalism)?" The new is an eruption of a barbaric kernel of economic life, which the old has masked in veils of culture and refinement.

This book opened with the pondering of some contemporary economists over the persistence of monogamy: how is it that advanced capitalist societies maintain a socialist regime in the allocation of women? The club parties of the superrich are the practical counterpart of this question, staging an imaginary primeval scene of the powerful man who owns all women. This imaginary scene should be understood along the lines of Žižek's (1997) concept of fantasy, which is not simply opposed to reality, but is a disavowed kernel constituting reality. In the clubs, the reality of the fantasy is anchored in goods and money. There is a real dimension to the fantasy in the sense that it is expressed in unique uses of goods and money, perverse uses from the standpoint of economics. These uses eroticize goods and money in a way that resonates with how money becomes capital. The book argues that these perverse forms are the true forms of goods and money in capitalism, ingrained in their everyday manifestations.

Notes

Introduction

1 Notice that the economists' unusual reference to "rich men" rather than "rich persons" is not a slip of the pen but an integral part of the argument. If rich women could also marry multiple husbands, then the riddle would vanish, since theoretically everyone would be able find a spouse.

2 Unlike academics in other branches of the social sciences, Kuhn writes, economists are not much bothered by the question of whether their discipline is a science. Yet this fact has to do less with the content of their work and more with its social, institutional form: "Is that because economists know what science is? Or is it rather economics about which they agree?" ([1962] 1996, 161).

Chapter One

1 https://www.msn.com/en-nz/news/other/50-hottest-hollywood-bachelorettes/ss-BBuFFsP. (Accessed May 20, 2019)

2 This idea was more easily visible in Marx's days, when money could be conceived, rightly or wrongly, as grounded on gold. In a such a case, every transaction is an exchange of two products of human labor: the labor involved in the production of a good and the labor involved in digging gold. It would be wrong, however, to conclude that contemporary fiat money is produced with no investment of human labor. In such a case, the bodies issuing money would have ended up owning everything. In truth, money is mostly issued by banks against debt in loans. That means that money is produced by taking account of future labor. This indeed complicates the simple observation of Marx but does not change its basic meaning, that a price is a social relation.

3 The paradox of a puritan kernel within eroticized culture has intensified since Firestone's days. Critics today deplore the pornification of culture, while some studies show that young people are having less sex than a few decades ago. The cascade of images in which we are immersed—video clips, Instagram images, selfies, and advertising—confronts us with a heightened sense of eroticism. Yet *The Atlantic* cites various indications that, in person, millennials are in fact more prudish. As one observer says: in a gym "everyone under 30 will put their underwear on under the towel" (Julian 2018).

4 Ana has never kissed a man. When Grey discovers this, he concedes, against his nature, to initiate her into the world of sex with romantic "vanilla" lovemaking. His concession is important on various levels. That Ana is a virgin completes the articulation of ownership in sexual terms: it consummates the aspect of exclusivity inherent in ownership as such. The romantic sex they have mitigates the cruelty of this ideal form of sexual domination. It also makes possible the combination of romance and BDSM that qualifies the book as "mommy pornography." It fuels the romantic fantasies of Ana to make Grey a normal boyfriend. This narrative choice, however, can also be read as reflecting how domination and ownership are inner codes of romance.

Chapter Two

1 A partial word count in both texts demonstrates the different landscapes of Smith's and Mandeville's texts. The words *whore, strumpet, prostitute, harlot, courtesan, mistress*, and *concubine* appear in total 34 times in Mandeville and 3 in Smith. The words *baker, brewer*, and *butcher* appear 6 times in Mandeville and 106 in Smith.

2 Today we are surrounded by hedonimeters, which demonstrate the same paradox. An addictive feature of many smartphone apps is the possibility of self-measurement: how many songs we listened to, how many steps we stepped, how many miles we ran. The pleasure of measurement annuls the pleasures measured. One may enjoy listening to books in Audible. The measures of daily, monthly, and total listening time, and the indications of listening level achieved, from "Newbie" to "Master," point at a different kind of pleasure, the capitalist pleasure of acquiring assets.

3 If it was a pedagogic project of economics to "induce people to avoid all sorts of display of individual wealth" it miserably has failed since Marshall's time. Considering the increasing distance between Marshall's wishful thinking and economic reality, one might wonder how economists keep adhering to the theory he founded. The answer is simple: economists do not read the founding texts of their own discipline, but rather the textbook versions of them. That is an aspect of the scientific presumption of the discipline. As Kuhn has shown, reliance on textbooks distinguishes natural sciences from other fields of knowledge. It allows sciences to align around a paradigm. Textbooks also nurture historical shortsightedness: "Textbooks ... begin by truncating the scientist's sense of his discipline's history and then proceed to supply a substitute to what they have eliminated" (Kuhn [1962] 1996, 137).

Chapter Three

1 The subverted hierarchy informs today all gift giving. Giving a purely practical thing as a gift today is a sign of a true intimacy.

Chapter Four

1 Shulamith Firestone agrees that that idealization of the love object is typical of men. She gives it a direct economic explanation, economic in the narrow sense of the term: "A man must idealize one woman over the rest in order to justify his descent to a lower caste"; by contrast, women, who have to "capture" men, must be more realistic (1971, 131).

Chapter Five

1 Far from natural, the desire to express difference requires careful nurturing. In Israel, a sort of ritual preceding entrance to school is buying the right school bag. The bags are exactly the same in all respects, apart from a detachable cover displaying a branded figure from television or comics. Children invest much thought in choosing their own personal bag. In an experiment I have repeated three times, they violently reject any suggestion to buy something *really* different, such as a bag of another make.

Chapter Six

1 What intellectual gain is there in substituting the academic term *erotic capital* for the colloquial *sex appeal*? The concept taps into the plurality of forms of capital characteristic of contemporary sociological discourse, like cultural capital and social capital. It primarily resonates, however, with the concept of human capital, which is distinguished by its ideological significance. Concepts of social and cultural capital still retain the antagonistic view of society embedded in the original concept of capital, expanding it to further domains. They are mechanisms of exclusion: cultural capital singles out people who possess it—in the form of tacit knowledge of proper demeanor, style, tastes, etc.—from people who do not. It usually remains implicit, and its significance is most strongly felt when someone *lacks* it. The concept of human capital, by contrast, plays a central role in neoliberal ideology because it blurs the social antagonism embedded in the concept of capital. It substitutes the fundamental opposition between labour and capital with a view of society in which everyone, including laborers, is an owner of capital, and the only differences are in measure. Hakim's work brings to the extreme this ideological function. Replacing *sex appeal* with *erotic capital* conjures a semblance of objectivity, but also cleanses the idea of capitalism of dirty residues, of the shadow of prostitution that haunts any articulation of sex and economy. It is the intellectual way to make capitalism itself seem sexy.

References

Adshade, Marina. 2013. *Dirty Money: The Economics of Sex and Love.* London: Oneworld Books.
Ansari, Aziz, with Eric Klinenberg. 2015. *Modern Romance.* New York: Penguin.
Arendt, Hannah. (1958) 1998. *The Human Condition.* Chicago: University of Chicago Press.
Arvidsson, Adam. 2006. *Brands: Meaning and Value in Media Culture.* London: Routledge.
Austin, John Langshaw. 1975. *How to Do Things with Words.* Cambridge, MA: Harvard University Press.
Bataille, Georges. 1986. *Erotism: Death and Sensuality.* San Francisco: City Lights Books.
Bazin, André. (1954) 2014. "A Contribution to an *Erotologie* of Television." In *Andre Bazin's New Media*, ed. Dudley Andrew. Oakland: University of California Press.
Beauvoir, Simone de. 1956. *The Second Sex.* London: Jonathan Cape.
Becker, Gary S. 1976. *The Economic Approach to Human Behavior.* Chicago: University of Chicago Press.
Benjamin, Walter. (1968) 2007. *Illuminations.* New York: Schocken Books.
Benjamin, Walter. 1999. *The Arcades Project.* Cambridge, MA: Harvard University Press.
Boorstin, Daniel J. 1962. *The Image: A Guide to Pseudo-events in America.* New York: Vintage.
Bogle, Kathleen A. 2008. *Hooking Up.* New York: New York University Press.
Brandon, John. 2015. "8 Words That Totally Reveal You Are Not a Millennial." *Inc.*, November 24, 2015. https://www.inc.com/john-brandon/8-words-that-totally-reveal-you-are-not-a-millennial.html.

Breckman, Warren G. 1991. "Disciplining Consumption: The Debate about Luxury in Wilhelmine Germany, 1890–1914." *Journal of Social History* 24 (3): 485–505.
Bushnell, Candace. 2003. *Trading Up*. New York: Hyperion.
Bushnell, Candace, and Katie Cotugno. 2021. *Rules for Being a Girl*. New York: Balzer and Bray.
Coase, Ronald. 1937. "The Nature of the Firm." *Economica* 4 (16): 386–405.
Coontz, Stephanie. 2006. *Marriage, a History: How Love Conquered Marriage*. London: Penguin Books.
Cooper, Melinda. 2017. *Family Values: Between Neoliberalism and the New Social Conservatism*. Boston: MIT Press.
Dabhoiwala, Farmarez. 2013. *The Origins of Sex: A History of the First Sexual Revolution*. London: Penguin.
Debord, Guy. 2004. *Society of the Spectacle*. London: Rebel Press.
Defoe, Daniel. (1839) 1987. *The Complete English Tradesman*. Gloucester: Alan Sutton.
Deleuze, Gilles, and Leopold von Sacher-Masoch. 1989. *Masochism*. New York: Zone Books.
Dewey, Catlin. 2016. "Is Rule 34 Actually True?: An Investigation into the Internet's Most Risqué Law." *Washington Post*, April 6, 2016. https://www.washingtonpost.com/news/the-intersect/wp/2016/04/06/is-rule-34-actually-true-an-investigation-into-the-internets-most-risque-law/.
Dichter, Ernest. 1965. "Discovering the Inner Jones." *Harvard Business Review*. 43 (3): 6–10, 157.
Ditmore, Melissa Hope, Antonia Levy, and Alys Willman, eds. 2013. *Sex Work Matters: Exploring Money, Power, and Intimacy in the Sex Industry*. London: Bloomsbury Publishing.
Donovan, Blair. 2023. "How Much Should You Spend on an Engagement Ring?" *Brides*, October 25, 2023. https://www.brides.com/story/proper-cost-of-engagement-ring.
Dunn, Sarah. 2004. *The Big Love*. New York: Little Brown and Company.
Dworkin, Andrea. (1987) 2007. *Intercourse*. New York: Basic Books.
Edgeworth, F. Y. 1881. *Mathematical Psychics: An Essay on the Application of Mathematics to the Moral Sciences*. London: C. Kegan Paul & Co.
Ekis Ekman, Kajsa. 2013. *Being and Being Bought: Prostitution, Surrogacy and the Split Self*. North Melbourne: Spinifex Press.
Elster, Jon. 1991. "Envy in Social Life." In *Strategy and Choice*, ed. Richard Zeckhauser, 49–82. Cambridge, MA: MIT Press.
Engels, Friedrich. 1902. *The Origin of the Family, Private Property and the State*. Chicago: Charles H. Kerr and Co.
Firestone, Shulamith. 1971. *The Dialectic of Sex: The Case for Feminist Revolution*. New York: Bantam Books.
Flaubert, Gustave. 2004. *Madame Bovary*. Translated by Margaret Mauldon. New York: Oxford University Press.
Foucault, Michel. 1978. *The History of Sexuality, Volume 1: An Introduction*. New York: Pantheon Books

Frank, Thomas. 1998. *The Conquest of Cool: Business Culture, Counterculture, and the Rise of Hip Consumerism*. Chicago: University of Chicago Press.
Freud, Sigmund. (1905) 1981. "Three Essays on the Theory of Sexuality." In *The Standard Edition of the Complete Psychological Works of Sigmund Freud, Vol. 7*. London: Hogarth Press.
Freud, Sigmund. (1910) 1981. "A Special Type of Choice of Object Made by Men (Contributions to the Psychology of Love I)." In *The Standard Edition of the Complete Psychological Works of Sigmund Freud, Vol. 11*, 163–75. London: Hogarth Press.
Freud, Sigmund. (1912) 1981. "On the Universal Tendency to Debasement in the Sphere of Love (Contributions to the Psychology of Love II)." In *The Standard Edition of the Complete Psychological Works of Sigmund Freud, Vol. 6*, 157-70. London: Hogarth Press.
Freud, Sigmund. (1924) 1961. "The Economic Problem of Masochism." In *The Standard Edition of the Complete Psychological Works of Sigmund Freud, Vol. 11*, 177–90. London: Hogarth Press.
Friedan, Betty. 1963. *The Feminine Mystique*. New York: Dell Publishing House.
Gira Grant, Melissa. 2014. *Playing the Whore: The Work of Sex Work*. London: Verso.
Goffman, Erving. 1956. *The Presentation of Self in Everyday Life*. New York: Doubleday.
Hakim, Catherine. 2010. *Erotic Capital: The Power of Attraction in the Boardroom and the Bedroom*. New York: Basic Books.
Hardy, Janet W., and Dossie Easton. 2017. *The Ethical Slut*. New York: Ten Speed Press.
Hartley, James E. 2008. "The Chameleon Daniel Defoe: Public Writing in the Age before Economic Theory." In *Money, Power, and Print: Interdisciplinary Studies on the Financial Revolution in the British Isles*, ed. Charles Ivar McGrath and Christopher J. Fauske, 26–50. Plainsboro, NJ: Associated University Presses.
Harvey, David. 1989. *The Condition of Postmodernity*. Oxford: Blackwell.
Hayes, Adam. 2023. "Brand Equity: Definition, Importance, Effect on Profit Margin, and Examples." Investopedia, October 27, 2023. https://www.investopedia.com/terms/b/brandequity.asp.
Hirschman, Albert O. 1977. *The Passions and the Interests: Political Arguments for Capitalism before Its Triumph*. Princeton, NJ: Princeton University Press.
Hochschild, Arlie R. 1983. *The Managed Heart: Commercialization of Human Feeling*. Berkley: University of California Press.
Horne, Thomas A. 1981. "Envy and Commercial Society: Mandeville and Smith on Private Vices, Public Benefits." *Political Theory* 9 (4): 551–69.
Hosie, Rachel. 2021. "What is Findom? A Submissive Man Explains Financial Domination." *Independent*, September 6, 2021. https://www.independent.co.uk/life-style/love-sex/findom-fetish-money-financial-domination-b1915084.html.
Illouz, Eva. 2019. *The End of Love: A Sociology of Negative Relations*. Oxford: Oxford University Press.
Ingham, Geoffrey. 2013. *The Nature of Money*. Hoboken, NJ: John Wiley & Sons.
James, E. L. 2012. *Fifty Shades of Grey*. Naperville, IL: Bloom Books
James, Henry. (1877) 2005. *The American*. San Diego: ICON.

Julian, Kate. 2018. "Why Are Young People Having So Little Sex?" *The Atlantic*, December 2018.

Klein, Naomi. 2009. *No Logo: Taking Aim at Brand Bullies*. New York: Picador.

Kondo, Marie. 2014. *The Life-Changing Magic of Tidying Up: The Japanese Art of Decluttering and Organizing*. Emeryville, CA: Ten Speed Press.

Krugman, Paul. 1994. *Peddling Prosperity: Economic Sense and Nonsense in the Age of Diminished Expectations*. New York: W. W. Norton.

Krugman, Paul. 2010. "The Conscience of a Liberal." *New York Times*, October 30, 2010. https://krugman.blogs.nytimes.com/2010/10/30/sex-and-drugs-and-markets-role/.

Kuhn, Thomas. (1962) 1996. *The Structure of Scientific Revolutions*. Chicago: University of Chicago Press.

Lacan, Jacques. 2013. "The Symbolic, the Imaginary and the Real." In *On the Names of the Father*. Cambridge: Polity Press.

Laplanche, Jean, and Jean-Bertrand Pontalis. 1988. *The Language of Psychoanalysis*. London: Karnac Books.

Le Goff, Jacques. 1990. *Your Money or Your Life: Economy and Religion in the Middle Ages*. New York: Zone Books.

Lears, Jackson. 1995. *Fables of Abundance: A Cultural History of Advertising in America*. New York: Basic Books.

Lévi-Strauss, Claude. 1969. *The Elementary Structures of Kinship*. Boston: Beacon Press.

Levin, Hanoch. 2003. "The Whore from Ohio." In *The Labor of Life: Selected Plays*, 173–210. Stanford, CA: Stanford University Press.

Levy, Ariel. 2010. *Female Chauvinist Pigs: Women and the Rise of Raunch Culture*. Black Inc.

Lombroso, Cesare, and Guglielmo Ferrero. 2004. *Criminal Woman, the Prostitute, and the Normal Woman*. Durham, NC: Duke University Press.

Mac, Juno, and Molly Smith. 2018. *Revolting Prostitutes: The Fight for Sex Workers' Rights*. London: Verso.

MacKinnon, Catherine A. 2011. "Trafficking, Prostitution, and Inequality." *Harvard Civil Rights Civil Liberties Law Review* 46: 271–309.

Maine, Henry J. S. 1861. *Ancient Law: Its Connection with the Early History of Society, and Its Relation to Modern Ideas*. London: John Murray.

Mandeville, Bernard. 1962. *The Fable of the Bees; or, Private Vices, Publick Benefits*. New York: Capricorn Books.

Marshall, Alfred. (1890) 2013. *Principles of Economics*. London: Palgrave Macmillan.

Marshall, P. David. 2014. *Celebrity and Power: Fame in Contemporary Culture*. Minneapolis: University of Minnesota Press.

Marx, Karl. (1959) 1977. *The Economic and Philosophical Manuscripts of 1844*. Moscow: Progress Publishers.

Marx, Karl. 1973. *Grundrisse*. New York: Vintage Books.

Marx, Karl. 1975. "The German Ideology." In *Karl Marx and Frederick Engels: Collected Works*, vol. 5. New York: International Publishers.

Marx, Karl. 1976. *Capital: A Critique of Political Economy*, vol. 1. New York: Penguin Books.
Marx, Karl, and Frederick Engels. 1965. *Manifesto of the Communist Party*. Peking: Foreign Languages Press.
Massey, Alana. 2015. "Against Chill," *Matter*, April 1, 2015. https://medium.com/matter/against-chill-930dfb60a577.
McLuhan, Marshall. 1964. *Understanding Media: The Extensions of Man*. London: Routledge & Kegan Paul.
Mears, Ashley. 2020. *Very Important People: Status and Beauty in the Global Party Circuit*. Princeton, NJ: Princeton University Press.
Michaels, Walter Benn. 1987. *The Gold Standard and the Logic of Naturalism: American Literature at the Turn of the Century*. Berkley: University of California Press.
Mill, John Stuart. (1869) 2009. *The Subjection of Women*. Floating Press.
Millett, Kate. (1970) 2016. *Sexual Politics*. New York: Columbia University Press.
Mitchell, Wesley C. 1912. "The Backward Art of Spending Money." *American Economic Review* 2 (2): 269–81.
Montaigne, Michel de. 1958. *The Complete Essays of Montaigne*. Stanford, CA: Stanford University Press.
Nilsson, Patricia, and Alex Barker. 2022. *Hot Money: Porn, Power and Profit* (podcast). *Financial Times*, July 29, 2022. https://www.ft.com/content/762e4648-06d7-4abd-8d1e-ccefb74b3244.
Nussbaum, Martha C. 1998. "'Whether from Reason or Prejudice': Taking Money for Bodily Services." *Journal of Legal Studies* 27 (2): 693–723.
Orenstein, Peggy. 2017. *Girls and Sex: Navigating the Complicated New Landscape*. New York: Simon and Schuster.
Parent-Duchâtelet, Alexandre J. P. 1845. *Prostitution in Paris, Considered Morally, Politically, and Medically*. Boston: C. H. Brainard.
Paul, Pamela. 2007. *Pornified: How Pornography Is Transforming Our Lives, Our Relationships, and Our Families*. New York: Macmillan.
Pine, B. Joseph, and James H. Gilmore. 1999. *The Experience Economy: Work Is Theatre and Every Business a Stage*. Boston: Harvard Business Press.
Pine, B. Joseph, and James H. Gilmore. 2000. *Markets of One: Creating Customer-Unique Value through Mass Customization*. Boston: Harvard Business School Press.
Pine, B. Joseph, and James H. Gilmore. 2007. *Authenticity: What Consumers Really Want*. Boston: Harvard Business Press.
Polanyi, Karl. (1944) 2001. *The Great Transformation: The Political and Economic Origins of Our Time*. Boston: Beacon Press.
Posner, Richard A. 1992. *Sex and Reason*. Cambridge, MA: Harvard University Press.
Pountain, Dick, and David Robins. 2000. *Cool Rules: Anatomy of an Attitude*. London: Reaktion Books.
Ronson, Jon. 2017. "The Fallow Years between Teen and Milf." *The Butterfly Effect* (podcast). Audible, October 24, 2017. https://www.audible.com/podcast/The-Butterfly-Effect/B08DDD6299.

Rosenberg, Anat. 2017. *Liberalizing Contracts: Nineteenth-Century Promises through Literature, Law and History*. New York: Routledge.
Samman, Amin. 2019. *History in Financial Times*. Stanford, CA: Stanford University Press.
Sahlins, Marshall. 2017. *Stone Age Economics*. London: Routledge.
Sandel, Michael J. 2013. *What Money Can't Buy: The Moral Limits of Markets*. New York: Farrar, Straus and Giroux.
Saussure, Ferdinand de. 2011. *Course in General Linguistics*. New York: Columbia University Press, 2011.
Smith, Adam. (1759) 1984. *The Theory of Moral Sentiments*. Indianapolis: Liberty Fund.
Smith, Adam. (1776) 2007. *An Inquiry into the Nature and Causes of the Wealth of Nations*. New York: Cosimo.
Sombart, Werner. 1967. *Luxury and Capitalism*. Ann Arbor: University of Michigan Press.
Sowell, Thomas. 2002. *Controversial Essays*. Stanford, CA: Hoover Institution Press.
Stiglitz, Joseph E. 2012. *The Price of Inequality*. New York: W. W. Norton.
Strauss, Neil. 2005. *The Game: Penetrating the Secret Society of Pick-Up Artists*. New York: Harper Collins.
Srinivasan, Amia. 2022. *The Right to Sex*. London: Bloomsbury Publishing.
Thiel, Peter, and Blake Masters. 2014. *Zero to One: Notes on Startups, or How to Build the Future*. New York: Currency.
Trollope, Anthony. (1875) 2012. *The Way We Live Now*. London: Vintage.
Turner, Graeme. 2010. *Ordinary People and the Media: The Demotic Turn*. Thousand Oaks, CA: Sage.
Veblen, Thorstein. (1899) 2007. *The Theory of the Leisure Class: An Economic Study of Institutions*. Oxford: Oxford University Press. First published by Macmillan.
Veblen, Thorstein. 1908. "On the Nature of Capital." *Quarterly Journal of Economics* 22 (4): 517–42.
Waller, Willard. 1937. "The Rating and Dating Complex." *American Sociological Review* 2 (5): 727–34.
Weber, Max. (1930) 1992. *The Protestant Ethic and the Spirit of Capitalism*. London and New York: Routledge. First published by Allen and Unwin.
Weber, Max. 1978. *Economy and Society: An Outline of Interpretive Sociology*. Berkley: University of California Press
Wharton, Edith. (1905) 1997. *The House of Mirth*. Hertfordshire: Wordsworth Classics.
Witt, Emily. 2017. *Future Sex*. Média Diffusion.
Wollstonecraft, Mary. (1790) 1995. *A Vindication of the Rights of Men*. Cambridge: Cambridge University Press.
Zelizer, Viviana A. 2005. *The Purchase of Intimacy*. Princeton, NJ: Princeton University Press.
Žižek, Slavoj. (1989) 2008. *The Sublime Object of Ideology*. London: Verso.
Žižek, Slavoj. 1997. *The Plague of Fantasies*. London: Verso.
Zola, Emile. 2013. *The Ladies' Paradise*. London: Sovereign Classics.
Zupančič, Alenka. 2017. *What Is Sex?* Boston: MIT Press.

Index

abstinence, 80, 81
Adshade, Marina, 2, 3, 4–5, 6, 10
advertising: internet advertising, 194; Jaguar advertising, 35–37, 42, 43; luxury advertising, 56; Marlboro advertising, 186; meaning of words in, 16, 31; on merging attractions of woman and attractions of commodity, 46; mock commercial for "Second Cheapest Wine," 60–61; play of seduction and exaggerated expectations as permeating, 94; promises of, 15, 56; revolution in, 176, 178–81, 184–85; seductive photographs of food dishes in, 98; as visualizing Marx's erotic metaphors, 37, 39; Volkswagen ad campaign, 179, 180; "you deserve this" formula, 115
The American (James), 158–59, 173
The American Meme (film), 191
analogies, use of, 39, 43, 84, 85, 98, 120, 121, 144, 156, 167, 182. *See also* metaphors

Anastasia "Ana" Steele (fictional character in *Fifty Shades* trilogy), 53–54
Ansari, Aziz, 167
Apple marketing, 189
Arcades Project (Benjamin), 45
Arendt, Hannah, 92
Arvidsson, Adam, 176–77, 186
aura, according to Benjamin, 193–94
Austin, John, 121
authenticity, 28, 129, 187–89

"The Backward Art of Spending Money" (Mitchell), 7
balanced systems, and systematic imbalance, 77–79
Bataille, Georges, 48, 130
Bazin, Andre, 191
Becker, Gary, 67, 95, 96, 97, 169
Belfort, Jordan, 152, 159
Benjamin, Walter, 45–46, 56–57, 59, 65, 154, 183, 193
Big Brother, 187–88, 189
The Big Love (Dunn), 196–98, 201

Bobby Axelrod (fictional character in *Billions*), 21
Boccaccio, Giovanni, 103
Bogle, Kathleen, 183, 199–200, 202
Boorstin, Daniel, 190
The Bourgeois Gentleman (Molière), 173
branding, modern branding, 176, 186, 189. *See also* advertising
Brandon, John, 183
Brontsatski (fictional character in *The Whore from Ohio*), 164
Burnet, Bishop, 24
Bushnell, Candace, 84, 146, 148

capital: erotic capital, 196, 221n1; as erotic relation to money, 160; origin of, 63–64; women and, 195–217
Capital (Marx), 37, 40, 42–43, 161
capitalism: according to Sombart, 112; according to Weber, 112; economic theory of, 1–2, 12, 13, 23, 45; as historical economic regime, 14; luxury and, 102–8; money as means of debasement of exchange in, 29; patriarchy and, 12, 23; Sombart's search for historical cause for emergence of, 105–6
capitalist, defined, 116
capitalist economy: antisocial, dehumanizing tendencies attributed to, 87; commodity as basic object of, 38; as compared to traditional economy, 105; as distinguished by its unique forms of desire, 13–14; and finance, 157; inner split within, 10; as not identical to market, 16, 30; obscene supplement of, 28; popular culture outlooks on, 68; and prostitution, 17, 35, 139, 143, 145; relation of sex to unique topology of, 32; rise of, 104; of sex, 122; topology of, 14, 20–65; value as innermost principle of, 38
carceral feminism, 136, 141
celebrities, 189–91, 192, 193, 210
chill attitude, 201
Christian Grey (fictional character in *Fifty Shades* trilogy), 53–56
Christopher Newman (fictional character in *The American*), 158–59, 173
Claire de Cintré (fictional character in *The American*), 158–59, 173
Cline, Victor B., 205
club economy, 210, 211, 212, 213–14
club scene, 210–13, 216, 217
C-M-C, 42
Coase, Ronald, 144
CollegeHumor, 60
Communist Manifesto (Marx and Engels), 103, 105, 195
The Complete English Tradesman (Defoe), 113, 119, 121–22
The Conquest of Cool (Frank), 176, 178
conspicuous consumption, 18, 115, 150, 171, 172, 173, 174, 175, 177, 217
conspicuous leisure, 18, 149, 150, 171–72, 173, 174, 175, 176, 177–78, 181, 217
consumer rebellion, 185
consumption: eroticization of, 17, 46, 130, 166–94; excluding of from scope of economic knowledge, 44–45; and failure to be oneself, 187–94
cool style/coolness, 175–82, 183, 184
Coontz, Stephanie, 21, 100, 129
Cooper, Melinda, 6–7, 11
Cotugno, Katie, 84
credit: love and, 123–28; sex and, 119–23; as supplement to money, 120

Dabhoiwala, Faramerz, 24, 26, 129–30
Dante Alighiere, 117
de Beauvoir, Simone, 5–6, 12, 96–97, 202
Debord, Guy, 174–75
Defoe, Daniel, 107, 113, 119, 120, 121–22, 124
Deleuze, Gilles, 13
desire, disavowal of, 93–95
Dichter, Ernest, 185, 186, 187
"Discovering the Inner Jones" (Dichter), 185
double standard, 195, 198–99, 200
Dunn, Sarah, 196–98, 201
Dunton, John, 26
Dworkin, Andrea, 22–23

Easton, Dossie, 133–34
Economic and Philosophical Manuscripts (Marx), 30, 161
economic imperialism, 2, 16, 67, 90, 95–99
"The Economic Problem of Masochism" (Freud), 98
economic theory: banishment of objects from, 92; of capitalism, 1–2, 12, 13, 23, 45; challenge posed by economy of sex for, 28, 56; moralist tendency of, 93; of Edgeworth, 88; of Mandeville, 70; sex as enlisted in service of, 97
economic thought: basic components of, 65; canonical tradition of, 44, 62; history of, 14–15; what money cannot buy as reorienting, 170
economy: according to Mandeville, 69–70; according to Smith, 69; club economy, 210, 211, 212, 213–14; of eroticism, 197; eroticized economy, 20–21, 34–37, 59, 63, 65, 122; "the experience economy," 138; expression of in culture, 45–46; intermingling of eroticism with, 54; libidinal economy, 13, 40; and marriage, 17, 27–28; "models and bottles" economy, 209, 214; of nonbuying, 1, 208–17; real economy, 38, 79, 80, 157, 206, 211–13
Edgeworth, Francis Ysidro, 88–90, 91
Edward Lewis (fictional character in *Pretty Woman*), 156
Ekis Ekman, Kajsa, 137–38, 139, 142
Elster, Jon, 76
Emma Bovary (fictional character in *Madame Bovary*), 124–25
emotional labor, 23, 138
Engels, Friedrich, 5–6, 103, 105, 195, 196, 200
erotic capital, 196, 221n1
eroticism: changes in, 46; commodity fetishism as informing, 47; described, 48–49; economy of, 197; financial eroticism, 130, 158–63; intermingling of with economy, 54; and perverted exchange, 61; notions of, 25, 51, 52, 184; relation of capitalist money to, 119; as secret code of ownership, 200; widening gap between sex and, 196, 210, 214
eroticization: of aspects of economic life, 14, 35, 36–37; of consumption, 17, 46, 130, 166–94; of luxury, 183; of money, 123, 214–15; of ownership, 49–56, 85
eroticized economy, 20–21, 34–37, 59, 63, 65, 122
erotic monogamy, 48–49
The Ethical Slut (Hardy and Eaton), 133–34
exchange: according to Mandeville, 70–73; according to Smith, 70–71; of people, objects, and passions, 70–73
"the experience economy," 138

The Fable of the Bees (Mandeville), 66, 67, 68, 107
Facebook, 165
family: crisis of, 7, 10; reinvention of through lagging, 8, 11, 12
Family Values (Cooper), 6
fantasy: according to Žižek, 217; erotic fantasy, 191; of the market, 141–45; pornographic fantasy, 202, 203
Faust (Goethe), 203
Felix (fictional character in *The Way We Live Now*), 126
Female Chauvinist Pigs (Levy), 161
feminism: carceral feminism, 136, 141; on conjoining marriage and prostitution, 96; as exposing secret dimension of continuity between patriarchal and liberal societies, 12; on love as continuation of patriarchy through other means, 22, 23, 100; on objectification and female submissiveness involved in prostitution, 138; as showing how patriarchal notion of possession of women permeates everyday life, 22–23
Fifty Shades (James), 53–56
finance: capitalist economy and, 157; prostitution and, 135–65; use value of money, 151–58
financial domination (findom), 155
financial eroticism, 130, 158–63
financial soul, and pleasures of imagination, 79–82
Firestone, Shulamith, 12, 22, 47–48, 49, 163
Flaubert, Gustave, 128
food porn, 98
Ford, Henry, 169
formal rationality, 9
Foucault, Michel, 32–33
Frank, Thomas, 176, 178, 179, 181

Franklin, Benjamin, 113, 116–17, 118, 120
Freud, Sigmund, 32, 33–34, 39, 98, 99, 123, 160, 162–63, 184, 205
Friedan, Betty, 12, 22

The Game (Strauss), 203
Generation Wealth (Greenfield), 26–27
The German Ideology (Marx), 160
Gilmore, James, 138, 169
Gira Grant, Melissa, 138–39
Girls and Sex (Orenstein), 198
Goethe, Johann Wolfgang von, 203
Goffman, Erving, 188
Gordon Gekko (fictional character in *Wall Street*), 68, 69, 81
Greenfield, Lauren, 26–27
Grundrisse (Marx), 7, 32
Guattari, Félix, 13
Gus Trenor (fictional character in *The House of Mirth*), 146–47

Hakim, Catherine, 196
Hardy, Janet, 133–34
Harvey, David, 169
Haters Back Off (mockumentary), 192
Hayek, Friedrich, 158, 169
hedonimeter, 88, 90, 91
Hetta (fictional character in *The Way We Live Now*), 125, 126, 127–28
Hirschman, Albert, 57, 67, 71
Hochschild, Arlie, 12, 23, 138
Hoibitter (fictional character in *The Whore from Ohio*), 164
homemaker, use of term, 10
homo economicus, 70
hook-up scene, 183, 199, 200
Horne, Thomas, 67
The House of Mirth (Wharton), 146–47
housewife: as offensive term, 10; *The Real Housewives* (TV series), 10–11

Ida (fictional character in *Sexus*), 202
Illouz, Eva, 123
The Image (Boorstin), 190
imaginary, according to Mandeville, 80, 81
imagination, pleasures of, financial soul and, 79–82
imperialism, economic. *See* economic imperialism
influencers, 189–93, 194
Ingham, Geoffrey, 118
Instagram, 174
"the invisible hand," 68
iPhone marketing, 189

Jaguar advertising, 35–37, 42, 43
James, E. L., 53
James, Henry, 158, 173
James Morse (fictional character in *Pretty Woman*), 156
Janey Wilcox (fictional character in *Trading Up*), 146, 148, 150

Klein, Naomi, 189
Klinenberg, Eric, 167
Kondo, Marie, 182, 187
Krugman, Paul, 79, 151
Kuhn, Thomas, 14

Lacan, Jacques, 40, 94, 205, 212
Ladies' Paradise (Zola), 108–11
Lady Carbury (fictional character in *The Way We Live*), 125
Lawrence Selden (fictional character in *The House of Mirth*), 149
Lears, Jackson, 129
Le Goff, Jacques, 117
leisure, conspicuous. *See* conspicuous leisure
Levin, Hanoch, 163–64, 165
Lévi-Strauss, Claude, 24, 25
Levy, Ariel, 161–62, 163
libidinal economy, 13, 40

libido, 39–40
Lily Bart (fictional character in *The House of Mirth*), 146–47, 148–50, 165
Lobbying, 61–63
Lois, George, 178
Lombroso, Cesare, 140
love: according to feminist tradition, 22; as continuation of patriarchy, 22; and credit, 123–28; economy of, 100–101; and marriage, 100–134; secularization of, 102–3
Luther, Martin, 81–82, 114
luxury: according to Mandeville, 74, 75, 76; according to Marshall, 93; according to Smith, 74–75; and capitalism, 102–8; eroticization of, 183; neoclassical economics' suspicion of, 92; place of in economy, 73–76
Luxury and Capitalism (Sombart), 102, 112
Lyotard, Jean-François, 13

Mac, Juno, 136–37, 139, 141, 143–44
MacKinnon, Catherine, 34–35, 36, 57, 59, 154
Madame Bovary (Flaubert), 119–20, 124–26
Maine, Henry, 21
Mandeville, Bernard, 14, 16, 17, 66–67, 68, 69, 70, 74, 82–83, 84, 86, 87–88, 93, 94, 99, 107, 183
Marcuse, Herbert, 13
market: fantasy of, 141–45; and its outside, 167–70; markets of one, 169
marketing: and failure to be oneself, 187–94; iPhone marketing, 189; revolution in, 185. *See also* advertising
Marlboro advertising, 186

marriage: according to Becker, 96; according to de Beauvoir, 96; capitalism as conferring new forms on patriarchal tradition of, 12; as economic institution, 25; economy and, 17, 27–28; as heritage of patriarchy, 158; as legal prostitution, 25; love and, 100–34; mercenary marriage, 129–30; neo-marriages, 133; renunciation of, 200; as shadow that haunts sex, 200–202; shift from companionate to passionate marriage, 167, 168, 169–70
Marro, Antonio, 96
Marshall, Alfred, 30, 80, 91–92, 93, 117
Marshall, Gary, 155–56
Marx, Karl, 7, 14, 30–31, 32, 36–39, 40–46, 47, 49, 52, 56, 63, 64, 65, 85, 90, 103, 105, 115–16, 118, 119, 145, 151, 157, 160, 161, 162, 195, 196, 197, 200, 201–2, 203, 209
masochism, 50–51, 98
Massey, Alana, 201
McLuhan, Marshall, 152
M-C-M', 42, 116, 157
Mears, Ashley, 209–13, 215, 216, 217
media personas, 189–92
men: as acting in public sphere of politics and economy, 129; businessman tasks, 9; and rational art of making money, 10; and women and money, 145–50
Mercier, Louis Sebastien, 108
metaphors, use of, 27, 32, 37, 39, 43–44, 56, 57, 58, 59, 60, 62, 63, 64, 65, 80, 81, 101, 119–20, 122, 141, 154, 161, 197, 203, 209. *See also* analogies
Michael, Walter Benn, 49–50
Mill, John Stuart, 200
Miller, Henry, 202

Millet, Kate, 198
Miranda (fictional character in *Haters Back Off*), 192
Mitchell, Wesley C., 7–10, 12, 13
models, 211
"models and bottles" economy, 209, 214
Modern Romance (Ansari and Klinenberg), 167
Molière, 173
mommy pornography, 53
money: according to Smith, 59; backwardness of art of spending, 7–10; commodity money, 118–19; credit money, 121; eroticization of, 123, 214–15; erotic money and financial eroticism, 158–63; as ethical substance, 115–19; gendered nature of, 11; as hedonimeter, 89, 90; history of as entangled with history of family, 128–29; libidinal view of, 41; Marx's conception of, 40–44; men, women, and, 145–50; new money, 150, 163, 172, 174, 175, 217; obscene money, 59; old money, 18, 149, 150, 159, 163, 165, 172, 173, 175, 217; as playing dramatic role in literature, 128; prostitution and, 26–27, 57, 136–41; as universal equalizer, 12–13, 59–60; use value of, 151–58; what it can't buy, 27–34
money shot, 208–9
monogamy: economic explanations of, 5–7; erotic monogamy, 48–49; hysterization of, 168; persistence of, 2–5, 12; as private property regime and sexual regime, 12; resilience of, 133
Montaigne, Michel de, 48–49, 103
morals, macroeconomics of, 111–15

Mr. Jourdain (fictional character in *The Bourgeois Gentleman*), 173
Mr. Melmotte (fictional character in *The Way We Live Now*), 125–26, 127

"The Nature of the Firm" (Coase), 144
neoclassical economics: and moralistic imperative, 93–94; as objectless theory, 91–92; rise of, 90–91
neoliberalism, impact of on economic concept of choice, 168–69
Nilsson, Patricia, 207
Ninety-Five Theses (Luther), 114
Nussbaum, Martha, 142–43, 144

objectless theory, 91–92
obscenity: according to Mandeville, 70; as theoretical choice, 67–70
Octave Mouret (fictional character in *Ladies' Paradise*), 108–11
OnlyFans, 207
"On the Sexual Theories of Children" (Freud), 33–34
Orenstein, Peggy, 198, 204, 206
The Origin of the Family, Private Property and the State (Engels), 5
Orwell, George, 187
Ostrovsky, Josh, 191

Parent-Duchâtelet, Alexandre, 140
Pateman, Carole, 12
patriarchy: and capitalism, 12, 23, 84; continuity between patriarchal and liberal societies, 12, 22, 23; as encompassing wives in circle of ownership, 6; eroticization of women as last line of defense of, 47–48; loves as continuation of, 22, 52, 100; marriage as heritage of, 158; traditional patriarchy. *See* traditional patriarchy

Paul, Pamela, 205–6
Paul Montague (fictional character in *The Way We Live Now*), 125, 126–27
paying for paying, 59, 60, 61
pick-up artists (PUAs), 203–4
Pine, Joseph, 138, 169
Playing with Fire (film), 207
pleasure measurement, 90
polyamory, 133–34
Polyani, Karl, 86–87
pornography: food porn, 98; mommy pornography, 53; as objectifying women, 202–8
Posner, Richard, 97, 98
potlatch, 216
Pountain, Dick, 175–76
Pretty Woman (film), 155–57, 158
primal repression, 67–88
private property: according to Veblen, 170; rethinking notion of, 12
private sphere, women as acting in, 129
prostitution: according to Benjamin, 57; according to de Beauvoir, 202; according to MacKinnon, 34–35, 57; according to Smith, 57–59; capitalist economy and, 17, 35, 139, 143, 145; economic status of, 25–27; economies underlying, 17; and finance, 135–65; finance and, 154–55; marriage as legal prostitution, 25; as metaphor, 32; and money, 57; money and, 136–41; public prostitution, 57, 58, 62–63, 101; repugnance toward, 26; use of term, 27
The Protestant Ethic and the Spirit of Capitalism (Weber), 112
public sphere, men as acting in, 129
Puritanism, prurient Puritanism, 198–200

Quasar, Mike, 207

raunch culture, 162
real economy, 38, 79, 80, 157, 206, 211–13
The Real Housewives (TV series), 10–11
Revolting Prostitutes (Mac and Smith), 136
Robins, David, 175–76
Roger Carbury (fictional character in *The Way We Live Now*), 125, 126, 127, 128
romantic value theory, 196–98
Ronson, Jon, 207
Rosenberg, Anat, 125
Rules for Being a Girl (Bushnell and Cotugno), 84

Samman, Amin, 68–69
Sandel, Michael, 28, 29
Saussure, Ferdinand de, 182
Scorsese, Martin, 152
The Second Sex (de Beauvoir), 5
Selden Rose (fictional character in *Trading Up*), 149
Severin (fictional character in *Venus in Furs*), 49–52
sex: analogy of to eating, 97–98; capitalist economy of, 122; and credit, 119–23; and the department store, 108–11; in economic thought, 16, 66–99; economy of, 21–25; as enlisted in service of economic theory, 97; erotic disavowal of, 88–91; interest of economics in, 97; marriage as shadow that haunts sex, 200–202; relation of to unique topology of capitalist economy, 32; repression of, 95–99; widening gap between sex and eroticism, 196, 210, 214
Sex and Reason (Posner), 97
sex appeal, 46, 221n1

sex privatization, 49
sexual culture, economy of current sexual culture, 18
sexual economics, 56–65
sexual economy: according to Mandeville, 82–83, 84, 86, 87–88; according to Smith, 82–83, 85–86; as characterized by conceptual triad of marriage, love, and prostitution, 135; as contrasted with libidinal economy, 13; notion of, 13; as theme of nineteenth-century realist literature, 108; use of term, 20
sexual overvaluation, 162, 163
sexual prohibitions, 32–33
Sexus (Miller), 202
sex work, 27, 135–45, 148, 155
Shakespeare, William, 161
Shaw, George Bernard, 140
Smith, Adam, 16, 17, 30, 40, 41, 57–60, 61, 62, 63, 64, 65, 66, 67–68, 69, 70, 73, 74–75, 82–83, 85–86, 87–88, 92, 94–95, 101, 154
Smith, Molly, 136–37, 139, 141, 143–44
Sombart, Werner, 14, 17, 30, 102–8, 111–12, 113, 114, 115, 183
Sowell, Thomas, 76
spouse choice, 167, 168, 169
Srinivasan, Amia, 141
stars, as different from celebrities, 191
Stiglitz, Joseph, 61–62
Stone, Oliver, 68
Strauss, Neil, 203
surplus value, 63, 64, 90, 157, 160
systems: according to Mandeville, 77, 78, 79; according to Smith, 77

Theory of the Leisure Class (Veblen), 149, 170
The Theory of Moral Sentiments (Smith), 70, 85

Thiel, Peter, 165
Three Essays on the Theory of Sexuality (Freud), 33, 163
Timon of Athens (Shakespeare), 161
topology, of capitalist economy, 14, 20–65
Trading Up (Bushnell), 146
traditional patriarchy, 10, 11–12, 21, 101, 102, 164, 197, 201
Trollope, Anthony, 125, 127, 128
Turner, Graeme, 190
Twilight (Meyer), 53

usury, condemnation of, 117
utility, concept of, 91, 95, 96

Val (fictional character in *Sexus*), 202, 203
Veblen, Thorstein, 14, 17–18, 30, 60, 149, 150, 170–75, 177, 182, 183–84, 185, 217
Venus in Furs (von Sacher-Masoch), 49–52
Very Important People (Mears), 209
Vivian Ward (fictional character in *Pretty Woman*), 155–56, 157
Volkswagen ad campaign, 179, 180
von Sacher-Masoch, Leopold, 49–52

Waller, Willard, 130–32
Wall Street (Stone), 68–69
Wanda (fictional character in *Venus in Furs*), 49–52
The Way We Live Now (Trollope), 119–20, 125–28
The Wealth of Nations (Smith), 57, 58, 66, 70, 74, 85, 92
Weber, Max, 9, 14, 30, 81, 112–13, 114, 115, 116, 204
Weldon, Jo, 136
Wendy Rhoades (fictional character in *Billions*), 21
Wharton, Edith, 146
What Money Can't Buy (Sandel), 28, 29
The White Lotus (TV series), 11
whore, gift of, 163–65
The Whore from Ohio (Levin), 163–65
Witt, Emily, 132–33
The Wolf of Wall Street (film), 152–54, 155, 158, 159–60
Wollstonecraft, Mary, 25

Zelizer, Viviana, 101–2, 122
zero to one, 165
Žižek, Slavoj, 50, 52, 73, 145, 217
Zola, Emile, 108–11
Zupančič, Alenka, 122–23, 147, 185, 206

CURRENCIES

New Thinking for Financial Times
STEFAN EICH AND MARTIJN KONINGS, EDITORS

Joscha Wullweber, *Central Bank Capitalism: Monetary Policy in Times of Crisis*

Eli Jelly-Schapiro, *Moments of Capital: World Theory, World Literature*

Jakob Feinig, *Moral Economies of Money: Politics and the Monetary Constitution of Society*

Charly Coleman, *The Spirit of French Capitalism: Economic Theology in the Age of Enlightenment*

Amin Samman, *History in Financial Times*

Thomas Biebricher, *The Political Theory of Neoliberalism*

Lisa Adkins, *The Time of Money*

Martijn Konings, *Capital and Time: For a New Critique of Neoliberal Reason*

The authorized representative in the EU for product safety and compliance is:
Mare Nostrum Group
B.V Doelen 72
4831 GR Breda
The Netherlands

www.ingramcontent.com/pod-product-compliance
Lightning Source LLC
Chambersburg PA
CBHW022006220426
43663CB00007B/984